To my grandmother ...

And to my friends F, D(7), B, M, K, J, P, M(Blackhole) ...

`mapt.io`

Mapt is an online digital library that gives you full access to over 5,000 books and videos, as well as industry leading tools to help you plan your personal development and advance your career. For more information, please visit our website.

Why subscribe?

- Spend less time learning and more time coding with practical eBooks and Videos from over 4,000 industry professionals

- Improve your learning with Skill Plans built especially for you

- Get a free eBook or video every month

- Mapt is fully searchable

- Copy and paste, print, and bookmark content

PacktPub.com

Did you know that Packt offers eBook versions of every book published, with PDF and ePub files available? You can upgrade to the eBook version at `www.PacktPub.com` and as a print book customer, you are entitled to a discount on the eBook copy. Get in touch with us at `service@packtpub.com` for more details.

At `www.PacktPub.com`, you can also read a collection of free technical articles, sign up for a range of free newsletters, and receive exclusive discounts and offers on Packt books and eBooks.

Voice User Interface Projects

Build voice-enabled applications using Dialogflow for Google
Home and Alexa Skills Kit for Amazon Echo

Henry Lee

BIRMINGHAM - MUMBAI

Voice User Interface Projects

Commissioning Editor: Kunal Chaudhari
Acquisition Editor: Nigel Fernandes
Content Development Editor: Francis Carneiro
Technical Editor: Akhil Nair
Copy Editor: Safis Editing
Project Coordinator: Sheejal Shah
Proofreader: Safis Editing
Indexer: Rekha Nair
Graphics: Jason Monteiro
Production Coordinator: Nilesh Mohite

First published: July 2018

Production reference: 1300718

Published by Packt Publishing Ltd.
Livery Place
35 Livery Street
Birmingham
B3 2PB, UK.

ISBN 978-1-78847-335-4

www.packtpub.com

Contributors

About the author

Henry Lee has over 18 years of experience in software engineering. His passion for software engineering has led him to work at various start-ups. Currently, he works as the principal architect responsible for the R&D and the digital strategies. In his spare time, He loves to travel and snowboard, and enjoys discussing the latest technology trends over a cigar! Also, he authored three books at Apress on mobile development.

Thank God for being there no matter what!

I dedicate this book to my grandmother who gave me guidance and love when I was young.

My friends are the family I chose. Thank you, guys!

Thank you, Packt and all who were involved in the publishing process because I could not have done without your support!

Special thanks to Fernando Coto (Zepto Segundo) for the podcast materials and Rocky Ace Turbeaux for the cigars.

About the reviewer

Fernando Coto comes from the Graphic Design background and started as a Web Designer back in 2001. He trained himself to become what we know today as a UI/UX specialist and has followed the development and evolution of this field since its early days. Fernando has worked as a UI Designer since 2007 mostly for the Banking and Finance industries. He decided to participate in this project in order to evaluate the impact of voice interfaces and what he expects will be a transformation from User Interface Design to Human Interaction Design, involving visuals, voice, and gestures.

I'd like to thank the author for the opportunity to become directly involved in a new and fresh approach to human-machine communication, and for the multiple learning opportunities, I have enjoyed during our projects together, not only in technical aspects but also on everyday life experiences. I'd also like to thank Sheejal Shah at Packt Publishing for her work and patience managing the review process.

Packt is searching for authors like you

If you're interested in becoming an author for Packt, please visit authors.packtpub.com and apply today. We have worked with thousands of developers and tech professionals, just like you, to help them share their insight with the global tech community. You can make a general application, apply for a specific hot topic that we are recruiting an author for, or submit your own idea.

Table of Contents

Preface

Today the voice technology is being integrated into many mobile devices such as iOS Siri, Android Google Assistant and Windows Phone Cortana allowing you to perform mobile phone tasks using the voice commands. The voice technology is even coming into our home through Amazon Echo and Google Home allowing you to control home appliances like bedroom lights or opening the garage door. Also you can use your voice in your car allowing you to perform hands free tasks like making a call, texting and playing a music.

This book is designed to help you understand and create voice user interfaces for Google Assistant, Google Home, Android Auto and Amazon Echo. It will help you understand the natural language processing platforms like Alexa and Dialogflow and create Node.js middle tier REST API that will fulfill the platforms' requests. Furthermore, you will take advantage of the cloud technology to deliver your infrastructure back-end needs in order to help deliver your application faster and reliably.

Who this book is for

This is book designed for the developer with a basic knowledge of any programming language. This book will utilize Node.js, C# and Xamarin Android, and if you are not familiar with any of these language you can start with basics tutorials from the following web sites:

- Node.js - https://www.w3schools.com/nodejs/
- C# - https://docs.microsoft.com/en-us/dotnet/csharp/quick-starts/
- Xamarin - https://docs.microsoft.com/en-us/xamarin/android/
- Android - https://developer.android.com/guide/

What this book covers

Chapter 1, *Introduction*, covers the history of the voice user interfaces (VUIs) and discusses what VUIs are. The chapter will help you understand the roles the natural language processing platforms play in the development of VUIs. Also, the chapter will introduce modern voice enabled applications such as the chat bots, the personal digital assistant devices (Amazon Echo and Google Home), and the automobile virtual assistant system and how the VUIs can be beneficial to these applications.

Chapter 2, *Building an FAQs Chatbot*, helps you understand and program in Dialogflow, a natural language processing platform from Google. You will utilize the concepts like entities, intent, context and actions to create a chatbot. Then learn to deploy and test your chatbot using Google Assistant using Android and iOS.

Chapter 3, *Building a Fortune Cookie Application*, starts by creating the voice user interfaces in Dialogflow for the fortune cookie application that tells the famous people's quotes. Then you will be creating the webhook in Node.js to handle the incoming Dialogflow fulfillment requests. In Node.js, you will learn to trigger follow up or custom intents, create a visual response if the device supports visual elements, build speech synthesis markup language and integrate audio files in response. Finally, you will learn to work with Dialogflow analytics.

Chapter 4, *Hosting, Securing, and Testing Fortune Cookie in the Cloud*, teaches about Microsoft Azure cloud platform. And you will learn to deploy Node.js to Microsoft App Service and deploy the data to CosmoDB. You will learn apply the security to the Node.js REST API and finally you will be using Dialogflow SDK to create functional test.

Chapter 5, *Deploying the Fortune Cookie App to Google Home*, teaches your how to set up Google Home and then deploy development version of your cooking application. Then you will learn about the Google Home application certification process and submit your cooking application to the Google marketplace.

Chapter 6, *Building a Cooking Application Using Alexa*, teaches about using Alexa to build cooking application for the Amazon Echo devices. You will learn to use Alex Skills Kit to create the voice user interfaces for the cooking application. This chapter will cover basic Alex concepts like intent, slots and utterances required for building the voice user interfaces. Finally, you will build back-end Node.js webhook to process Alexa requests.

Chapter 7, *Using Advanced Alexa Features for the Cooking App*, teaches you how to log application events and errors to the Microsoft Azure storage. Then you will further enhance the cooking application by using built-in intents and managing your own application state in Redis. Finally, you will learn to submit your application to Amazon marketplace.

Chapter 8, *Migrating the Alexa Cooking Application to Google Home*, covers how to migrate Alexa skill to Dialogflow agent. Learning to convert Alexa skill to Dialogflow agent will help you reach wide ranges of audiences from multiple devices. Finally, you will learn to write Node.js webhook that can handle both Alexa and Dialogflow requests.

Chapter 9, *Building a Voice-Enabled Podcast for the Car*, teaches your how to create MusicService, MediaPlayer and MusicProvider that are needed for Android Auto to allow users to browse through the media content and play the podcast. You will be creating Android mobile media player UI in order to test MusicService.

Chapter 10, *Hosting and Enhancing the Android Auto Podcast*, teaches you how to simulate podcast application your wrote in previous chapter using desktop header unit to simulate in Android Auto. Then you will learn to test the podcast application using a real car. Finally, you will learn some basic voice commands for the Android Auto.

To get the most out of this book

1. It will help to have basic understanding of any programming language but knowing JavaScript will help the most
2. Here are some tutorial resources that you can take a look to help learn about the languages covered in this book:
   - Node.js - https://www.w3schools.com/nodejs/
   - C# - https://docs.microsoft.com/en-us/dotnet/csharp/quick-starts/
   - Xamarin - https://docs.microsoft.com/en-us/xamarin/android/
   - Android - https://developer.android.com/guide/

Download the example code files

You can download the example code files for this book from your account at www.packtpub.com. If you purchased this book elsewhere, you can visit www.packtpub.com/support and register to have the files emailed directly to you.

You can download the code files by following these steps:

1. Log in or register at www.packtpub.com.
2. Select the **SUPPORT** tab.
3. Click on **Code Downloads & Errata**.
4. Enter the name of the book in the **Search** box and follow the onscreen instructions.

Once the file is downloaded, please make sure that you unzip or extract the folder using the latest version of:

- WinRAR/7-Zip for Windows
- Zipeg/iZip/UnRarX for Mac
- 7-Zip/PeaZip for Linux

The code bundle for the book is also hosted on GitHub at https://github.com/ PacktPublishing/Voice-User-Interface-Projects. Check them out!

We also have other code bundles from our rich catalog of books and videos available at https://github.com/PacktPublishing/. Check them out!

Conventions used

There are a number of text conventions used throughout this book.

CodeInText: Indicates code words in text, database table names, folder names, filenames, file extensions, pathnames, dummy URLs, user input, and Twitter handles. Here is an example: "Let's create a sendResponse function that will respond with a simple response."

A block of code is set as follows:

```
var request, response;
exports.dialogflowFirebaseFulfillment =
firebase.https.onRequest((req, res) => {
 request = req;
 response = res;
 console.log('Fortune Cookie Request headers: ' +
JSON.stringify(request.headers));
 console.log('Fortune Cookie Request body: ' +
JSON.stringify(request.body));
 if (request.body.queryResult) {
 processV2Request();
 } else {
 console.log('Invalid Request');
 return response.status(400).end('Invalid Webhook Request');
 }
});
```

When we wish to draw your attention to a particular part of a code block, the relevant lines or items are set in bold:

```
var request, response, parameters;
```

Bold: Indicates a new term, an important word, or words that you see onscreen. For example, words in menus or dialog boxes appear in the text like this. Here is an example: "Click **Add follow-up intent** and select **custom intent**."

Warnings or important notes appear like this.

 Tips and tricks appear like this.

Get in touch

Feedback from our readers is always welcome.

General feedback: Email `feedback@packtpub.com` and mention the book title in the subject of your message. If you have questions about any aspect of this book, please email us at `questions@packtpub.com`.

Errata: Although we have taken every care to ensure the accuracy of our content, mistakes do happen. If you have found a mistake in this book, we would be grateful if you would report this to us. Please visit `www.packtpub.com/submit-errata`, selecting your book, clicking on the Errata Submission Form link, and entering the details.

Piracy: If you come across any illegal copies of our works in any form on the Internet, we would be grateful if you would provide us with the location address or website name. Please contact us at `copyright@packtpub.com` with a link to the material.

If you are interested in becoming an author: If there is a topic that you have expertise in and you are interested in either writing or contributing to a book, please visit `authors.packtpub.com`.

Reviews

Please leave a review. Once you have read and used this book, why not leave a review on the site that you purchased it from? Potential readers can then see and use your unbiased opinion to make purchase decisions, we at Packt can understand what you think about our products, and our authors can see your feedback on their book. Thank you!

For more information about Packt, please visit `packtpub.com`.

Introduction 1

In the future, user interfaces will move away from being touch-based and mouse-clicking web interfaces to voice and conversation-based user interfaces. On average, a person speaks about 20,000 words a day (`http://bit.ly/2GYZ1du`), which is the equivalent of reading half a book, and voice commands are 5 times faster to process (`http://hci.stanford.edu/research/speech/index.html`) than web user interfaces or typing. The huge efficiency of voice commands is attributed to the fact that speaking is natural to everyone. The technological leaps in **natural language processing (NLP)**, thanks to **machine learning (ML)** and **artificial intelligence (AI)**, and increased computing power has made it possible to accurately understand and process complex human voices and speech patterns. This book will teach developers how to create voice-enabled applications using NLP platforms such as Google's Dialogflow and Amazon's Alexa Skills Skit, and deploy them to personal digital assistant devices, such as Google Home, Amazon Echo, and Google's Android Auto.

This chapter covers the history of **voice user interfaces (VUIs)** and discusses what VUIs are. It will help you understand the roles NLP platforms play in the development of VUIs. The chapter also introduces modern voice-enabled applications such as chatbots, personal digital assistant devices, and automobile virtual assistant systems, and how VUIs can be beneficial to such applications. You will then learn about user experience and design principles to deliver compelling voice-enabled applications to consumers. Finally, this chapter ends by looking at both current and predicted future capabilities of digital personal assistant devices.

This chapter will cover the following topics:

- History of VUIs
- Basic concepts of VUIs
- NLP platforms
- Benefits of VUIs
- Chatbots, Amazon Echo, Google Home, and automobile virtual assistant systems
- Best practices, design principles, and user experiences when creating VUIs
- Current and predicted future capabilities of digital personal assistant devices

Technological advancement of VUIs

In 1952, at Bell Labs, the engineers Davis, Biddulph, and Balashek built the **Automatic Digit Recognizer (Audrey)**, a rudimentary voice recognition system. Audrey was limited by the technology of the time but was able to recognize the numbers 0 to 9. The Audrey system, which processed the 10 digits through voice recognition, was 6 feet tall and covered the walls of Bell Labs, containing large numbers of analog circuits with capacitors, amplifiers, and filters. Audrey did the following three things:

- The Audrey system took the user's voice as input and put the voice into the machine's memory. The voice input was classified and pattern matching was performed against the predefined classes of voices for the numbers 0 to 9. Finally, the identified number was stored in memory.
- It flashed a light that represented the matching number.
- It was also able to communicate selected digits over the telephone.

 Audrey performed what's known today as NLP, using ML with AI.

Although Audrey recognized voice input with an accuracy of 97% to 99%, it was very expensive and large in size, and it was extremely difficult to maintain its complex electronics. Thus, Audrey could not be commercialized. However, since the inception of Audrey, voice technology and research has continued to leap forward.

First-generation VUIs

The big break came in 1984, when SpeechWorks and Nuance introduced **interactive voice response (IVR)** systems. IVR systems were able to recognize human voices over the telephone and carried out tasks given to them (Roberto Pieraccini and Lawrence Rabiner 2012, *The Voice in the Machine: Building Computers That Understand Speech*). You will be able to recognize IVR systems today when you call major companies for support. For example, when you call to make a hotel reservation, you will be familiar with "Press *1* or say *reservation*, Press 2 or say *check reservation*, Press 3 or say *cancel reservation*, Press # or say *main menu*." In the '90s, I remember working on my first VUIs in an IVR system. To develop the IVR system, I had to work with the **Microsoft Speech API (SAPI)**, http://bit.ly/2osJpdM. With SAPI, I was able to perform **text to speech (TTS)**, where the voice received from the user was translated into text in order to evaluate the user's intent; then, after evaluating the user's intent, a text message was created and converted back to the voice to relay the message to the user on the telephone.

Boom of VUIs

In order to really appreciate the start of the emerging voice technology, first let's look at the year 2005. In 2005, Web 2.0 contributed to the increase in the volume of data. This increase brought about the creation of Hadoop and big data in order to meet the demand for storing, processing, and understanding data. Big data helps to advance data analytics, ML, and AI in order to identify patterns in data in business contexts. The same techniques as those used for big data, such as ML and AI, have helped in advancing NLP to recognize speech patterns and VUIs. The Web 2.0 big data boom kick-started the boom in the use of VUIs on smart phones, in the home, and in automobiles.

History of VUIs on mobile devices

In 2006, Apple introduced the concept of Siri, which allows users to interact with machines using their voice. In 2007, Google followed Apple and introduced voice searches. In 2011, Apple finally brought Siri concepts into reality by integrating Siri into iOS and iPhones. But unfortunately, with Steve Jobs' death that same year, the voice innovations from Apple slowed down, allowing others, such as Google and Amazon, to catch up. In 2015, Microsoft introduced Cortana for the Windows 10 operating system and smart phones (refer to the following screenshot). In 2016, Google introduced *Google Assistant* (refer to the following screenshot) to mobile devices. Later, from Chapter 3, *Build a Fortune Cookie Application*, to Chapter 5, *Deploying the Fortune Cookie App to Google Home*, you will learn how to create voice assistant applications for mobile devices. One of the major advantages of writing applications for Google Assistant is that the same applications you write for Google Assistant can also be deployed to Google Home.

The following illustration depicts screenshots of the mobile voice assistants Cortana, Siri, and Google Assistant:

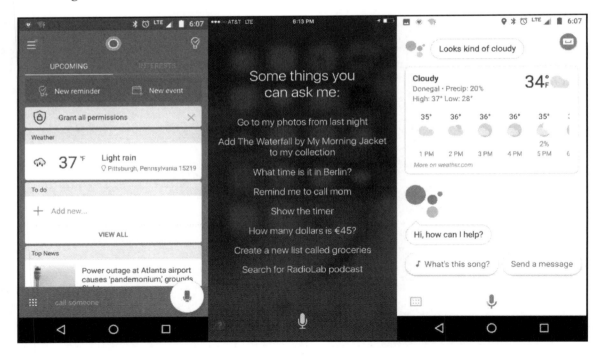

Mobile voice assistants—Cortana, Siri, and Google Assistant

History of VUIs for Google Home

In 2014, Amazon introduced Amazon Echo (refer to the following screenshot), the first VUI device designed for consumers' home. In 2016, Google released Google Home (refer to the following screenshot). In 2017, Amazon and Google continued to compete against each other in the consumer marketplace with the Amazon Echo and Google Home devices. The competition between Amazon and Google with these home devices shared similarities with the competition between Apple's iPhone and Google's Android. Currently, these home devices lack the third party applications the consumers can use and, as such, huge start-up and entrepreneurial opportunities exist. Remember *Angry Birds* for iPhone and Android? What could be the next big hit in this untapped marketplace? Later, from `Chapter 3`, *Building a Fortune Cookie Application*, through `Chapter 8`, *Migrating the Alexa Cooking Application to Google Home*, you will learn how to develop applications for Amazon Echo and Google Home devices.

The following photo shows Amazon Echo:

Amazon Echo

The following is a photo of Google Home:

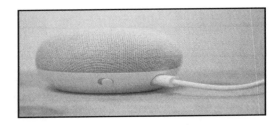

Google Home

History of VUIs in cars

In 2007, Microsoft partnered with Ford and integrated Microsoft Sync Framework, giving drivers hands-free interaction with their car's features of the car. In 2013, Apple introduced CarPlay for the cars, but only limited number of car manufacturers were willing to adopt CarPlay (`https://www.apple.com/ios/carplay/`). On the other hand, in 2018, major car manufacturers adopted Google Auto (`https://www.android.com/auto/`) because Google Auto is based on the Android operating system and already has huge developer ecosystems in the Android marketplace. Later, in `Chapter 9`, *Building a Voice Enabled Podcast for the Car*, and `Chapter 10`, *Hosting and Enhancing the Android Auto Podcast*, you will learn how to create your own podcast and stream your own content to cars through car dashboards that support Google Auto.

The following photo shows the voice assistant from Apple's CarPlay:

Apple CarPlay

The following screenshot shows Google Auto:

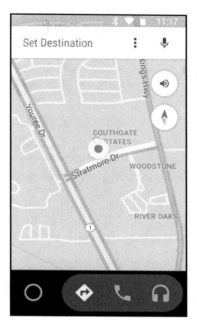

Google Auto

Basic design fundamentals of VUIs

There are a plethora of VUI design principles scattered across the internet and in books. I have aggregated the most common and the most important topics in this section, which are useful when developing VUIs. Before diving into the topics, let's first discuss what VUIs are and why they are important.

What are VUIs and why are they important?

VUIs allow you to interact with machines through conversation. If you have ever used the voice-enabled features of Apple's Siri or Google Assistant, you will be well aware of the capabilities they provide, such as asking about today's weather, getting the directions to nearby restaurants, or asking about last night's football scores for your favorite team.

Why is VUI important? Because user interfaces are moving away from touch-based interfaces and more toward conversational interfaces. According to Dr. Mehl from the University of Arizona, on average, humans speak anywhere between 15,000 and 47,000 words a day—equivalent to reading half a book! (http://bit.ly/29hmvcr) The importance and ubiquity of the spoken word in our daily lives will transform next-generation user interfaces from being touch-based to being VUIs.

Let's look at the advantages of VUIs:

- **Speed**: Processing voice inquiries is 5 to 10 times faster than typing and searching with the browser using search engines such as Google or Yahoo.

- **Intuitive**: Every day, people engage in conversations with other people, and simply asking questions is something that everyone can do without having to learn a new skill.

- **Hands-free**: VUIs can eliminate the need for touchscreens. For example, while driving or cooking, you can interact with an application with your voice.

- **Personal**: The ability to engage with machines through conversation brings a sense of closeness and almost human-like interactions. This can be a good thing when you want to engage users on a more personal level.

Role of NLP in VUIs

In 1950, Alan Turing published his famous paper entitled *Computing Machinery and Intelligence*. The paper proposed a way to test whether machines are artificially intelligent. Turing stated that if a machine could trick a human into thinking that they were talking to another human, then that machine is artificially intelligent. Today, this test is known as the **Turing Test** (https://plato.stanford.edu/entries/turing-test/). In order to pass the Turing Test, machines must understand and speak a human language, and this is known as **Natural Language Processing (NLP)**.

The role of NLP in VUIs is paramount because NLP parses human language so that machines can understand it. In this book, you will be using Node.js, which is, in a sense, a language that machines understand, but Node.js does not understand the human language. This is where NLP comes in, translating spoken language into a language that machines can understand, which in this case is Node.js.

The following is a question and answer, which NLP will be applied to in order to parse it into a language the machine can understand:

```
Question: When is my son's birthday?
Answer: Your son's birth is on January 1st, 1968.
```

The following JSON is the result of parsing the preceding question and answer using NLP:

```
{
    "responseId": "a48eecdd-a9d9-4378-8100-2eeec1d95367",
    "queryResult": {
      "queryText": "When is my son's birthday?",
      "parameters": {
        "family": "son"
      },
      "allRequiredParamsPresent": true,
      "fulfillmentText": "Your son's birth is on January 1st, 1968.",
      "fulfillmentMessages": [{
          "text": {
            "text": [ "Your son's birth is on January 1st, 1968."]
          }
      }],
      "intent": {
        "name": "projects/test-34631/agent/intents/376d04d6-c929-4485-b701-
  b6083948a054",
        "displayName": "birthday"
      },
      "intentDetectionConfidence": 1,
      "diagnosticInfo": { },
      "languageCode": "en"
    }
}
```

Note that Google's NLP platform, Dialogflow, parses the question and sends a JSON request that can be processed in a Node.js middle-tier server, as shown previously. In the preceding JSON request, there is the `intent.displayName` field, which describes the type of question the user asked, and in the Node.js middle-tier server, you can use the intent name to process the request accordingly and respond to the user with the answer.

Furthermore, in the preceding JSON request, there is the `queryResult.parameters[0].family` field, which describes whose birthday the user was asking about. In NLP combined with ML, you can create a template for the question, allowing the machine to learn variations of possible questions that the user might ask. This is useful because there are many ways to ask about someone's birthday. For example, refer to the italicized words, which will create a template matching pattern for the machine to learn:

- Do you know my son's birthday?
- Can you tell me when my son's birthday is?
- Tell me the birthday of my son.

VUI design platforms

VUI design platforms are those that can handle NLP. In this book, you will be introduced to two of the most popular NLP platforms: Google's Dialogflow and **Amazon's Alexa Skills Kit (ASK)**. You will be using Dialogflow to build a chatbot, Google Assistant, Google Home, and Google Auto. Using ASK, you will learn how to build a voice application for Amazon Echo.

Principles of conversation

In this section, you will learn about the fundamentals of conversation, because a good conversation in VUIs can bring a compelling user experience to an application. You will utilize the design principles covered in this section to build a chatbot in Chapter 2, *Building an FAQs Chatbot*, home assistant devices such as Google Home in Chapter 3, *Building a Fortune Cookie Application*, Amazon Echo in Chapter 6, *Building a Cooking Application Using Alexa*, and a voice-enabled application for cars using Google Auto in Chapter 9, *Building a Voice Enabled Podcast for the Car*.

Turn taking

A conversation is all about taking turns when people are speaking to each other. There is one who speaks and there is one who listens, and during each turn, the listener should not interrupt the speaker. Look at a simple conversation with MyApp:

```
Me: Where is the nearest gas station?
MyApp: Here is what I found 1300 Coraopolist Heights Rd
```

Flow

A conversation can contain multiple turns, exchanging words on specific topics in a very short and concise manner. Avoid using one-dimensional script with predefined one-off questions and answers, where the conversation can quickly turn boring and unnatural. A good example of this is the system IVR, where the user has to wait and listen to all of "Press 1 or say `reservation`, Press 2 or say `check reservation`, Press 3 or say `cancel reservation`, Press # or say `main menu`." However, nowadays, the user would simply press `0000000000000`, which typically sends the user to the operator. To give it a more conversational flow, you should try to anticipate the user's intention and engage with the user.

The following example shows the flow of conversation:

```
support: How can I help you today?
user: I need cancel my reservation.
support: Would you like to speak to the operator or would you like to do it
over the phone?
user: phone
support: Do you have the reservation number?
user: no
support: Then i can look it up by your name and date of the reservation.
What is your name and reservation date?
```

Having the conversation flow makes the user feel like they are having a conversation with a real person whereas in the IVR system the user did not engage with the user but presented all of the options, including options the user did not care about.

Context

In order to create an effective conversation flow, you will need to have contextual knowledge. A context starts with simply asking about the weather. Then, I ask MyApp if I can go snowboarding. MyApp wishes that it would snow so that I could go snowboarding today. MyApp understood the context of my question—that I want to go snowboarding—and responded in a thoughtful way. As we begin to design VUIs, it will be critical to capture the context of the conversation in order to properly process the user's intent and deliver a correct and appropriate answer:

```
Me: What's weather like today?
MyApp: Cloudy with a chance of snow!
Me: Do you think I will be able to go snowboarding today?
MyApp: I hope it snows!
```

Verbal confirmation

It is important to let the user know that you have understood their question during the conversation. In the following conversation, note how MyApp responds with *Let's see* and *Here you go* before giving the answers to my questions to let me know that MyApp understood my questions:

```
Me: What time is it?
MyApp: Let's see. It is 3:14 PM.
Me: Do I have any appointment?
MyApp: Here you go. You have one at 5:00 PM.
```

How about when you are about to process business critical functions, such as ordering candy online? In the following conversation, I begin by ordering candy. Then, MyApp confirms my order by asking whether or not I really want to place an order. Upon saying Yes, MyApp lets me know that my order has been placed. This kind of confirmation reassures the user that their intent has been processed by the system. However, there is a downside to using this kind of confirmation because, if overused, the conversation can become repetitive and annoying to the user. In order to avoid this, we provide a confirmation response based on confidence. Confidence is used in ML in such a way that for every voice that is recognized, the matching algorithm gives a confidence level of how accurate the match is. In the case of the following example, MyApp has a confidence level of 90% that what I asked is about buying 10 candy in order to skip the question that asks whether I really want to buy the candy, and simply responds with a confirmation that my order has been placed. If the confidence level is below the threshold of 90%, MyApp can ask the confirmation question about whether I want to buy 10 candies and request further confirmation:

```
Me: I would like to order 10 M&M candies.
MyApp: Would you like to buy 10 M&M for $10?
Me: Yes
MyApp: Order has been processed.
```

Visual confirmation

Sometimes, verbal confirmation will not suffice, and we require visual confirmation to be presented to the user. For example, when asking Google for the nearest gas station, Google will not say out loud the exact address of the gas station, because it would not make sense at all. Instead, you will see that Google provides a clickable visual card and the address opens on Google Maps.

The following screenshot shows the visual card confirmation:

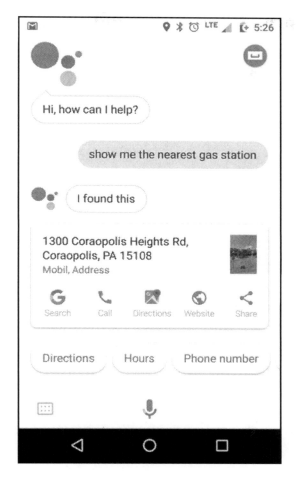

Visual response showing Google Maps

Error handling

When the errors occur in a voice application, the errors must be handled properly and the application must resume where it left off. Let's look at different types of errors in VUIs one at a time. First, imagine that you are talking to your friend and suddenly your friend stops talking in the middle of a sentence. Do you say nothing and wait for hours for your friend to talk and reengage in the conversation? Most likely, you would ask your friend if they are OK and try to reengage them in the conversation. The same is true for VUIs. If no response is provided in a given time frame, the voice application will need to recover and will try to reengage with the user. What if the voice application cannot understand the user's intent? In this case, the application would need to re-ask the question and ensure it doesn't blame the user in any way for any kind of error. Lastly, the user might continuously make the same mistakes in an attempt to provide information. In such cases, every new attempt to get the correct information from the user, the application needs to provide more detailed instruction as to how in hopes that the user can provide the correct intent.

Session awareness

Every time the user engages VUIs, there is specific data the application needs to remember. A good example of this would be the name of the user so that the application addresses the user by their first name. Another good example is the cooking voice application that you will build in Chapter 6, *Building a Cooking Application Using Alexa*. When a user is making use of cooking app, there are times when the application asks the user to saute the chopped onions till brown. Five minutes later, the user might come back and ask for the next step. The cooking application needs to be smart enough to understand that each step can take minutes to carry out and that the user's session must be maintained in order to correctly interact with the user.

Providing help

The VUIs do not have any visual representation, thus the user might not know what to do and ask for help. The application needs to visually and/or verbally provide help. When providing help, it's a good idea to use examples such as the following one, where, in order to see the photos on the phone, you have to say, Show my photos from last weekend.

The following screenshot shows an example of providing help for the user:

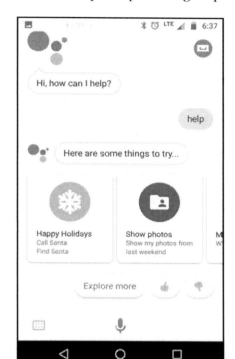

Providing help

Response time

When designing VUIs, the response time is a very important factor. A slow response time can jeopardize the user experience and the quality of the application. Note that here is a set limitation for Alexa and Google on how long the response time should be. For Alexa, the response must be received within 8 seconds, and for Google, the response must be received within 5 seconds. If the response from the backend server does not arrive within the given limit, Alexa and Google will send an exception back to the server. Consider factors that can affect responding to the user's intent, as follows:

- Slow internet speed, which can cause delays for the users in terms of sending their verbal intent and receiving the response from the server

- Slow backend server and database can cause slow latency issues when sending the instruction back to the application which in turn delays the responds sent to the users

Empathy

When creating VUIs, you want to make the user feel as though they are talking to a real person. This develops empathy by making a connection with the user. First, empathy can be achieved by allowing the user to choose the voice they want to use. For example, in Google Assistant, the user can choose either a male or female voice by navigating to **Settings** | **Preferences** | **Assistant voice**, shown as follows:

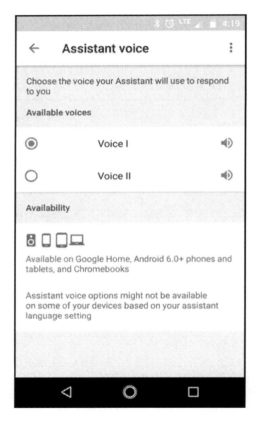

Changing Google Assistant's voice

A second way is to programmatically control the voice using **Speech Synthesis Markup Language (SSML)**, `https://www.w3.org/TR/speech-synthesis/`, which has been developed to generate synthetic voices for websites and other applications. With SSML, the response to the user can be controlled. Both Amazon Alexa and Google Dialogflow platforms support the use of SSML. Here are the most commonly used SSML tags and their usages in brief:

- `<break time="0.2s" />`: Introduces a short pause between sentences.
- `<emphasis level="strong">Come here now!</emphasis>`: Create speech that increases in volume and slows down, or decreases in volume and speeds up.
- `<prosody pitch="medium" rate="slow">great!!</prosody>`: Used to customize the pitch, speech rate, and volume.
- `<p> Some paragraph goes here </p>`: Similar to adding a long break between paragraphs.
- `<s> Some sentence goes here </s>`: The equivalent of putting a period at the end to denote the end of the sentence in order to give a short pause.
- `<say-as interpret-as="cardinal">123</say-as>`: Indicates the type of text. For example, the cardinal number `123` will be read as one hundred and twenty three. As for the ordinal number `123`, it will be read as first, second, and third.

 Both Amazon Alexa and Google Dialogflow support limited sets of SSML tags. Ensure that you check the SSML references for Amazon Alexa at `http://amzn.to/2BGLt4M` and Google Dialogflow at `http://bit.ly/2BHBQmq`. You will learn more in greater detail in `Chapter 2`, *Building an FAQs Chatbot*.

Using SSML, let's create a speech that shows some excitement. You would not want the voice to be monotonous and boring. For example, sometimes you might want to show excitement, and to create such excitement, you can use prosody with a high pitch and slow rate, shown as follows. Also, when you emphasize the word *love*, you will be able to convey a sense of happiness. You can copy and paste the following SSML code at the *Watson Text to Speech* service interface, found at `http://bit.ly/2AlAc9d`. Enter the SSML and the voice will be played back:

```
<speak>
  <p>
    <s>
      OK <prosody pitch="medium" rate="slow">great!!</prosody>
    </s>
  </p>
  <break time="0.2s" />
```

```
<p>
  <s>
    I <emphasis level="strong">love</emphasis> to see you tomorrow!
  </s>
</p>
</speak>
```

 In order to test the SSML using `http://bit.ly/2AlAc9d`, it is best to use either the Firefox or Chrome browser.

Voice-enabled applications

This section discusses the voice-enabled devices that are available today. These include home assistant devices such as the Amazon Echo, and Google Home, which can integrate with other voice-activated home appliances such as lights, garages, thermostats, televisions, stereo systems, and more. Finally, this section will also cover voice-enabled virtual car assistants.

Home assistant devices

These home assistant devices are literally invading homes today. Home assistant devices such as Amazon Echo and Google Home can control security cameras, the dishwasher, dryers, lights, power outlets, switches, door locks, and thermostats. For example, Amazon Echo and Google Home can turn lights on and off, control air conditioning and heating, and open and close garage doors.

There are three assistant devices from Amazon—Echo Plus (`http://amzn.to/2CBLfeu`), Echo (`http://amzn.to/2CcIFey`), and Echo Dot (`http://amzn.to/2yVB5mA`)—shown as follows. All three Amazon Echos have features such as set alarm, play music, search online, call Uber, order pizza, and integrate with other home assistant devices, such as WeMo, TP-Link, Sony, Insteon, ecobee, and others.

The only difference between Amazon Echo and Echo Plus is that Amazon Echo Plus has a built-in home assistant hub that allows the other home assistant devices to connect directly to Echo Plus without needing a hub. For Amazon Echo and Echo Dot, you would need to purchase a hub, such as Samsung's SmartThings Smart Home Hub ($73.49, `http://amzn.to/2oHkiDV`), in order to control other home assistant appliances.

The following photo shows a Smart Home device controlling home appliances:

Smart Home Hub

In the Amazon Echo family, there are two devices that come with a screen, which can be used to display pictures, a clock, and play videos: Amazon Echo Show ($149.00, `http://amzn.to/2sJVoRF`) and Spot ($129.00, `http://amzn.to/2jxEfeR`). Similarly, many of the home assistant devices that integrate with Amazon Echo can also be integrated and controlled through Google Home ($79.00, `http://bit.ly/2eYZq4D`), shown as follows. Many of these devices can be found on the Google support page at `http://bit.ly/2yV3NnA`.

Google Home is shown here:

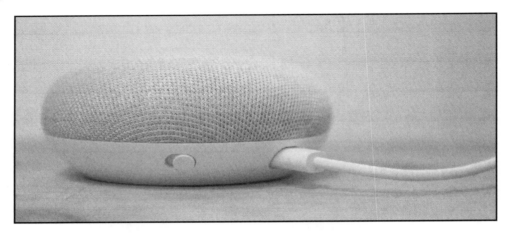

Google Home

Automobile virtual assistant devices

Nowadays, almost every car's dashboard comes with a voice recognition system, which enables drivers to control music volumes, change radio stations, add Bluetooth devices, turn inside lights on and off, and more. Since Microsoft Sync introduced the VUI in Ford cars in 2007, there has not been much technological advancement. In 2007, Microsoft Sync was ahead of the times, introducing the first of its kind voice-enabled features in cars, but designing VUIs for Ford had some challenges. First, there was the noise factor while driving at high speed, which hindered the driver's voice from being recognized. Second, being able to upgrade required bringing the car in to a dealer. Third, the car operating system was usually proprietary, hence it was difficult to write programs to introduce new features or enhance existing features.

In 2017, many challenges faced by Microsoft Sync were eliminated. Many cars had more soundproof bodies, which eliminated many of the road noises. Tesla has shown us that, with the right design, a car's system software can be upgraded via Wi-Fi, and many manufacturers have begun to allow car systems to be remotely upgraded. In 2018, many manufacturers began to integrate Google Auto and Apple CarPlay by taking advantage of the Android and iOS operating systems, which have proven track records in the mobile space. Also, car manufacturers taking advantage of Android and iOS brings entire ecosystems of developers together, who can bring innovation by developing voice-enabled applications for cars. For example, there is a project on GitHub (`http://bit.ly/2D83MjI`) that integrates the Tesla API into Google Home and into mobile devices via Google Assistant, which allows you to check the battery charge level, door status, flash the lights, and honk the horn. Just as developers have brought innovations through applications in the Android and iOS marketplaces, you will see a huge surge in voice-enabled applications in the Google Auto and Apple CarPlay marketplaces. Besides car manufacturers, in 2018, you will begin to see many car stereo manufacturers, such as Pioneer, Alpine, JVC, Kenwood, Sony, and others, begin to support Google Auto as well.

Chatbots

Chatbots have been around for a long time, since the days of **internet relay chat (IRC)**, the popular chat room. Back then, chatbots were used by the chatroom owner to send commands to kick users out, ban users, promote products, provide news news updates, and add more chat room members. However, now, with NLP, chatbots are more than just text-based and are becoming very popular with companies for promoting their products and providing support for them and **frequently asked questions (FAQs)**.

The following screenshot shows a chatbot by Patrón on Twitter:

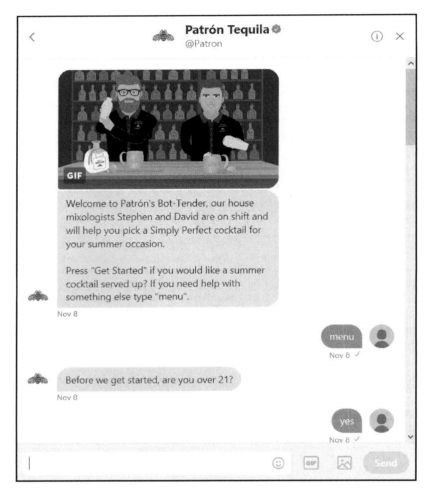

Patrón Twitter chatbot

Converting existing text-based chat into voice-enabled chat is simple because text-based chats are designed to answer the user's questions. In Chapter 2, *Building an FAQs Chatbot*, the chatbot will be used to demonstrate the basic functionalities of the NLP platform, and you will learn how to create a chatbot's VUIs. The chat you will create in Chapter 2, *Building an FAQs Chatbot*, can be used on mobile through Google Assistant or integrated into an existing mobile application.

Future of VUIs

VUIs are more than a technological advancement in the voice technology era. VUIs are the next **Internet of Things (IoT)**, ready to skyrocket into a untapped market for the software developers. Amazon Echo and Google Home interconnect home appliances, play music using Spotify, play podcasts of radio stations, stream Netflix movies on demand with a voice command, send messages to friends and family without the use of mobile phones, start a hot shower during the winter, brew a pot of coffee, ask a Samsung refrigerator what needs to be restocked, ask the home air conditioning system to set the heater to 74 degrees in 20 minutes after coming home from a long vacation, and more. The sky's the limit!

Currently, in Amazon Alexa, there are 15,000 voice applications, and Google Home has around 1,000. Many of these voice applications are not even in production yet; you will see a boom in voice applications in the coming year 2019. Many of the big players, such as Twitter, Facebook, Airbnb, and Snapchat have not released any voice applications yet. Look at Logitech releasing the automobile voice interfaces (`http://engt.co/2khYV5z`) for Ford, Volkswagen, and Volvo. Watch the Samsung and LG refrigerators utilizing VUIs closely (`http://on.mash.to/2B4Oj2i`). Take a look at Google Pixel Buds (`http://bit.ly/2kSP7Uo`), which can translate Spanish to English. Imagine a Spanish speaker talking to an English speaker while both wearing Google Pixel Buds; they would be able to communicate with each other. What will companies who create dating applications such as Tinder, Match, OkCupid, and POF bring to the world of voice? What about the educational sector? How about the transportation sector? How about voice-enabled gaming? How about voice-enabled ticketing systems for movie theaters? The possibilities are endless. I hope this book will help fuel your imagination and allow you to catch the wave of the voice era!

Summary

In this chapter, you learned about the history and basic fundamentals of VUIs, and about the importance and role of natural language processing in creating VUIs. You also learned best practices, design principles, and the user experience design principals involved in creating compelling VUIs. Then, you learned about various devices, such as Amazon Echo, Google Home, and Auto, where you can deploy your voice-enabled applications. Finally, you should now understand the future of VUIs and where they are heading.

In the next chapter, you will learn how to build you first voice-enabled application, a chatbot, utilizing the Dialogflow NLP platform from Google.

Building an FAQs Chatbot

2

This chapter introduces Dialogflow, which is the cornerstone of creating voice-enabled applications. In order to demonstrate Dialogflow's functionalities, you will learn how to build a voice-enabled **Frequently Asked Questions (FAQs)** chatbot. Dialogflow is a platform that processes the natural language spoken by a user and then converts it into intents so that a programming language, such as Node.js, Java, or C#, can understand it. In order to build voice-enabled applications for Google Home, Google Assistant, and Google Auto, Dialogflow will be used exclusively. In a similar way, later in this chapter, you will learn about Amazon's natural language processing platform, **Alexa Skills Kit (ASK)**, in order to build a voice application for Amazon Echo products.

You will first learn how to set up a project in Dialogflow, then be familiarized with Dialogflow's development environment, and will create an agent in Dialogflow. Then, you will learn how to program the FAQs chatbot's conversations using Dialogflow's intents, entities, context, and actions. This chapter will also teach you how to debug and test the chatbot's conversational flow in Dialogflow. Once the voice-enabled FAQs chatbot's conversations have been created using Dialogflow, the chatbot will be deployed to Google Assistant on Android and iOS. Finally, while testing the FAQs chatbot, developers will learn how to update a machine learning algorithm in Dialogflow, thereby improving the FAQs chatbot's ability to understand conversations.

This chapter will cover the following topics:

- Introduction to Dialogflow
- Dialogflow development setup
- Dialogflow intents, entities, context, and actions
- Programming and debugging in Dialogflow
- Google Assistant on Android and iOS
- Machine learning and natural language processing in Dialogflow

Why an FAQs chatbot?

FAQs are typically text-based, with questions and their answers. The questions most frequently posed to companies by their customers are usually posted, along with the company's answers, on the company website or mobile application, in the help page section, for other customers to be able to search through them. Sometimes, the company provides a search function on the website, allowing customers to type in keywords related to their questions, which displays the answers as search results. However, none of the preceding methods can compete with the speed and efficiency voice-enabled FAQs can provide. For example, take a look at a typical FAQs section in the GEICO insurance mobile application, which is shown in the following screenshot. There are 11 categories, and there are between 2 to 12 questions per category. It would take a long time for customers to seek out the answers to their questions, and they would probably end up calling the customer service department.

The following screenshot shows a number of question categories in GEICO's **FAQs**, which the user would have to search through, like finding a needle in a haystack:

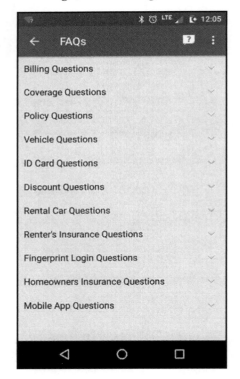

GEICO FAQs in the mobile application

When customers are self-served, fewer customers call customer service phone lines and fewer resources are needed in terms of customer service representatives, ultimately saving companies money. This is why FAQs have been around for a long time, and now, being able to add voice-enabled FAQs means that customers can actually have a conversation with an FAQs chatbot as if they are actually talking to a customer service representative on the phone. Also, talking to a chatbot is easier than typing in keywords or browsing and reading through questions.

The following screenshot shows the recently added voice-enabled chatbot in the GEICO mobile application, which is designed to make customers' lives easier:

GEICO's voice-enabled FAQs chatbot

Introduction to Dialogflow

Here's a brief history of Dialogflow. In 2012, Speaktoit received venture capital to create a platform for building natural language user interfaces. In 2014, Speaktoit released Api.ai, allowing developers to build voice user interfaces for Android, iOS, HTML5, and Cordova (https://en.wikipedia.org/wiki/Dialogflow). In 2016, Google acquired Api.ai and in 2017, Api.ai was rebranded to Dialogflow. Since then, Dialogflow has continued to add new features at lightning speed in order to compete with the counterpart technology of Amazon's Alexa. Dialogflow's strength lies in its ability to perform natural language processing through the use of machine learning and artificial intelligence, the core engine behind creating voice user interfaces. As a developer, you will never have to worry about the complexity of natural language processing, machine learning, or artificial intelligence aspects, because that is what Dialogflow handles behind the scenes, allowing you as a developer to focus on creating the voice user interfaces for your applications. Going forward, all Google voice applications (Google Assistant, Google Home, and Google Auto) covered in this book will use Dialogflow as the backbone engine for creating voice user interfaces.

Setting up a Dialogflow account

The following points describe the steps to create and set up a Dialogflow account:

1. Before creating voice user interfaces for the FAQs application, you will need to create a Dialogflow account. Go to https://accounts.google.com/SignUp and create a Google account. If you already have one, you can use that.

2. After creating a Google account, go to https://dialogflow.com and sign in using the Google account that you created. During this process, you will link the Google account to Dialogflow.

3. Once the Dialogflow account has been created and linked to the Google account, go to https://myaccount.google.com/activitycontrols and enable **Voice & Audio Activity**.

The following screenshot shows enabled **Voice & Audio Activity**, which will allow you to later test and debug the FAQs application using your voice:

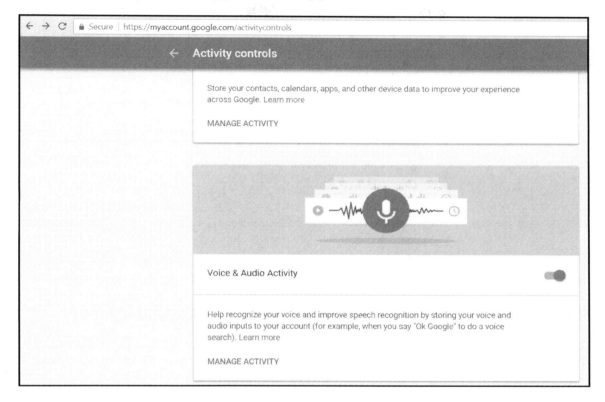

Enabling voice and audio activity

Creating your first agent

Now, you are ready to create the FAQs chatbot. Let's navigate back to Dialogflow. Then, log into Dialogflow and create an agent called `FaqChatBot`. Ensure that you enable **API VERSION** to **Dialogflow V2 API**.

The following screenshot shows the Dialogflow development interface, where you can start creating an agent:

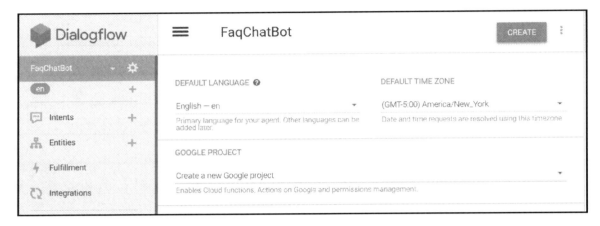

Creating a Dialogflow agent

You can think of a Dialogflow agent as a voice translator that receives the user's voice from a device such as a mobile phone or Google Home, and then applies natural language processing to it, converting the user's voice into JSON format so that the user's request can be processed by the backend application server. Then, the backend application server will respond to the Dialogflow agent in JSON format, containing an instruction as to how to respond to the user. Upon receiving the message, the Dialogflow agent will send it back to the device along with the instructions of what to say to the user, and the device will speak to the user with the response.

The following chart shows the process flow of a Dialogflow agent:

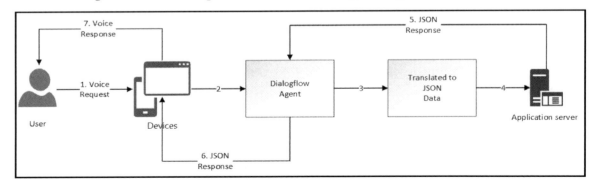

Dialogflow agent process flow

Once the `FaqChatBot` agent has been created, we can take a look at the agent's settings. First, in the **General** settings, take a note of the **API KEYS** section; you will need the client access token and developer access token later, in `Chapter 4`, *Hosting, Securing, and Testing Fortune Cookie in the Cloud*, to programmatically access the Dialogflow agent using the Dialogflow SDK.

The following screenshot shows the `FaqChatBot` agent settings:

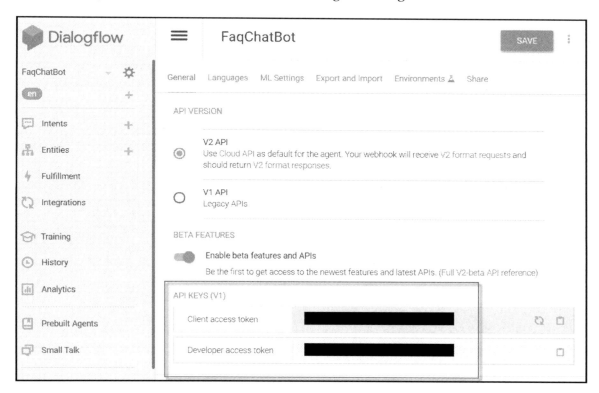

FaqChatBot agent settings-general

The following are the different sections of an `FaqChatBot` agent:

- **Languages**: In the **Languages** section, you can add multiple languages that the `FaqChatBot` can understand and translate and, for the purpose of this book, we will be using English.

- **ML Settings**: If you look at the **ML Settings** tab, you will notice the **ML CLASSIFICATION THRESHOLD** setting. The **ML CLASSIFICATION THRESHOLD** can be set between 0 and 1, and the default value is set at 0.3. You can think of the ML classification threshold as how confident the FaqChatBot agent is that the agent understood what the user just said. If the agent understood the user request, it will know how to respond; if not, it will tell the user that it did not understand what they said. You will learn more about the **ML CLASSIFICATION THRESHOLD** in the *What are Intents?* section of this chapter.

- **Export and Import**: In this section, the FaqChatBot can be backed up into the .zip file, restored from the .zip file by replacing the old version of the FaqChatBot agent, and can be imported from the .zip file, whereby the old one will be completely removed and restored from the .zip file.

- **Share**: In the **Share** section, you can give permissions to other developers of the FaqChatBot. This is useful if you have many developers working on a very large project in order to divide the work.

The following screenshot shows the **Export and Import** section of the FaqChatBot agent:

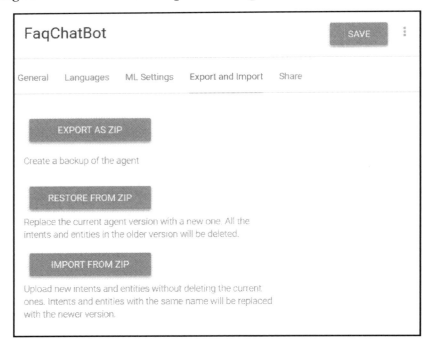

FaqChatBot agent settings - export and import

The following screenshot shows the **Share** section of the `FaqChatBot` agent:

FaqChatBot agent settings - share

About an FAQs chatbot

For the FAQs chatbot, I will choose the Presidents of the USA as a topic. I will gather various fun facts about U.S. Presidents from `https://millercenter.org/president` and turn them into questions and answers that the user can ask the FAQs chatbot. Later, in the following section where you create your first intent, you will learn how to build templates to generalize user questions for the FAQs in order to create intents.

The following are sample facts about the first U.S. President, George Washington:

```
{
    "fullName": "George Washington",
    "birthDate": "February 22, 1732",
    "dateDate": "December 14, 1799",
    "birthPlace": "Pope's Creek, Virginia",
    "education": "The equivalent of an elementary school education",
    "religion": "Episcopalian",
    "career": "Soldier, Planter",
    "politicalParty": "Federalist",
    "nickName": "Father of His Country"
    "marriage": "January 6, 1759, to Martha Dandridge Custis (1731-
        1802)"
    "children": "None",
    "inaugurationDate": "April 30, 1789",
    "dateEnded": "March 4, 1797",
    "presidentNumber": "1",
    "burialPlace": "Family vault, Mount Vernon, Virginia"
}
```

What are intents?

Dialogflow is a platform with complicated machine learning and artificial intelligence capabilities that matches what the user said to the **intent**. You can think of intents as questions that users will be asking about U.S. Presidents. When you first start with the FaqChatBot agent in Dialogflow, you will see two default intents: the **Welcome Intent** and the **Fallback Intent**, as shown in the following flowchart. The **Welcome Intent** gets triggered when the user first starts to interact with the FaqChatBot. Then, the user will start to ask questions and those questions will be matched against the intents, and if no matching intents are found then the **Fallback Intent** will be triggered and the FaqChatBot will respond with, **I didn't get that. Can you say it again?**.

The following flowchart shows the process flow of how intents are processed in Dialogflow:

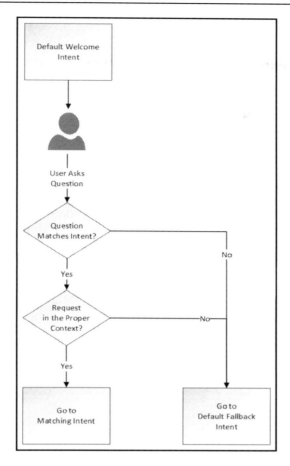

Intent process flow

The following screenshot shows the default intents that are created by Dialogflow:

Default intents

ML classification sets the level of confidence of the matching algorithm identifying the user voice input to the intents. For example, if the user asks the `FaqChatBot` agent, `Who is the first president of the United States?`, the agent will attempt to match the voice against any defined intents in the system. When Dialogflow matches the voice against the existing intent in the system, a confidence threshold of 30% will be used. If the confidence level is above 30%, the `FaqChatBot` agent will process the user's request using the matched intent, however, if the confidence level is below 30%, the agent will reroute the request to the **Default Fallback Intent**, where all unidentifiable requests are processed. Another way to look at this is when your friend asks you a question over the phone and you cannot hear well, so you cannot understand what your friend said. But, sometimes, based on a partial understanding of the voice coming through the phone, you can predict or guess what your friend said. If you want to increase the accuracy of the matching algorithm, you can increase the default value from `0.3` to a much higher value in the agent settings. But for the purpose of this book, we will keep this set as the default.

The following screenshot shows the `FaqChatBot` app's **ML Settings**:

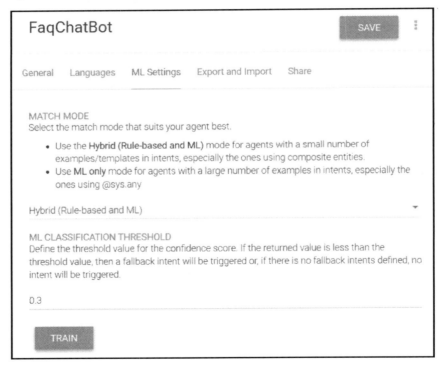

FaqChatBot agent settings - ML settings

Creating your first intent

Let's create our first FAQ question in this section: `who is the first president of USA?`. Click on **Intents (+)** and name it `First-President`. **Enter** `Who is the first president of USA?` into the **User says** box, and enter `The first president of USA is George Washington` into the text response box.

The following screenshot shows the `First-President` intent that was created in Dialogflow:

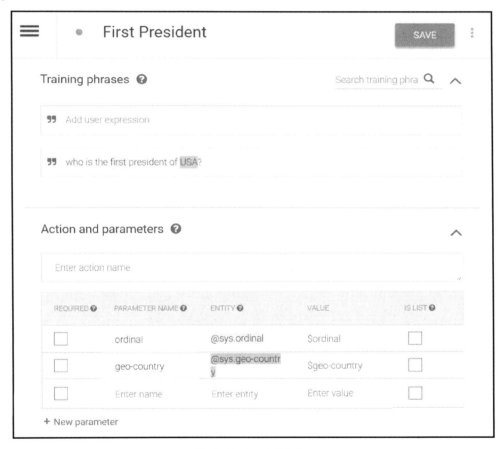

First President intent in Dialogflow

First, notice that when you enter Who is the first president of USA? into the **User says** input box, the words first and USA are highlighted in yellow and orange, respectively. Dialogflow automatically identifies the word first as the type ordinal (@sys.ordinal) and the word USA as the type geo-country (@sys.geo-country) and basically creates a templatized question. The FaqChatBot agent will use those parameters to match against the user's question. You can think of the parameters as the keywords that you will be using to search with Google's search engine and the search engine returning a result relevant to the search terms. In the case of FaqChatBot, the agent will match the intent First-President to the user's inquiry and respond to the user with the text you entered in the **Text response** box.

The following screenshot shows debugging in the virtual Google Assistant in Dialogflow:

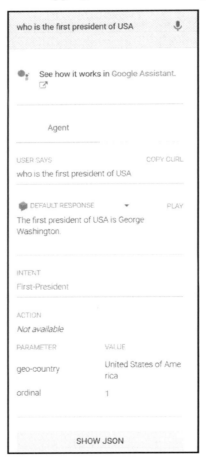

Dialogflow Virtual Google Assistant

When you type who is the first president of USA?, it shows the matching intent name First-President, and two parameters, geo-country as United States of America and ordinal 1, which are used to match the intent. It also shows the answer to the intent that you previously entered in the **Default Response** and you can play the voice output by clicking on the **PLAY** button. All this metadata about the found intent is converted into JSON, which the backend server can use. You will learn more about this in Chapter 3, *Building a Fortune Cookie Application*. When you click on the **SHOW JSON** button, you will see the request data in the JSON format.

Important properties that are useful to observe in the given JSON are queryResult.parameters.geo-country and queryResult.parameters.ordinal, which contain extracted values that map to the entities automatically defined by Dialogflow. Also, queryResult.intent.displayName contains the matching intent name. With this information, the backend server will be able to properly process the user requests. We will cover this in Chapter 3, *Building a Fortune Cookie Application*.

The following code shows the request data in JSON:

```
{
  "responseId": "0c50fd61-dd7e-4c91-a11a-eaebdaa1a412",
  "queryResult": {
    "queryText": "who is the first president of USA?",
    "parameters": {
      "geo-country": "United States of America",
      "ordinal": 1
    },
    "allRequiredParamsPresent": true,
    "fulfillmentText": "The first president of USA is George Washington.",
    "fulfillmentMessages": [
      {
        "text": {
          "text": [
            "The first president of USA is George Washington."
          ]
        }
      }
    ],
    "intent": {
      "name":
"projects/faqchatbot-9417a/agent/intents/40991159-4a3e-4cfe-95ac-9be610220f
51",
      "displayName": "First President"
    },
    "intentDetectionConfidence": 0.75,
    "diagnosticInfo": {},
    "languageCode": "en"
```

```
        }
    }
```

Lastly, if you enter `who is the second president of USA?`, you will notice that you get the exact same response, except the ordinal will be 2 and the response you get is George Washington as the second president, which is not the correct answer. In the next section, you will learn how to utilize entities to address this problem.

What are entities?

Entities are like keywords that are used to extract values from voice input. As seen in the previous section, *Creating your first intent*, the intent used the Dialogflow system entities `@sys.ordinal` and `@sys.geo-county` to extract the values 1 and USA from the voice input. The entities also help to create templatized questions so that you do not have to enter multiple variations of questions that result in the same answer. Similarly, Dialogflow's natural language processing engine uses entities to train data to become smarter at matching voice input to intents.

Using entities

In the `First-President` intent, you noticed that the intent had a problem answering the question `who is the second president of USA?` because the response was static, only replying with the first president, George Washington, and not the second president, John Adams, regardless of which ordinal positions were given by the user. Let's address this issue by dynamically creating the response using an entity:

1. Let's start by creating an entity called `president-number`. In the first column, add the presidents' names, and in the second column, add the ordinals that match the president. The following screenshot shows the `president-number` entity:

Creating a president-number entity

2. Now, create a new intent called `Find President`. Enter `who is the first president of USA?` in the **User says** textbox and then highlight the words `first president` and you will see that a drop-down pops out, where you can search and select the entity that you created, called `president-number`. The following screenshot shows the process of mapping the entity to the highlighted word:

Mapping an entity to a word

By accessing the entity value within the response, you have the ability to create a dynamic response that can map the ordinal value to the president's name. `$president-number.original` refers to the user's ordinal input, `first president`, and `$president-number` refers to the ordinal value mapped to the name George Washington in the president-name entity. The response `The $president-number.original of $geo-country is $president-number` creates a proper answer to the user's question about who was the first or second President of the USA. When you test this in Google Assistant in Dialogflow, you will see that the proper response gets returned: **The second president of USA is John Adams**.

3. Now, create a second question that does not have a geo-country, USA: `Who is first president?`, and create an equivalent response `The $president-number.original is $president-number.` The `FaqChatBot` agent will be smart enough to figure out that if the geo-country is omitted in the question, the agent will use the response that does not have `$geo-country`. The following screenshot shows the completed **Find President** intent:

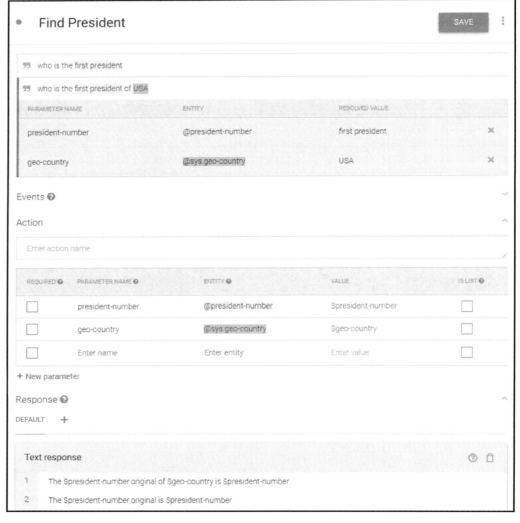

Find President intent

Using JSON to create entities

In the previous section, only two presidents were added to the `president-number` entity. For the `FaqChatBot`, you would need to add 45 entries, and adding one by one using the Dialogflow graphical user interface would be time consuming. Dialogflow provides an easier mechanism, where JSON content can be copied and pasted into the textbox. In the `president-number` intent, change from editor mode to raw mode.

The following screenshot shows editor mode in the entity editor:

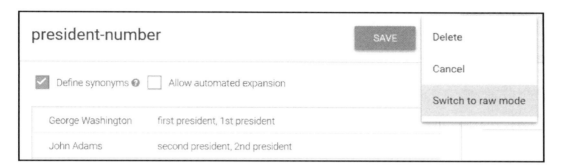

Editor mode in the entity editor

The following screenshot shows raw mode in the entity editor:

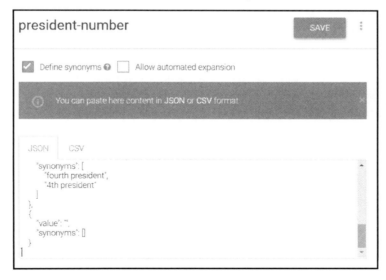

Raw mode in entity editor

Once in raw mode, copy and paste the JSON, similar to the following format. I have not included a JSON that contains 45 entries, but you can find a JSON that contains all 45 President entries on my GitHub.

The following code shows the JSON data of the `president-number` entity:

```
[
    {
        "value": "George Washington",
        "synonyms": ["first president","1st president"]
    },
    {
        "value": "John Adams",
        "synonyms": ["second president","2nd president"]
    },
    {
        "value": "Thomas Jefferson",
        "synonyms": ["third president","3rd president"]
    },
    {
        "value": "James Madison",
        "synonyms": ["fourth president","4th president"]
    }
]
```

About action

Action in Dialogflow is a rather simple concept. In the previous section, you created an intent using the template `who is the first president?`. Action in the `FaqChatbot` agent is responsible for extracting parameters such as `@president-number` and `@sys.geo-country` from the intent. Typically, you do not have to define the name of the action, as Dialogflow will automatically add the action name, but you can also give the action name manually, `president_number`, as shown:

The following screenshot shows the action:

Action

In the next section, you will learn how to create a context using an action. Using context, the action can extract values, not only from the current intent, but also from external intents, allowing current intents to access parameters from other intents.

What is context?

Context is like a session, where previous session information is maintained so that the next context can have access to that session information. For example, upon meeting a stranger in a bar, you initiate a conversation, asking the name of the person you are speaking with. From that point on, you know his or her name and you might use his or her name during the conversation. Another example is during a conversation, where you are asked the ambiguous question, "When is his birthday?" by a friend, but you do not know who "he" refers to, in which case, you might ask your friend who he or she is referring to. When your friend explains that they are asking about John Doe's birthday, you have successfully established the context that "he" refers to John Doe.

In Dialogflow, contexts can also be used to establish and control conversational flow, allowing only a specific intent to be triggered if specific contextual requirements are met. For example, during the checkout process in an e-commerce store, you only allow the user to buy an item if all the necessary requirements are gathered, such as credit card information and a shipping address.

Creating your first context

In this section, you will learn how to incorporate contexts into intents.

The following flowchart shows the conversational flow that you will learn to build for `FaqChatBot`, which is asking about the Presidents' birthdays:

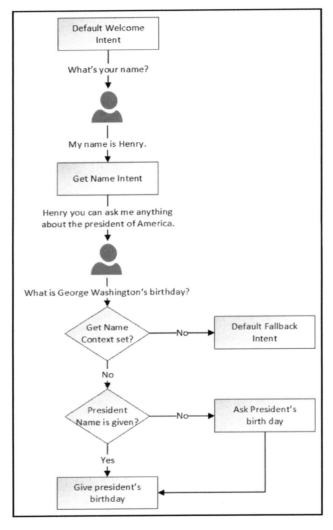

President Birthday Context flow diagram

1. In `FaqChatBot`, you will find the list of intents created by Dialogflow: **Default Fallback Intent** and **Default Welcome Intent**. The following screenshot shows the default welcome and fallback intents:

Default welcome and fallback intents

2. The **Default Welcome Intent** is triggered the very first time the user uses `FaqChatBot`. Modify the **Default Welcome Intent** by changing the text response to `Hi! Welcome to FAQ Chatbot. What is your name?` so that the user will be greeted and asked what his or her name is. The following screenshot shows the modified **Default Welcome Intent** text response:

Modified default welcome intent text response

3. Create **Get Name** and, in the **Contexts** section, type in GET_NAME in the **Add output context** textbox. GET_NAME can now be used as the input context in other intents, allowing other intents to access all the parameters captured by the **Get Name** intent.

4. From the @sys.given-name:username template or my name is @sys.given-name:username, the intent will extract the username @sys.given-name:username and store it in the $username variable.

5. Create a personalized text response using the user's name stored in the $username variable, $username you can ask me anything about the president of America. The following image shows the **Get Name** intent, which gets triggered when the user responds with his or her name:

Get name intent context and user says

The following screenshot shows the username variable, which contains the captured username found in the **Action** section of the **Get Name** intent:

REQUIRED	PARAMETER NAME	ENTITY	VALUE
☐	username	@sys.given-name	$username
☐	Enter name	Enter entity	Enter value

Action

Enter action name

\+ New parameter

Response

DEFAULT \+

Text response

1 $username you can ask me anything about the president of America

2 Enter a text response variant

ADD MESSAGE CONTENT

Get name intent action and response

Notice that there is a number 5 next to the GET_NAME context. This number defines the lifespan of the context. The number **5** means that the context will be available for the next 5 requests or for the next 10 minutes after the time context is activated. You can simply increase the lifespan number by editing the number to something greater. This will all depend on the use cases for the context.

6. Before we can start creating the intent that can use the GET_NAME context, let's create a new entity for the Presidents' birthdays, called president-birthday, using JSON.

The following code shows the president-birthday entity:

```
[
    {
        "value": "December 14, 1799",
        "synonyms": [ "George Washington" ]
    },
    {
        "value": "October 30, 1735",
        "synonyms": [ "John Adams" ]
    }
]
```

7. Once the president-birthday entity has been created, you can create the **Get President Birthday** intent, as shown in the following screenshot. Notice that, in the **Contexts** section, there is the GET_NAME context as the input context, which comes from the output context of the **Get Name** intent. By adding the GET_NAME context as the input, the **Get President Birthday** intent has access to all the parameters in the Get_Name intent.

8. In the **Action** section, you can add the parameter called username, which maps to the parameter from the **Get Name** intent, #GET_NAME.username.

The following screenshot shows the get **President Birthday** intent, which shows the username variable mapping to #GET_NAME.username:

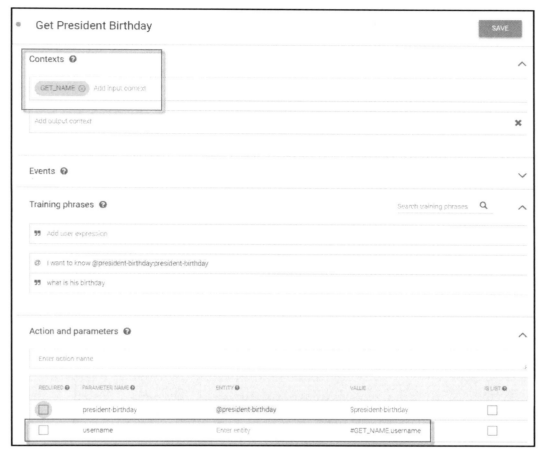

Get President Birthday intent

9. You can create the text response using the $username variable, making the response more personable by using $username $president-birthday.original's birthday is on $president-birthday.

Contexts are a very powerful way to persist data across requests, but they come with drawbacks. First, if the intent contains the context, the intent will only get triggered if the request contains the required context and what the user says matches the intent template. For example, in the case of the **Get President Birthday** intent, the request must contain the GET_NAME context, and what the user says must also match the what is his birthday? or I want to know @president-birthday:president-birthday template. Lastly, the context lifespan can be limited to 10 minutes or the context can only be available through *n* number of requests. But an expiring context is not really ideal in a real-world application because you would not want to ask a user their name every time they use the voice application. In fact, you would want to recognize the user and greet them by their name. In Chapter 4, *Hosting, Securing, and Testing Fortune Cookie in the Cloud*, you will learn how to manage your own context without relying on Dialogflow contexts by creating your own persistence.

No context

In the previous section, we used the context from the external intent **Get Name** to get the data needed for the **Get President Birthday** intent. What if you do not always want to use the context, but simply want to ask the user for the missing data?

1. In the **User says** section, add I want to know @president-birthday:president-birthday. Notice that the president-birthday parameter in the **Action** section is automatically added.
2. Have a **REQUIRED** checkbox checked for president-birthday.
3. Click on the **Define prompts** link that appears in the **PROMPTS** column.
4. Enter the prompt that asks, **Which president's birthday would you like to know?**.

The following screenshot shows steps 2 to 4 with the required parameter, `president-birthday`:

No context

The following screenshot shows the default prompt if the required parameter, president name, is not given:

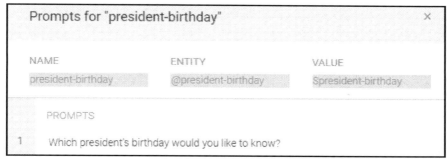

Default prompt for the required parameter

When the user asks `what is his birthday?`, the **Get President Birthday** intent will get triggered, but since no `president-birthday` entity is captured from the user's request, the intent will prompt the user with **Which president's birthday would you like to know?** As soon as the user gives the answer, the intent will provide a response.

Testing context and no context scenarios

Let's test the context using Google Assistant simulator from the Dialogflow console. In the Try it now textbox, enter `my name is Henry` and you will see the response, **Henry you can ask me anything about the president of America**. Notice that, in the **Contexts** section, it shows that the GET_NAME context is set and also has the username parameter value of `Henry`.

The following screenshot shows us testing the get_name context:

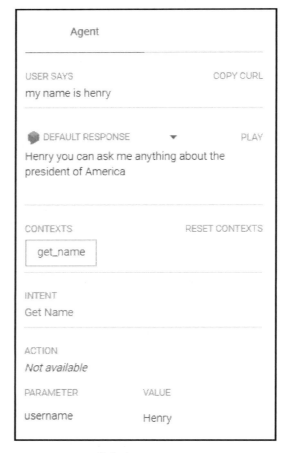

Testing the get_name context

If you enter the next question, I want to know John Adams' birthday, you will see that the response contains the username when responding about the president's birthday.

The following screenshot shows the debugger showing the **Get President Birthday** intent with the get_name context:

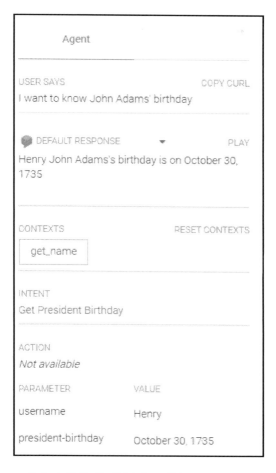

Agent

USER SAYS   COPY CURL
I want to know John Adams' birthday

🔵 DEFAULT RESPONSE   ▼   PLAY
Henry John Adams's birthday is on October 30,
1735

CONTEXTS   RESET CONTEXTS
get_name

INTENT
Get President Birthday

ACTION
Not available

PARAMETER   VALUE

username   Henry

president-birthday   October 30, 1735

Testing the Get President Birthday intent with the get_name context

Test out the no context scenario by typing in, What is his birthday?. The intent will trigger the prompt, asking **Which president's birthday would you like to know?** When you respond with George Washington, the response returns George Washington's birthday.

The following screenshot shows the intent triggering the prompt, asking the user which president's birthday they would like to know about:

Testing no context

The following screenshot shows the chatbot providing the president's name as a response to **Get President Birthday**:

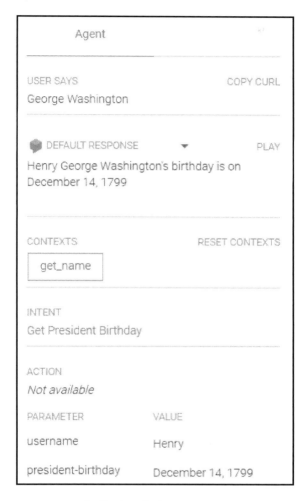

Providing the president's name as a response

In the following section, you will learn how to actually test `FaqChatBot` using your iPhone or Android mobile device.

What is Google Assistant?

Google Assistant is a platform where you can create and deploy voice-enabled applications. Google Assistant is available on all Android 6.0 devices or higher, including mobile phones, tablets, Google Home, and Google Auto. For all new Android devices, Google Assistant comes pre-installed. In this section, you will learn how to deploy and test `FaqChatBot` on your iPhone or Android phones.

Installing Google Assistant on iPhone and Android

Follow the Google instructions on installing Google Assistant on your iPhone or Android device at `http://bit.ly/2sEKMXS`. After installing Google Assistant, link your Google account that you used to set up your Dialogflow account to Google Assistant. First, open Google Assistant and then click on the Google Assistant settings, located in the top-right corner.

The following screenshot shows the location of the Google Assistant settings button:

Google Assistant settings

Notice here that for Android devices, you can start Google Assistant by clicking the middle circle button located at the bottom of the phone screen, as shown in the preceding screenshot. For iPhone, you must click on the Google Assistant application.

Now, click on the Google Assistant settings menu and click on **Account**. Add the Google Account that you used to log in to Dialogflow.

The following screenshot shows a menu to link the Google account to Google Assistant:

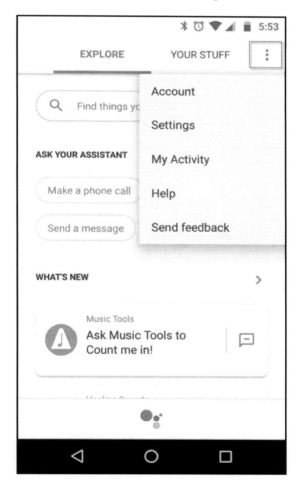

Google Assistant account linking menu

The following screenshot shows choosing a Google account to link to Google Assistant:

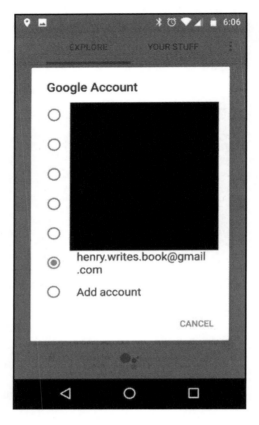

Google Assistant account linking menu

Configuring Google Assistant on Android and iPhone

In this section, I will help you configure Google Assistant. First, let's change the Google Assistant voice. Personally, I prefer a female voice, so that is what I have chosen on my phone, by going to **Google Assistant Settings** | **Preferences** | **Assistant voice**. Choose the voice that you would like to use.

The following screenshot shows the Google Assistant voice settings:

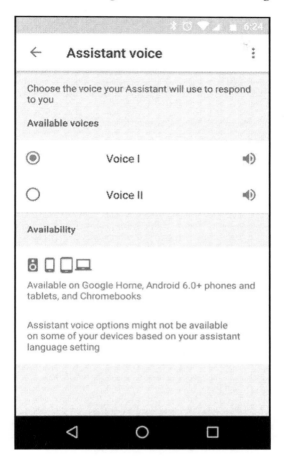

Google Assistant voice settings

Next, configure Google Assistant so that, instead of needing to click on the Google Assistant application to start it, you can activate Google Assistant hands-free by simply saying Ok Google or Hey Google to your phone. To configure Google Assistant hands-free, go to **Google Assistant Settings | Phone |** Enable **"Ok Google" detection** and you will go through a series of steps, in which Google Assistant will record your voice to create your voice signature. This only works on Android devices; iPhone requires the user to click on the Google Assistant application.

The following screenshot shows the Google Assistant's hands-free settings:

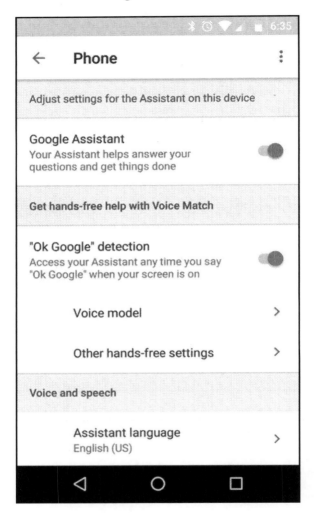

Google Assistant hands-free settings

Deploying FaqChatBot to Google Assistant

1. Since you have configured Google Assistant on your phone, you can now deploy the FaqChatBot to your phone. Go to the Dialogflow FaqChatBot agent, and then go to Integrations and click on the **INTEGRATION SETTINGS** link. The following screenshot shows the Dialogflow integration setting:

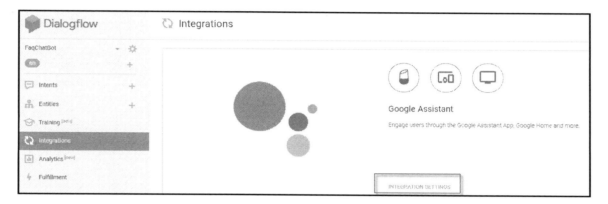

Dialogflow integration setting

2. You will see **Google Assistant Setting** pop up. Here, notice by default that Explicit Invocation triggers **Default Welcome Intent** of the FaqChatBot. Set the **Auto-preview changes** so that you do not have to constantly deploy the voice application whenever you make changes in the Dialogflow agent. Click **TEST** to go to the Google Assistant simulator. The following is the Google Assistant settings pop-up window:

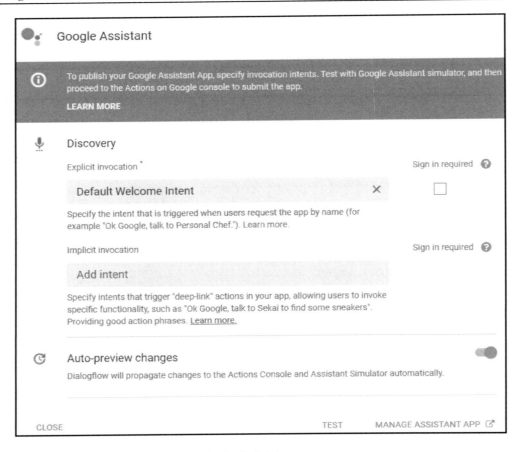

Dialogflow Google Assistant settings

Note here that there is an implicit invocation where certain user requests can trigger an intent that will return a "deep-link" that can open the Application. Imagine saying "OK, Google. Start my application cooking app". Google Assistant would open your mobile application. Deep linking to an Android application is out of the scope of this book, but you can find more information as to how to create and trigger your application using your voice at http://bit.ly/2zrhxIi.

3. You will be redirected to the **Actions on the Google** website, where you will see a virtual simulator that you can use to test all of your Dialogflow agents in the future. In the **Surface** column, there is the phone icon or the Google Home icon, which you can select in order to simulate Google Assistant or Google Home. In the middle, you will see an actual simulator, where you can type or talk to test your agent. On the right-hand side, notice that there are the **REQUEST** and **RESPONSE** tabs, where you can extract JSON, which you will need to understand and use in later chapters. There is also the **DEBUG** tab, which displays even more information about the intent that got triggered.

4. I would suggest going ahead and testing the questions that you have built in the simulator so far. The following screenshot shows the **Actions on the Google** user interface:

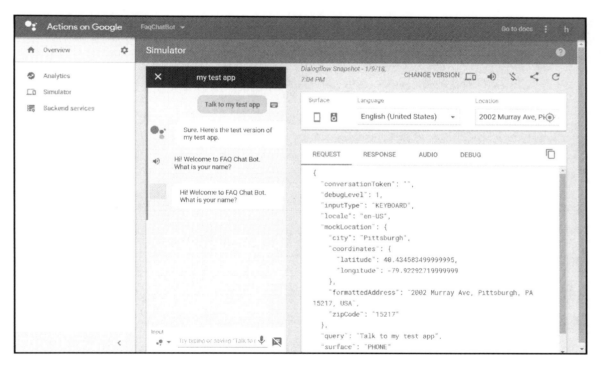

Actions on the Google user interface

5. Now, go to your mobile device and say `OK Google, talk to my test app`, and Google Assistant will launch your `FaqChatBot`. Congratulations—you have successfully deployed your first voice application!

After interacting with your voice application, you will want to exit from it, because you might want to launch a different voice application. For example, if you try to launch a cooking application by saying `Talk to my cooking app` while you're still in `FaqChatBot`, there will be no such intent that can map to `Talk to my cooking app`. To exit the current voice application in session, simply say `goodbye`.

Configuring FaqChatBot

Let's customize this properly so that you can say `OK Google, test Henry's FaqChatBot`:

1. In **Actions on Google**, go to **Overview**, then click on **App information** and click **Edit**. You will see **App information**.
2. First, start by editing the **Name** section by entering your application name, `Henry's FaqChatBot`.
3. In the **Pronunciation** section, enter `Henry's f a q Chat Bot`. Because Google Assistant will pronounce `f a q` exactly as it appears, you want to correct this behavior by putting spaces in-between the letters `faq`, which will force Google Assistant to pronounce the individual letters, `f`, `a`, and `q`. The following screenshot shows the **App Information Name** section:

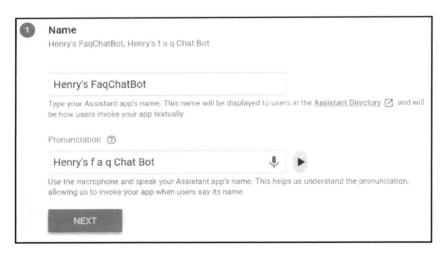

App information name

4. Now, fill out the application's details. In the description section, try to describe the type of questions that the user can ask. The **Sample invocation** section should match your application name section, because if the invocation cannot be understood by Google Assistant, deployment to the marketplace will fail. The following screenshot shows the **Application Details** section:

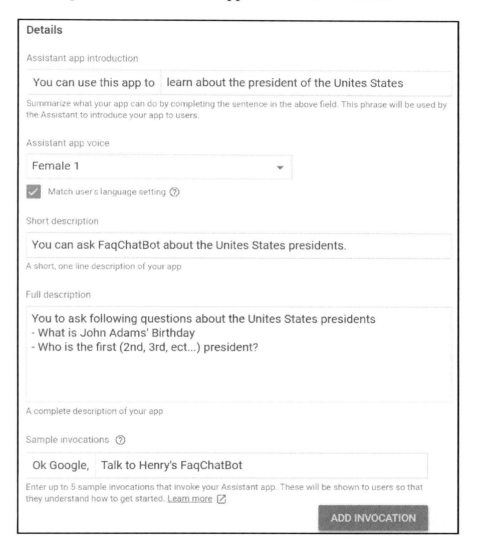

Application details

5. Upload the banner and the logo that will be used in the marketplace. They should be images in PNG format, 1,920 by 1,080 and 192 by 192, respectively. The following screenshot shows the **Application Images** section:

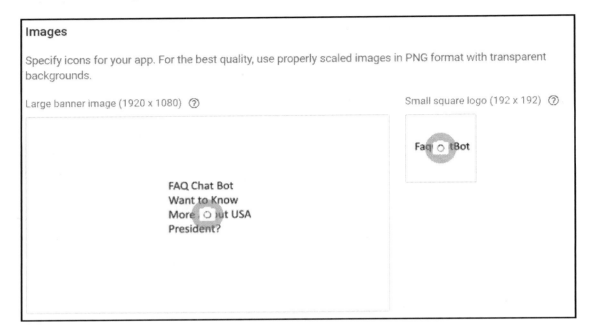

Application images

6. Finally, fill in the **Contact details** section in case the user requires support or has questions, and in the additional information section, categorize `FaqChatBot` in the **Education & reference** group. The following screenshot shows **Contact details**:

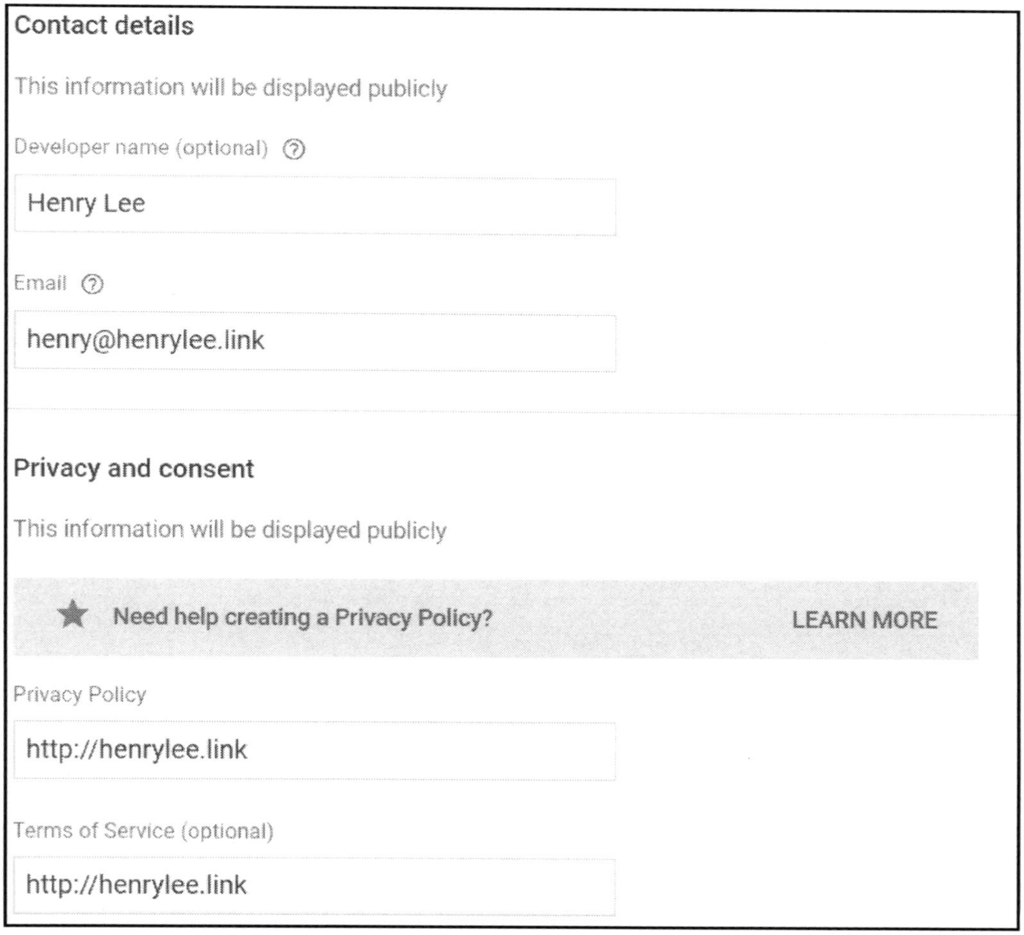

Contact details

This information will be displayed publicly

Developer name (optional) ⑦

Henry Lee

Email ⑦

henry@henrylee.link

Privacy and consent

This information will be displayed publicly

⭐ Need help creating a Privacy Policy?   LEARN MORE

Privacy Policy

http://henrylee.link

Terms of Service (optional)

http://henrylee.link

Contact details

The following screenshot shows the **Additional Information** section:

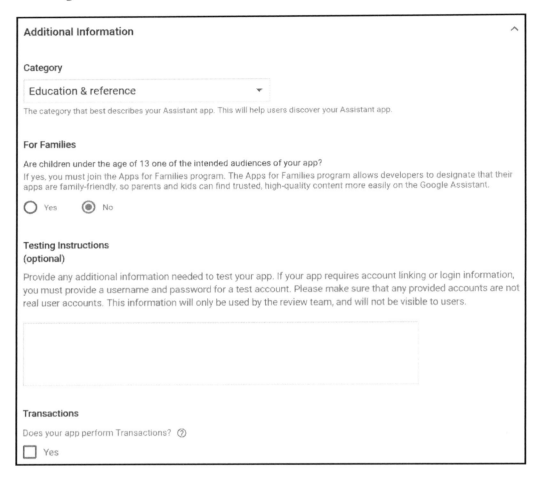

Additional information

Once you have saved this information, you will be able to go back to Google Assistant on your phone and say OK Google, Talk to Henry's FaqChatBot.

In order for these section changes to take effect, you must close **Actions** on the Google website, then go back to Dialogflow and go to **Integration** | **INTEGRATION SETTINGS** | **TEST**.

Machine learning in Dialogflow

Processing human conversation into something that machines can understand is challenging. Even today, with all the technology that's available, natural language processing is still a big challenge. Google has been in the business of natural language processing since day one, through Google Search. Google Search is all about natural language processing, where keywords or phrases are converted into meaningful machine-understandable forms, and then the backend server returns search query results to the user. Similarly, Dialogflow takes care of all the complexities of machine learning behind the scenes to process natural language and even add artificial intelligence to train data so that machines can become smarter over time. For example, whenever a user speaks, their voice is transcribed and then processed by Dialogflow and then matched against the existing intent, where the request data in a JSON is passed to the server to be processed. In fact, you have witnessed this in this chapter when you created `FaqChatBot` and tested it with Google Assistant.

Even though many complex machine learning concepts are hidden in Dialogflow, Dialogflow provides options for tweaking settings, such as the machine learning classification threshold, and also allows data to be properly trained so that agents like `FaqChatBot` can become smarter. In the next section, you will learn more about the machine learning classification threshold and the training of data.

Machine learning classification threshold

The **machine learning classification threshold** basically defines the confidence level percentage that the user request matches the intent. In Dialogflow, you can find this by clicking on the `FaqChatBot` agent setting and going to **ML Settings**. By default, the machine learning classification threshold in Dialogflow is set to `0.3`. You might want to increase the confidence level of the intent matched, especially if you are dealing with a business critical voice application, for example, an e-commerce voice application, where it is important to take the right order. In the **match** mode, there is a **hybrid** mode or an **ML only** mode. The **hybrid** mode is recommended for a small number of intents, but for a large number of intents, the **ML only** mode should be used. Personally, even for large projects that I have worked on, I have not run into a situation where I needed to run Dialogflow agent in the **ML only mode**.

The following screenshot shows the **ML Settings** section of the `FaqChatBot` agent:

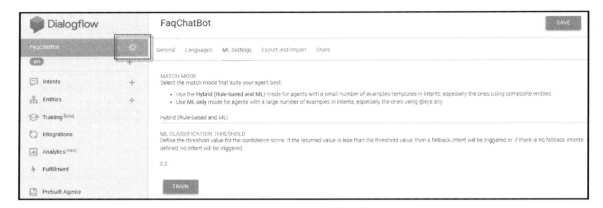

Machine learning classification threshold

Lastly, if you look at the request in the simulator, when you say or type I am Henry, you will see the following JSON with the `queryResult.intentDetectionConfidence` with a match of 1 or 100%. In `Chapter 1`, *Introduction*, you learned that you can use this confidence level to dynamically deliver a response where you ask the user the question back in order to validate what they said. For example, let's assume that the user says I want an apple and the confidence level is 0.3. Although the agent matched the I want an apple intent, since the default ML setting is 0.3, you decide you want to confirm with the user by saying Are you sure you want an apple?, because you decided that in the backend server you will only accept 0.5, but still want the user's request to come through.

The following JSON data shows the `intentDetectionConfidence` of 1:

```
{
   "responseId": "f3e78d40-2737-4832-bdda-7f6aa11136ab",
   "queryResult": {
     "queryText": "i am Henry",
     //omitted to shorten the JSON result ...
     "intent": {
       "name": "projects/faqchatbot-9417a/agent/intents/035fc2f3-586e-4df2-
bc0f-0899e0edecde",
       "displayName": "Get Name"
     },
     "intentDetectionConfidence": 1,
     "diagnosticInfo": {},
     "languageCode": "en"
   }
}
```

Training data

Machine learning is all about using data to train the model via artificial intelligence. For example, let's assume you tell your child that apples are red and, at some point, your child goes to the grocery store and finds a green apple. Your child asks you, "Can apples be green as well?" and you confirm, "Yes." Your child has just learned that the color of an apple can be red or green. The same analogy will apply to the Dialogflow agent where, over time, the user will say things that no intents will match. So, what do you do with those that did not have any intents to match? Rather than ignoring unknown requests, send them back into the system to train the Dialogflow agent.

Let's see this in the following example. Go to the simulator and say I am Henry, and the returned response will show that the intent is unknown. The following screenshot shows the unknown input:

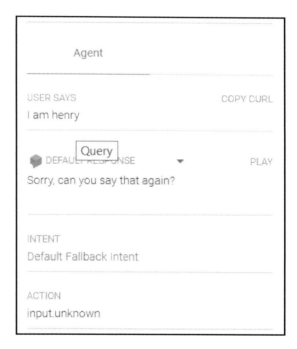

Unknown input

In Dialogflow, click **Training**[beta], and you will notice that it lists unknown inputs where no matching intents are found.

The following screenshot shows the training data list, where you can find unknown inputs:

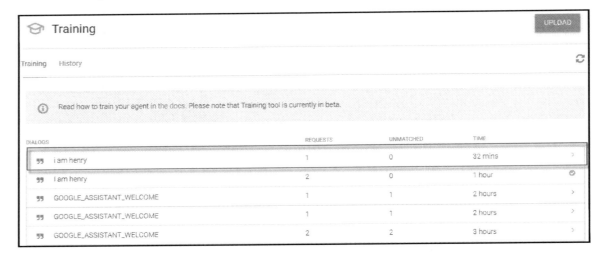

Training data list

One of the inputs is `i am henry`. If you click on `i am henry`, you will see that it requires approval and also requires the proper intent to be assigned. So, go ahead and assign the **Get Name** intent and approve it. Once approved, you will see a green checkmark.

The following screenshot shows the window where you can approve and assign an unknown input to an existing intent:

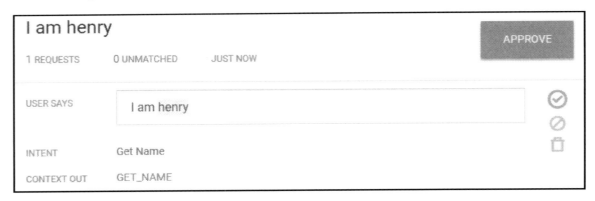

Approving and assigning the "I am Henry" input to the Get Name intent

Now, go to the **Get name** intent and you will notice that I am henry is matched with the proper entity applied. Over time, you can monitor the **Training** section data and learn what users are asking, and then you can create or update intents. Over time, the Dialogflow agent will become smart enough to handle multiple variations of questions, but asked differently. Having to anticipate every possible combination is not humanly possible. Although it is difficult, the ability to train a machine to learn and anticipate the future is as simple as being a few mouse clicks away in Dialogflow. The following screenshot shows an unknown input assigned to the **Get Name** intent:

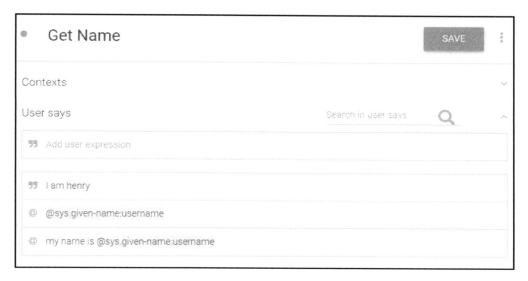

Unknown input assigned to Get Name intent

Summary

In this chapter, you learned about Google's natural language processing platform and applied it to building voice user interfaces for FaqChatBot. Then, you learned how to configure and deploy to Google Assistant on iPhone or Android. Finally, you learned how to tweak machine learning configuration in Dialogflow, and also how to train data to make the Dialogflow agent smarter.

In the next chapter, you will learn how to build voice-enabled applications using a built-in Node.js server in Dialogflow. You will also learn about new Dialogflow features, such as webhooks and fulfillment, and more advanced topics on context and entities will be introduced.

3
Building a Fortune Cookie Application

Over the course of the next three chapters, you will build a more complex voice-enabled application that tells users fortune-cookie-style quotes. Using the previous chapter's technique, you will build conversations in Dialogflow that will respond to users' inquiries about the fortune cookie quotes. First, you will be introduced to the fulfillment and webhook concepts in Dialogflow. Using fulfillments and webhooks will help you understand how to dynamically process and respond to intents received from Dialogflow with a built-in Node.js server. This chapter will also cover more advanced topics, such as triggering custom events and follow-up intents, and creating visual responses that the user can interact with. Furthermore, a more advanced customization technique using the **speech synthesis markup language (SSML)** will be covered, and you will also learn how to respond to users with sound effects. Finally, we will introduce the built-in Dialogflow analytic for viewing how your users are using your application.

This chapter will cover the following topics:

- Creating the webhook with Node.js in Dialogflow
- Triggering custom events
- Follow-up intents
- Creating a visual response
- Using SSML in a response
- Integrating an audio file
- Using Dialogflow analytics

About the Fortune Cookie project

I thought it would be fun to import a Unix-style command called `fortune` (`https://en.wikipedia.org/wiki/Fortune_(Unix)`) into the **voice user interface** (**VUI**) project. The Unix `fortune` command randomly displays quotations by famous people and, similarly, the Fortune Cookie voice application will randomly read out quotations to users. The Fortune Cookie application will be able to respond to the following set of remarks:

- Tell me a quote
- Give me a fortune cookie
- I feel sad/happy
- Show me authors

About webhook

In the previous chapter, intents were fulfilled statically by adding text responses. This is ideal if you already know the questions that will be asked and their answers, such as FAQs. But in real-world scenarios, the questions asked by users often require complex calculations; the answers might come from searching a database, or even hitting external web services in order to build responses. For example, if you were building a weather voice interface, you would most likely use the AccuWeather **application programming interfaces** (**APIs**) (`https://developer.accuweather.com/apis`). So, in order to achieve calling external APIs to build proper responses requires your own middle-tier server. In Dialogflow, the concept of allowing your middle-tier server to serve responses dynamically is called **fulfilling intents through webhook**. Dialogflow provides a built-in Node.js server to handle simple requests dynamically. In the next chapter, you will learn how to host your own Node.js server on the Microsoft Azure cloud in order to take full advantage of its cloud offerings and to take full control of your middle-tier servers.

The following flowchart shows a simple webhook architecture:

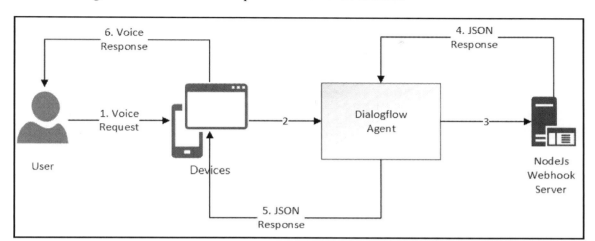

Webhook architecture

Installing Visual Studio Code

Before we can move on, go ahead and install the free Node.js editor Visual Studio Code (https://code.visualstudio.com/). Although Node.js code can be edited in Dialogflow's inline editor, it is much more efficient and convenient to use Visual Studio Code to write it and simply copy and paste it to Dialogflow. Also, using Visual Studio Code, you can pull down code from GitHub, which can save you time writing out code. There are other Node.js editors out there that you can choose to use—this is totally your choice.

Setting up an agent

First, log in to the Dialogflow website and a create new agent called FortuneCookie. Make sure to enable **Dialogflow V2 API** and leave the rest of the settings leave as their defaults.

The following screenshot shows the `FortuneCookie` agent creation settings:

Creating a FortuneCookie agent

Checking security and the service account

This section will delve much deeper into the workings of Dialogflow and how Dialogflow is closely integrated into Google Cloud Platform, where the built-in Node.js server will be deployed. All of this is done behind the scenes and is something you will never have to worry about, but it is important to understand it as we start to work on more advanced topics, and for troubleshooting issues. You will learn more about this later in this chapter. Here are the steps to check security and the service accounts.

1. Go to the `FortuneCookie` agent settings and you will notice the **Service Account** section. Click on the **Service Account** that Dialogflow automatically created when the agent was created.

The following screenshot shows you where to find the **Service Account** link:

The FortuneCookie agent's service account

2. Notice that when you click on **Service Account**, the browser will take you to Google Cloud Platform. Click on **IAM & admin** and notice that you will find the same **Service Account** on the list.

The following screenshot shows the service account used by the `FortuneCookie` agent with the permission to use **Dialogflow API Client**:

Service Account lists in IAM & admin

When the agent is created, the **Service Account** gets automatically created with the permission to access the **Dialogflow API**. This is how Dialogflow security is enforced so that not everyone can use the agent. This section is for informational purposes in order to help you understand how Dialogflow and Google Cloud Platform, which hosts Dialogflow, is connected. In the following section, when you use the built-in Node.js server in Dialogflow, the same **Service Account** will be used, allowing the Node.js server to receive requests and respond to Dialogflow. Again, all this is done automatically behind the scenes.

Enabling webhook

Before we start to build the Fortune Cookie application, let's enable the webhook feature of Dialogflow so that all intents can be routed to the Dialogflow Node.js server.

1. In Dialogflow, go to **Fulfillment** and enable **Inline Editor**. This will allow you to enter Node.js code into the editor.

The following screenshot shows enabling webhook in the Dialogflow fulfillment:

The text in this screenshot is not important. This image gives you an idea of how to enable webhook

2. Notice that there are default codes. First, let's replace those codes by declaring Google Cloud Functions for Firebase.

```
'use strict';
const firebase = require('firebase-functions');
```

Dialogflow's built-in Node.js server uses Google Cloud Functions for Firebase, which allows you to write code that intercepts HTTPS events. For example, when an intent is triggered, Dialogflow will send a HTTPS request to Firebase and allows Google Cloud Functions to execute. In this case, the Google Cloud Function triggered is the code that you will be writing in the Dialogflow **Inline Editor**.

3. Next, capture the HTTPS request and response. The request object will contain a Dialogflow request (http://bit.ly/2Gnj31K) and send back the response (http://bit.ly/2rNf0Zn) to Dialogflow so that it can properly answer the user's intent.

The following code intercepts the HTTPS request initiated by Dialogflow when the intent is triggered and the Firebase event is notified `firebase.https.onRequest`:

```
var request, response;
exports.dialogflowFirebaseFulfillment =
firebase.https.onRequest((req, res) => {
  request = req;
  response = res;
  console.log('Fortune Cookie Request headers: ' +
JSON.stringify(request.headers));
  console.log('Fortune Cookie Request body: ' +
JSON.stringify(request.body));
  if (request.body.queryResult) {
    processV2Request();
  } else {
    console.log('Invalid Request');
    return response.status(400).end('Invalid Webhook Request');
  }
});
```

When the HTTPS request (`firebase.https.onRequest`) is triggered, the request and the response object will be captured. Then, using `console.log`, the request header and the request body will be captured. In the previous chapter, when you were debugging `FAQChatBot` in the simulator, the simulator provided the request object. Similarly, you will see the Dialogflow request object that contains the important information about the intent so that you can write a proper response. If the request body contains the `queryResult`, the version 2 API can be used otherwise reject the request with invalid request error.

4. Now let's create intent handlers that will create proper responses to Dialogflow requesting that the server handles the user's intents. By default, two intents will always be created when the agent is created: **Default Fallback Intent** and **Default Welcome Intent**. In the previous chapter, we created a static text response in Dialogflow, but you will handle this in the code now.

The following code shows handlers that respond to the fallback (input.unknown) and the welcome intent (input.welcome):

```
const intentHandlers = {
  'input.welcome': () => {
    sendResponse('Hello, Welcome to Henry\'s Fortune Cookie!');
  },
  'input.unknown': () => {
    sendResponse('I\'m having trouble, can you try that again?');
  },
  'default': () => {
    sendResponse('This is Henry\'s Fortune Cookie!');
  }
};
```

An intent in Dialogflow is associated with an action and when Dialogflow sends a request to the Node.js server, the request body will contain queryResult.action, which will map to the intentHandlers functions, where the proper text response will be sent to the user. For the welcome intent, the Hello, Welcome to Henry's Fortune Cookie! response will be sent to Dialogflow and then to the user. For input.unknown, which is the fallback intent, the I'm having trouble, can you try that again? response will be sent back. If for some reason, the action is never sent by Dialogflow, the default intent handler will send the This is Henry's Fortune Cookie! response.

The following image shows the **Default Welcome Intent** with the **Action** name `input.welcome` used in the code and also, in the **Fulfillment** section, **Use webhook** is checked, which will allow the intent to be handled in the code:

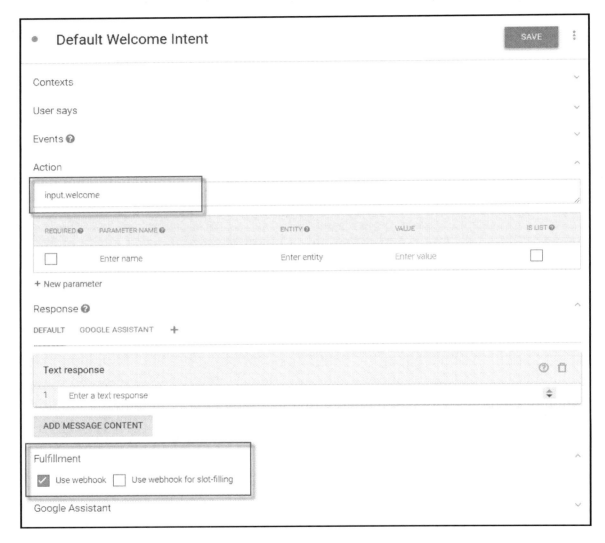

Default Welcome Intent with Action name and Enabling Webhook

5. Let's create a `sendResponse` function that will respond with a simple response. First, we need to build the Dialogflow response object that contains the `fulfillmentText` property. Finally, the response object will be logged and the response will be sent to Dialogflow. `fullfilmentText` will be used by Dialogflow to translate text into the voice and the response will be spoken to the user.

The following code describes the `sendResponse` function, which will build Dialogflow's simple text response, which will be translated into voice and sent to the user:

```
function sendResponse (responseToUser) {
  let responseJson = { fulfillmentText: responseToUser };
  console.log('Response to Fortune Cookie: ' +
JSON.stringify(responseJson));
  response.json(responseJson);
}
```

The following code stitches together everything we've built so far and processes the request by extracting the action from `request.body.queryResult.action` and sending the response back to Dialogflow by executing the intent handler:

```
function processV2Request () {
  let action = (request.body.queryResult.action) ?
request.body.queryResult.action : 'default';
  if (intentHandlers[action]) {
    intentHandlers[action]();
  }
  else {
    intentHandlers['default']();
  }
}
```

Deploying and testing webhook

If you used the Visual Studio Code editor to edit, then copy and paste the codes to the **Inline Editor** and click on the **Deploy** button. Once deployed, do not forget to go into **Default Welcome Intent** and **Default Fallback Intent** and check **Use webhook** in the **Fulfillment** section. In Dialogflow, go to the **Integrations** section and click on **Integration Settings**, then click **Test** to go to the Google Assistant simulator.

The following screenshot shows the the result of testing the `FortuneCookie` agent with the basic webhook handling the **Default Welcome Agent**:

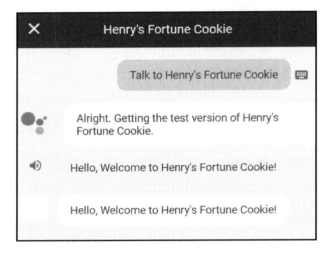

Test the Fortune Cookie Default Welcome Intent going through the webhook

Working with logs

In the code, you create a log entry whenever you write `console.log` (`some log goes here.`). These log entries are important for troubleshooting and debugging your Node.js code. You can view the log entries by going to Google Cloud Platform and the fastest way to go there is to click on the agent settings and then click on the **Service Account** link under the **GOOGLE PROJECT** section.

The following screenshot shows the **GOOGLE PROJECT** property in the agent settings:

Google Project in the agent settings

1. Clicking the **Service Account** link will take you to Google Cloud Platform for the Dialogflow agent
2. Select **Home | Logging | log**

The following screenshot shows the menu to go to in order to log the Dialogflow agent:

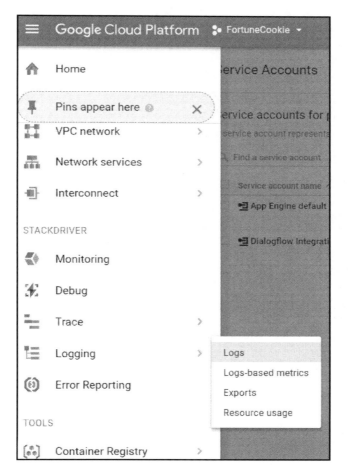

Logging the agent in Google Cloud Platform

You will see all the log entries entered using `console.log`. Here, you can search logs by keywords, time, function, and log level.

The following screenshot shows the agent log entries entered using the `console.log` function:

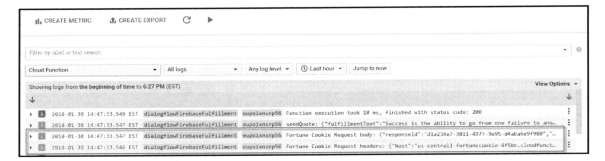

Agent log entries

Building Fortune Cookie VUIs

So far, what you have done is learn how to create what I call *plumbing* code. For example, when you build a bathroom, you always have to build the pipelines so that the bathroom can have water, and then you build sinks, toilets, and showers. If you tried to build pipelines after building the showers, it would be very difficult to put the pipes behind the shower through the concrete. In the previous section, you learned to build the webhook that will handle the **Default Welcome Intent**. Using this plumbing code, you can now add more complex scenarios to handle Fortune-Cookie-specific conversations.

Building a Get Quote intent

First, let's build an entity that contains the keywords `Fortune Cookie` and `Quote`. The following code shows the `Fortune` entity, which contains two keywords that will be used to match the user's request to the fortune cookie or the quote:

```
[
    {
        "value": "Fortune Cookie",
        "synonyms": [
            "Fortune Cookie",
            "Quote"
        ]
    }
]
```

Using the `Fortune` entity, create templatized questions for the **Get Quote** intent, as follows:

- @ Tell me a @Fortune.Fortune
- @ Give me @Fortune.Fortune

Now, a user will be able to ask a combination of questions using `Tell me` and the `Fortune` entity. For example, the user can say `Tell me a fortune cookie` or `Tell me a quote`. Now, give it an **Action** name, `input.fortune`, which will capture the HTTPS request event and map it to the `intentHandler`. Finally, in **Fulfillment**, enable the **Use webhook** option.

The following image shows the **Get Quote** intent settings:

Get Quote intent

Note that the **Get Quote** intent has an empty text response. From here on, all intents will be routed to the webhook and the response will be programmatically created in the middle-tier server.

Handling the Get Quote intent from the Webhook

You will be adding quotes to the **Inline Editor** that you just worked on. Go to **Fulfillment** in Dialogflow and add an array of nine quotes to the code. Notice here that there is author information and tags, which you will use to build the **Get Author Quote** intent.

The following variable array, named quotes, contains nine quotes, from which you will randomly select one and respond to the user when the **Get Quote** intent is triggered:

```
const quotes = [
  {
    "author": "T. S. Eliot", "tags": "happy",
    "quote": "Do not stop to ask what is it;  Let us go and make our
visit."
  },
  {
    "author": "J. B. White", "tags": "happy",
    "quote": "at least I thought I was dancing, til somebody stepped on my
hand."
  },
  {
    "author": "Dave Stutman", "tags": "happy",
    "quote": "Complacency is the enemy of progress."
  },
  {
    "author": "Winston Churchill", "tags": "happy",
    "quote": "Success is the ability to go from one failure to another with
no loss of enthusiasm."
  },
  {
    "author": "Woody Allen", "tags": "happy",
    "quote": "There's more to life than sitting around in the sun in your
underwear playing the clarinet."
  },
  {
    "author": "Confucius", "tags": "sad",
    "quote": "It does not matter how slowly you go so long as you do not
stop."
  },
  {
    "author": "Mark Twain", "tags": "sad",
```

```
    "quote": "It usually takes me more than three weeks to prepare a good
impromptu speech."
  },
  {
    "author": "Albert Einstein", "tags": "sad",
    "quote": "Imagination is more important than knowledge."
  },
  {
    "author": "Steven Wright", "tags": "sad",
    "quote": "You can't have everything. Where would you put it?"
  }
];
```

Now, in `intentHandler`, you will need to add the `input.fortune` action in order to handle the **Get Quote** intent.

The following code shows `input.fortune` added to `intentHandlers`, which calls the `sendQuote` function:

```
const intentHandlers = {
  'input.welcome': () => {
    sendResponse('Hello, Welcome to Henry\'s Fortune Cookie!');
  },
  'input.unknown': () => {
    sendResponse('I\'m having trouble, can you try that again?');
  },
  'input.fortune': () => {
    sendQuote();
  },
  'default': () => {
    sendResponse('This is Henry\'s Fortune Cookie!' );
  }
};
```

In the `sendQuote` function, a number between 0 and 9 will be randomly generated using `Math.random()`, and then that randomly generated number will be used to select a quote from the array of quotes. The Dialogflow `fulfillmentText` response will be assigned with `quotes[randomNumber].quote`.

The following code shows the `sendQuote` function, where the Dialogflow response will be generated and sent using one of the quotes:

```
function sendQuote () {
    var randomNumber = Math.floor(Math.random() * 9);
    let responseJson = { fulfillmentText: quotes[randomNumber].quote };
    console.log('sendQuote: ' + JSON.stringify(responseJson));
    response.json(responseJson);
}
```

Once the code has been modified, you can click on **Deploy** and then go to the **Google Assistant simulator** to test it out!

There are thousands of quotes that you can use, which can be found at `http://bit.ly/2njYCe6`. Also, in Chapter 3, *Building a Fortune Cookie Application*, in the GitHub repository, I have written a small program that will convert this Fortune Cookie data into JSON format for your convenience. For the purpose of the book, I am using nine quotes to keep things short. In Chapter 4, Hosting, Securing, and Testing Fortune Cookie in the Cloud, you will learn how to import an entire data file into the NoSQL database in order to query quotes. For this chapter, the quotes will remain static data in the code, without using the database.

Building a Get Quote based on the user feelings

In this section, you will learn how to build a `Feeling` intent, where you will take the user's current feelings as input and properly display appropriate quotes that will go with the user's feelings. For example, if the user feels sad, the quote that has `sad` in the tags property will be randomly selected, and if the user feels happy, one of the quotes that contains `happy` in the tags property will be selected. In order to do this, the user request will be routed to **Default Welcome Intent** and then randomly chosen to welcome the user or trigger the **Custom Welcome** intent. **Default Welcome Intent** will simply greet the user normally and will wait for the user to request the Fortune Cookie. However, in **Custom Welcome Intent**, after the user is greeted, they will be asked about how they are feeling. If the user answers that they are sad or happy, the response will trigger a follow-up intent called **Get Feeling** and a quote based on the user's feeling will be selected and sent to the user.

The following flowchart shows the flow of getting a quote based on the user's feeling:

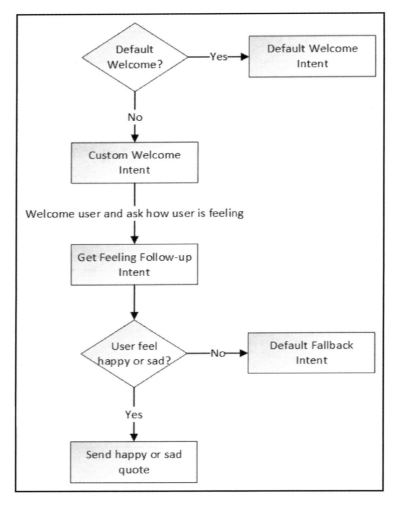

Get Quote based on Feeling flow

Building a Feeling entity

In order to create an intent template to match the user's feeling, create a **Feeling** entity with
happy and sad. The **Feeling** entity can be expanded to handle more diverse ranges of
emotions such as anger, frustration, and fear. For the purpose of keeping the project simple,
only two emotions will be added.

The following code shows the **Feeling** entity in JSON format, which can be imported into Dialogflow:

```
[
    {
        "value": "happy",
        "synonyms": [ "happy" ]
    },
    {
        "value": "sad",
        "synonyms": [ "sad" ]
    }
]
```

Building events to get Feeling-based quotes

So far, you have learned about triggering intents by matching user requests. You have also used entities to create templatized patterns for what the user will be saying in order to create the intent. Another way to trigger an intent is to use an event. In an intent, there is a section called **Events**, where you can enter your own custom events and then, in the code, you can trigger the intent by simply referencing the event name you entered for the intent.

Building a Custom Welcome intent

The **Custom Welcome** intent does not contain any User says properties because it will be triggered by the **Default Welcome** intent. There will be a 50/50 chance that the **Default Welcome** intent will proceed normally by greeting the user and will wait for the user request or the **Default Welcome** intent will trigger the **Custom Welcome** intent, which will greet the user and ask them how they feel today. Create a **Custom Welcome** intent and, in the **Events** box, enter custom_welcome_event. Then, in **Text response**, add Welcome to Henry's fortune cookie. How are you feeling today?

The following image shows the **Custom Welcome** intent settings:

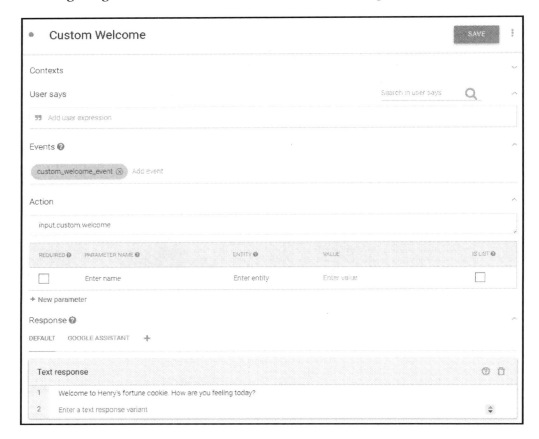

Custom Welcome intent

Building a get feeling custom follow-up intent

A follow-up intent is like any other intent you have created, the only difference being that a follow-up intent is chained after another intent as part of the follow-up conversation or to provide the user with confirmation. When creating a follow-up intent, you have the option to create a custom follow-up intent or use existing follow-up intents. Here are the pre-built follow-up intents that you can use (more information can be found at `http://bit.ly/2Gwr98h`):

- **yes**: Used for affirmation (yes, do it, sure, exactly, of course)

- **no**: Used for negation (no, don't do it, definitely not, I disagree)
- **later**: Doing something later (later, not yet, ask me later, next time)
- **cancel**: Used for canceling an action (cancel, stop, dismiss, skip)
- **more**: Asking for more information (more, more results, anything else, what else)
- **next**: Moving to the next item in a list (next, next page, show me next)
- **previous**: Moving to the previous item in a list (back, go back, previous page)
- **repeat**: Asking to do something again (repeat, come again, do it again)
- **select.number**: Selecting items from a list (third, I choose number 3, select the first one)

Let's now build a follow-up intent called `Get Feeling`. On the intent list screen, if you hover over the **Custom Welcome** intent, you will see the **Add follow-up intent** link.

The following screenshot shows the **Add follow-up intent** link when hovering over the **Custom Welcome** intent:

Add follow-up intent

1. Click **Add follow-up intent** and select **custom intent**. Name the follow-up intent `Get Feeling` and, in the **User says** section, add the following two templates, which utilize the **Feeling** entity:
   - I am feeling @Feeling:Feeling
   - I feel @Feeling:Feeling

   Notice that in the **Contexts** section, **CustomWelcome-followup** has already been created by Dialogflow. The `Get Feeling` intent is the follow-up of the **Custom Welcome** intent when the user responds to the question, `How are you feeling today?` and the **Custom Welcome** context will flow into the `Get Feeling` follow-up intent.

2. In the **Action** section, enter `input.feeling`, which will be used to identify which intent got triggered in the code in order to respond properly by selecting the `FortuneCookie` based on the user's emotion. Finally, enable the **Use webhook** in the **Fulfillment** section.

The following screenshot shows the `Get Feeling` follow-up intent settings:

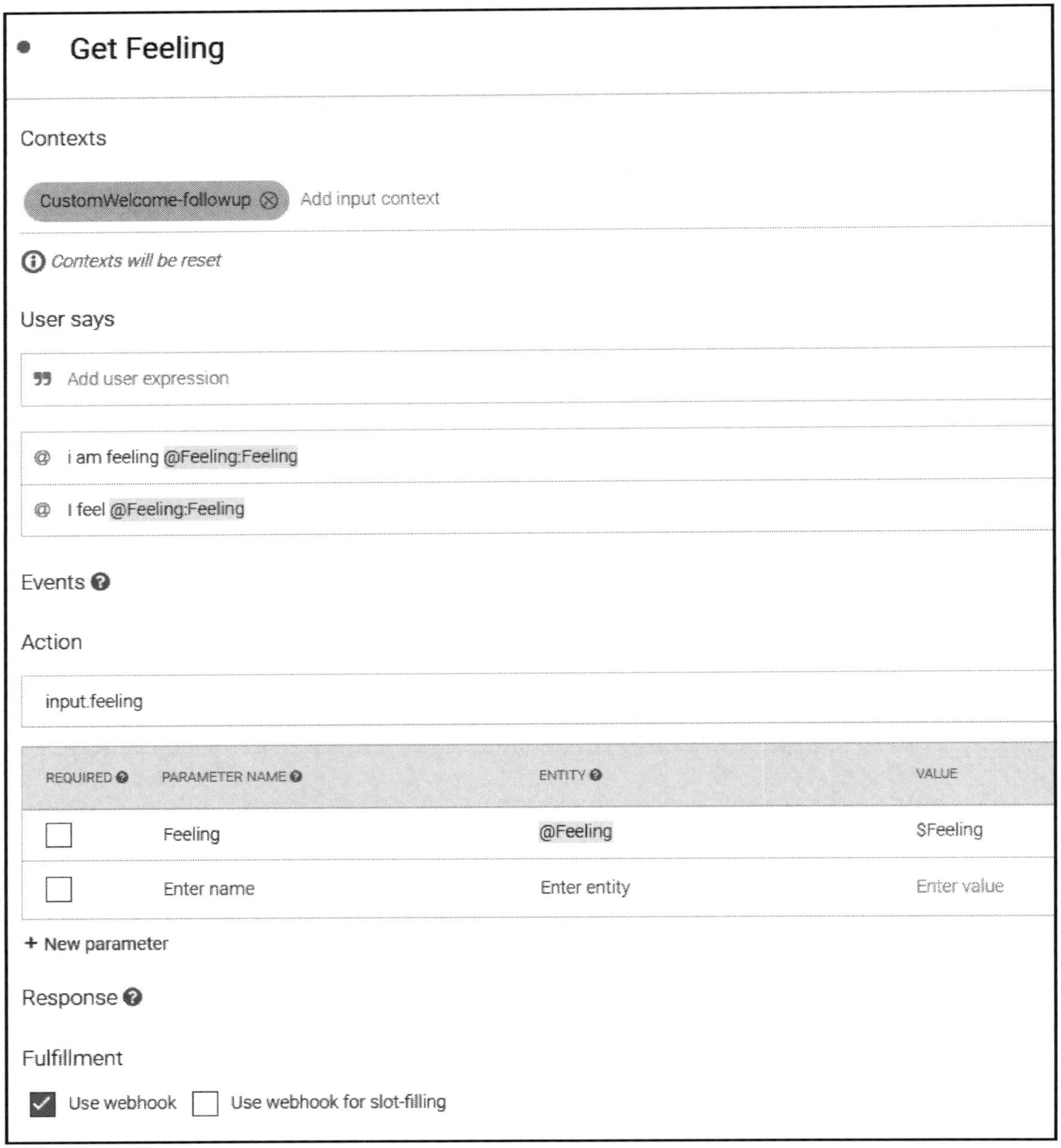

Get Feeling

Contexts

CustomWelcome-followup ⊗   Add input context

ⓘ *Contexts will be reset*

User says

99 Add user expression

@ i am feeling @Feeling:Feeling

@ I feel @Feeling:Feeling

Events ❓

Action

input.feeling

REQUIRED ❓	PARAMETER NAME ❓	ENTITY ❓	VALUE
☐	Feeling	@Feeling	$Feeling
☐	Enter name	Enter entity	Enter value

+ New parameter

Response ❓

Fulfillment

☑ Use webhook   ☐ Use webhook for slot-filling

Get Feeling follow-up intent

Writing code for a feeling custom follow-up intent

1. Let's first add and modify `intentHandlers`. Modify `sendWelcome` so that it does not take any arguments and add the `input.feeling` action in order to handle the `Get Feeling` custom follow-up intent.

   The following code shows the modified `sendWelcome` and a new intent handler, called `input.feeling`:

   ```
   const intentHandlers = {
     'input.welcome': () => {
       sendWelcome();
     },
     'input.unknown': () => {
       sendResponse('I\'m having trouble, can you try that again?');
     },
     'input.fortune': () => {
       sendQuote();
     },
     'input.feeling': () => {
       sendQuoteWithFeeling();
     },
     'default': () => {
       sendResponse('This is Henry\'s Fortune Cookie!' );
     }
   };
   ```

2. Modify the `sendWelcome` intent such that it will randomly redirect the user to `custom_welcome_event`, which is determined by `executeCustomWelcome = Math.random() >= 0.5`. Otherwise, the user will be greeted normally with `Hello, Welcome to Henry's Fortune Cookie!`. Notice that `followupEventInput` will be populated in the response with the name of the event to be executed.

The following code modifies the previously written `sendWelcome` method, triggering `custom_welcome_event` 50% of the time:

```
function sendWelcome () {
  let responseJson;
  let executeCustomWelcome = Math.random() >= 0.5;
  if(executeCustomWelcome) {
    responseJson = {
      followupEventInput: {
        name: "custom_welcome_event"
      }
    };
  }
  else {
    responseJson = { fulfillmentText: 'Hello, Welcome to Henry\'s
Fortune Cookie!' };
  }
  console.log('sendWelcome: ' + JSON.stringify(responseJson));
  response.json(responseJson);
}
```

3. Now let's write code to handle the `input.feeling` action, where a quote based on the user's feeling will be sent as a response. First, you need to capture parameters from the request, so add it to the global variable.

The following code declares the global variable parameters:

```
var request, response, parameters;
```

The following code captures the parameters from the request:

```
parameters = request.body.queryResult.parameters || {};
```

The following code shows the entire modified processV2Request function, which includes capturing the parameters value:

```
function processV2Request () {
  let action = (request.body.queryResult.action) ?
request.body.queryResult.action : 'default';
  parameters = request.body.queryResult.parameters || {};

  if (intentHandlers[action]) {
    intentHandlers[action]();
  }
  else {
    intentHandlers['default']();
  }
}
```

4. Since the parameters value containing the user's feeling is captured, you can go ahead and write the sendQuoteWithFeeling function, which will be executed when the request action is input.feeling. The Get Feeling Custom follow-up intent will contain the parameter called Feeling, which will come through the parameters.Feeling Dialogflow request object. After comparing parameters.Feeling to happy, if true, a random number will be selected from 0 to 5, or if not, a random number will be selected from 6 to 9 and then an appropriate quote corresponding to the feeling will be selected using quotes[randomNumber].quote.

The following code describes the sendQuoteWithFeeling function, which creates a Dialogflow response that sends the quote based on the user's feeling:

```
function sendQuoteWithFeeling () {
  let responseJson, randomNumber;
  if(parameters.Feeling === "happy"){
    randomNumber = Math.floor(Math.random() * 5)
  }
  else {
    randomNumber = Math.floor(Math.random() * 4) + 6
  }
  responseJson = { fulfillmentText: quotes[randomNumber].quote };
  console.log('sendQuoteWithFeeling: ' +
JSON.stringify(responseJson));
  response.json(responseJson);
}
```

Building a Get Fortune Cookie by an author

In this section, you will return a Fortune Cookie quote by an author. To accomplish this, you will learn how to display a list of authors on the user's phone, where the user can scroll through and select the author or say the author's name. Then, the response will return a quote by the selected author to the user.

Building an Author entity

Start by building the `Author` entity, which will be used by the **Get Author Quote** intent that matches the author's name in order to send a quote by that author

The following JSON data shows multiple ways to identify the author:

```
[
    { "value": "T. S. Eliot", "synonyms": [ "T. S. Eliot", "Eliot" ] },
    { "value": "J. B. White", "synonyms": [ "J. B. White", "White" ] },
    { "value": "Dave Stutman", "synonyms": [ "Dave Stutman", "Dave",
"Stutman" ] },
    { "value": "Winston Churchill", "synonyms": [ "Winston Churchill",
"Winston", "Churchill" ] },
    { "value": "Woody Allen", "synonyms": [ "Woody Allen", "Woody", "Allen"
] },
    { "value": "Confucius", "synonyms": [ "Confucius" ] },
    { "value": "Mark Twain", "synonyms": [ "Mark Twain", "Mark", "Twain" ]
},
    { "value": "Albert Einstein", "synonyms": [ "Albert Einstein",
"Albert", "Einstein" ] },
    { "value": "Steven Wright", "synonyms": [ "Steven Wright", "Steven",
"Wright" ] }
]
```

About rich response

Normally, when you send a response to the user, you create a response object with the `fulfillmentText` property set with what your user will hear. But rich response allows you to send hyperlinks, images, a list of items, and cards, where the user can not only see, but can also interact with the response. In order to send a rich response, create a response object with the `fulfillmentMessages` object that contains the rich message objects.

Creating a text response

A text message is similar to the response the intent will send to the user.

The following code shows a text message object that displays text to the user:

```
"text": {
    "text": [ "hi", "hello" ]
},
```

Creating an image response

If the user asks what a cat looks like, you can send an image of a cat, which will get displayed on the user's phone.

The following code shows an image message object:

```
"image": { "imageUri": "http://myweb.com/cat.png" }
```

Creating quick replies

Quick replies display a list of replies displayed on the screen that the user can click.

The following code shows a quickReplies object:

```
"quickReplies": { "title": "Select an option", "quickReplies": [ "option1",
"option2" ] }
```

Creating a card response

The card contains an image, a title, a subtitle, and a button that the user can click, which will open a web link. Ask Google Assistant on your phone where good Chinese restaurants near you are and it will display cards.

The following image shows card responses:

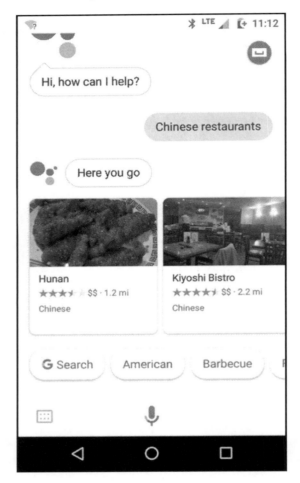

Card responses

The following code shows how to build a card response:

```
"card": {
  "title": "My Restaurant",
  "subtitle": "Chinese Food",
  "imageUri": "http://myweb.com/image.png",
  "buttons": [
      {
        "text": "my button",
        "postback": "text send to Dialogflow",
```

```
        }
    ]
}
```

Creating a listSelect response

A `listSelect` response allows you to respond to the user by displaying a list of items that the user can click. The clicked item will send to the Dialogflow. In this section, you will use this to list authors so that the user can choose an author, which will trigger an intent.

The following code shows how to build a `listSelect` response:

```
"listSelect": {
  "title": "Select an Author",
  "items": [
    { "info": { "key": "Eliot" }, "title": "T. S. Eliot"},
    { "info": { "key": "White" }, "title": "J. B. White"},
  ]
}
```

Note that you can find more rich responses at `http://bit.ly/2E0M58T`. I provided five of the most common ones and other rich responses are slight variations of what I have covered here.

Building a Get Authors intent

A `Get Authors` intent will be used to capture the user's request to display a list of authors. You will learn how to build a `listSelect` response, where the user can click the name of the author from the list. First, build a `Get Authors` intent by adding `show me authors` and `list authors` to the **User says** section. Name the **Action** `input.authors` so that you can identify the request from server. Finally, enable `Use webhook` in the **Fulfillment** section.

The following screenshot shows the Get Authors settings:

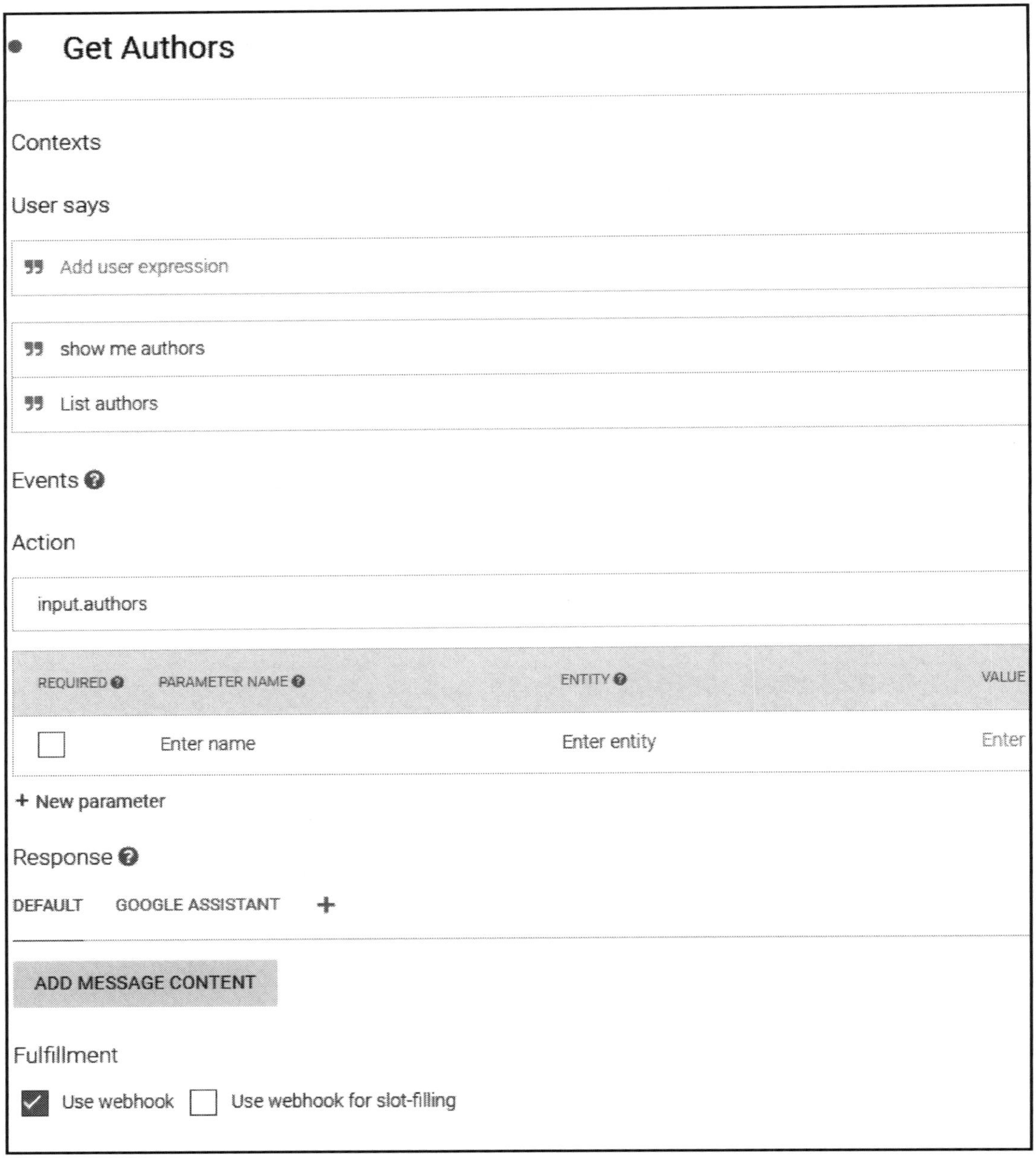

Get Authors

Contexts

User says

> 🙶 Add user expression

> 🙶 show me authors

> 🙶 List authors

Events ❷

Action

input.authors

REQUIRED ❷	PARAMETER NAME ❷	ENTITY ❷	VALUE
☐	Enter name	Enter entity	Enter

+ New parameter

Response ❷

DEFAULT   GOOGLE ASSISTANT   ✚

ADD MESSAGE CONTENT

Fulfillment

☑ Use webhook   ☐ Use webhook for slot-filling

Get Authors intent

Building a listSelect response in code

1. First, add to the `intentHandler`, which captures the **Action** named `input.authors`, which executes the `sendAuthors` function.

   The following code, which captures the `input.authors` action, is added to `intentHandler`:

   ```
   'input.authors': () => {
       sendAuthors();
   }
   ```

2. The next thing do is to create the `sendAuthors` function, where the `listSelect` response will be created. Setting `fulfillmentText` with `defaultText`, asking the user to say the author's name is important because not every device has capability to display response on the screen. For example, on Google Home there is no way to display a list of authors so it will default to simply saying `fulfillmentText`.

   The `listSelect` response is created and set to `fulfillmentMessages`. Notice here that the `fulfillmentMessages` property is an array of rich responses. This is because it depends on which platform you are using Dialogflow from and Dialogflow is smart enough to use rich response when appropriate. For example, one of the platforms supported is Facebook, and for Facebook you might not want to use the `listSelect` response, but instead want to use the card type of response. For Facebook then, you will add the card response and set the platform property to **FACEBOOK**. All of the platforms Dialogflow supports can be found at `http://bit.ly/2rUTUZ5`. The Fortune Cookie application only has one platform to support, which is **ACTIONS_ON_GOOGLE**, so set the platform property to **ACTIONS_ON_GOOGLE**. In the `listSelect` object, set the title to **Select an Author** and, in the **items** property, add the authors. The key value is sent to Dialogflow when the user clicks the item and the title is what gets displayed to the user.

The following code shows the completed `sendAuthors` function, which will send the `listSelect` response to the user:

```
function sendAuthors () {
    let defaultText = "Choose an author. T S Eliot, J B White, Dave
Stutman, Winston Churchill, ";
    defaultText = defaultText + "Woody Allen, Confucius, Mark Twain,
Albert Einstein, Steven Wright";
    let responseJson = {
        fulfillmentText: defaultText,
        fulfillmentMessages: [
        {
            platform: "ACTIONS_ON_GOOGLE",
            listSelect: {
                title: "Select an Author",
                items: [
                    { info: { key: "Eliot" }, title: "T. S. Eliot"},
                    { info: { key: "White" }, title: "J. B. White"},
                    { info: { key: "Stutman" }, title: "Dave Stutman"},
                    { info: { key: "Churchill" }, title: "Winston
                    Churchill"},
                    { info: { key: "Allen" }, title: "Woody Allen"},
                    { info: { key: "Confucius" }, title: "Confucius"},
                    { info: { key: "Twain" }, title: "Mark Twain"},
                    { info: { key: "Einstein" }, title: "Albert Einstein"},
                    { info: { key: "Wright" }, title: "Steven Wright"}
                ]
            }
        }
        ]
    };
    console.log('sendAuthors: ' + JSON.stringify(responseJson));
    response.json(responseJson);
}
```

3. Deploy the code and test the `list authors` command in the simulator and you will see that the list of authors will be displayed.

The following screenshot shows the displayed `listSelect` response, containing the author names:

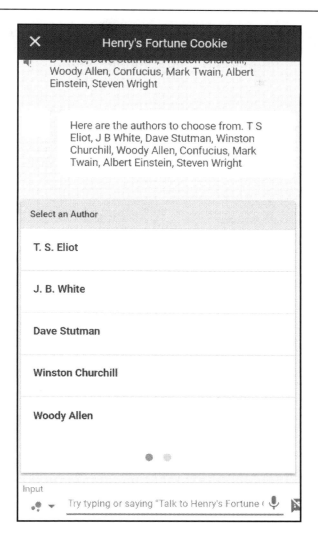

Building a Get Author Quote intent

When the user selects the author from the list, the author's name will be sent back to Dialogflow and you will want to build an intent that captures the authors and then selects a quote by that selected author. Using the Author entity, build an intent that gets triggered when the user says the author's name or the author's name is selected from the list. Create Get Author Quote and add @Author:Author to **User says** and enable **Use webhook**.

The following screenshot shows the Get Author Quote intent settings:

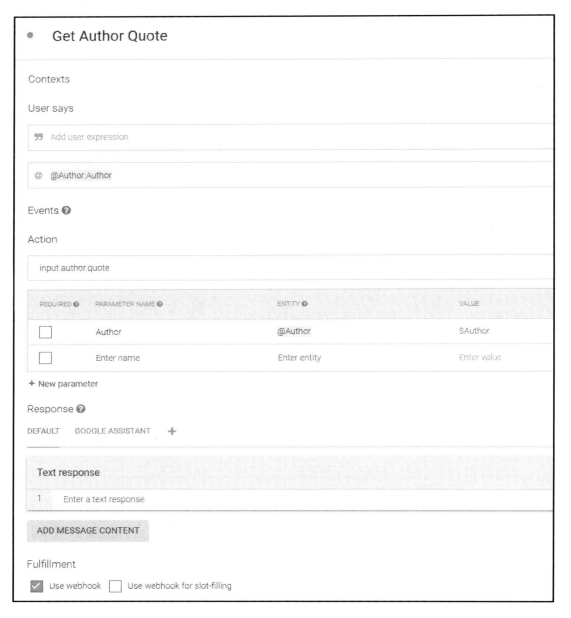

Get Author Quote intent

Building a Get Author Quote intent's webhook

1. When the `Get Author Quote` intent is triggered, the request will come into the webhook with the **Action** name `input.author.quote`, and `input.author.quote` needs to be added to `intentHandler`, which will execute the `sendAuthorQuote` function.

   The following code handles the request with the **Action** name `input.author.quote` triggered by the `Get Author Quote` intent and will execute the `sendAuthorQuote` function:

   ```
   'input.author.quote': () => {
     sendAuthorQuote();
   },
   ```

2. Now create a `sendAuthorQuote` function, which will build a response with the request author. When `Get Author Quote` is triggered, either by the user saying the author's name or by selecting from the list of the authors, the request will be sent with `parameters.Author`.

   The following line of code uses `parameters.Author` to search the quotes array and extract the author's quote:

   ```
   quotes.find(x =>
   x.author.toLowerCase().indexOf(parameters.Author.toLowerCase())>=0)
   .quote
   ```

3. Finally, the author's quote is set to `fulfillmentText` and sent as a response and the user will hear the author's quote.

   The following code shows the completed version of the `sendAuthorQuote` function:

   ```
   function sendAuthorQuote () {
     let authorQuote = quotes.find(x =>
   x.author.toLowerCase().indexOf(parameters.Author.toLowerCase())>=0)
   .quote;
     let responseJson = { fulfillmentText: authorQuote };
     console.log('sendAuthorQuote: ' + JSON.stringify(responseJson));
     response.json(responseJson);
   }
   ```

SSML and audio integration

Previously, in Chapter 1, *Introduction,* you used SSML to manipulate tone, rate, and pitch to make speech sound more human. In this section, you will modify the **Default Welcome** intent to sound more exciting and also introduce an opening sound, so that when the user first uses the FortuneCookie, they will hear a thunder sound and then the FortuneCookie will welcome the user with excitement. Using SSML and sound brings that *pop* to your application, making it more fun to engage with. You can find more information on SSML that Dialogflow supports at http://bit.ly/2BHBQmq.

Integrating SSML and audio to Default Welcome intent

Previously, **Default Welcome** intent simply greeted the user with Hello, Welcome to Henry's Fortune Cookie! by setting fulfillmentText in the response object. Let's enhance this by using the simpleResponses object in the fulfillmentMessages property of the response object. The simpleResponses object contains properties called ssml and displayText. The ssml property contains SSML speech and also part of SSML speech the audio sound can be incorporated. displayText is displayed if the device does not have the audio capability.

In ssml, the speech will start with the thunder sound <audio src="https://actions.google.com/sounds/v1/weather/thunder_crack.ogg" /> and then there will be a pause of 200 ms, <break time="200ms"/>. Finally, Hello Welcome to Henry's Fortune Cookie! will be inside <prosody rate="medium" pitch="+2st">, where the speech rate is set to medium with a slightly higher pitch, set at +2st.

Setting a high pitch with a medium speech rate will give the effect of being excited and happy.

The following code shows the `simpleResponse` object set with the SSML speech, which contains the audio in the `sendWelcome` function:

```
responseJson = {
      fulfillmentText: 'Hello, Welcome to Henry\'s Fortune Cookie!',
      fulfillmentMessages: [
        {
          platform: "ACTIONS_ON_GOOGLE",
          simpleResponses: {
            simpleResponses: [
              {
                ssml: `<speak>
                      <audio
src="https://actions.google.com/sounds/v1/weather/thunder_crack.ogg" />
                      <break time="200ms"/>
                      <prosody rate="medium" pitch="+2st">
                        Hello Welcome to Henry's Fortune Cookie!
                      </prosody>
                    </speak>`,
                displayText: "Hello, Welcome to Henry\'s Fortune Cookie!"
              } ] } } ]
};
```

Testing the default welcome intent SSML and audio sound

In order to come up with perfect-sounding speech, you will need to experiment with SSML. The best way to do this is by trial and error, using the simulator found in `Actions` on Google. In the simulator, there is an **AUDIO** section, where you can enter an SSML speech, then click the **UPDATE AND LISTEN** button to play back the SSML.

The following image shows the simulator's audio section, where SSML speech can be entered and tested:

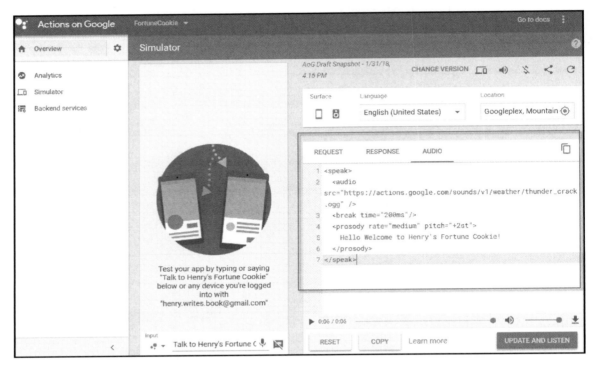

Testing SSML using the simulator

Using Analytics

In Dialogflow, there is an **Analytics** section, where you can see the performance of the agent. The following data metrics are collected:

- The number of queries per user session
- The number of times the intent was called
- The percentage of where user exited
- The average response time to user requests

One of the important metrics is the number of times the intent was called, because it gives us an insight into the most popular intent in your VUIs. Once you know which intent is popular, you can continue to improve it. Also, knowing the average response time to user requests provides important information, as you would not want your user to wait a long time for a response.

The following image shows you the all the metrics collected by Dialogflow Analytics:

Dialogflow Analytics

Summary

In this chapter, you learned how to use a built-in Node.js server, and Cloud Functions for Firebase provided by Dialogflow to handle fulfillments through webhooks. In the Firebase Node.js server, a user intent request is intercepted and then a response object is created. You learned how to trigger an intent using an event in the code and also built a follow-up intent to create a conversation. Then, you built more advanced response objects using selectList, SSML, and audio. Finally, you learned about the data metrics collected by Dialogflow in the agent analytics section. In the next chapter, you will learn how to deploy the Node.js middle tier to the Microsoft Azure cloud, thereby taking full control of your infrastructure environment.

4

Hosting, Securing, and Testing Fortune Cookie in the Cloud

In the previous chapter, the built-in Node.js server in Dialogflow was used to create a Fortune Cookie Webhook that responds to the user inquiries. In this chapter, you will learn how to deploy Node.js webhook code to the Microsoft Azure cloud. Traditionally, to build a server to deploy web application code required extensive knowledge of networking and server hardware. However, Microsoft Azure makes it very easy to build a virtual server with a click of a button, bypassing the need to build a physical server and set up complex networking. This chapter will cover various Microsoft Azure offerings in order to deploy Node.js code and, even as a novice, you will be able to perform complex network administrator tasks as if you were an expert. Learning how to use Microsoft Azure will give you a taste of what it's like to create a real-world enterprise-grade Node.js web service. You will also learn how to use Microsoft Azure's NoSQL database, known as Cosmos DB to store author quotes and dynamically query quotes. During the development process, you will learn about securing the Node.js RESTful API for DialogFlow webhooks. Finally, you will test the Fortune Cookie application using the Dialogflow client SDK.

This chapter will cover the following topics:

- Learning about Microsoft Azure
- Hosting the Node.js RESTful API in Microsoft Azure for Dialogflow webhooks
- Using Microsoft Azure Cosmos DB
- Securing the Node.js RESTful API
- Managing Microsoft Azure Cosmos DB and a Node.js service
- Testing Dialogflow using SDK

What is the Microsoft Azure cloud platform?

These days, you will hear a lot of buzz around cloud computing. There are many competing cloud platforms such as Microsoft Azure, **Amazon Web Services (AWS)**, Google Cloud Platform, and IBM Cloud. Today, it is very likely that you are already using some kind of cloud platform at home. For example, in the past, there was Blockbuster, where you had to walk into the store to rent and return movies. However, walking into a store and renting and returning movies could be very time consuming. Nowadays, you can simply pay a monthly flat fee to Netflix and watch as many movies as you like, in the comfort of your home. Similarly, in order to deploy a web service like the Fortune Cookie webhook, you would need to build a physical server, place the server in a data center, and route a network cable to the server. Obviously, I simplified the server deployment process, but the traditional approach is very time consuming, costly, and complex and not every developer would be able to do it. This is where cloud platforms like Microsoft Azure come into the picture, virtualizing that physical process into a simple process of clicking buttons on the Microsoft Azure website in order to build, create, and deploy a network to the web service server.

The following parameters explain why you would want to use the cloud platform to build your webhook in the cloud.

- **Cost**: Cloud platforms eliminate the need to buy physical hardware and software. Also, charges are based on usage, so if you do not use the server, you can simply turn it off and save money.
- **Fast time to market**: The server can be built and deployed by you in a minute, at the click of a button, and you simply focus on building an application.
- **Scalable**: Let's say that today you are targeting users in America, and tomorrow you need to target audiences in Asia. With cloud platforms, you can easily scale your web services globally.
- **Performance**: You never know—the voice application you build might do extremely well. For example, your voice application users might increase from 100 to 100,000 in a matter of days. With the increase in the amount of users using your voice application, the webhook must be able to support increases in usage. Cloud platforms allows you to quickly increase the performance of servers to accommodate demand.
- **Easy to maintain**: On a cloud platform, servers are easily maintained, allowing you to focus more on developing new features for your voice application. Also, because it is easy to maintain, maintenance costs will be low as well.

- **Reliability**: You would not want users to experience a critical error because your webhook went down. Cloud platforms bring highly available servers with redundancies and backups with a service level agreement of 99.9% to 99.99% uptime guarantees.

The following table details uptime percentages in terms of per year, per month, per week, and per day:

Availability %	Downtime per year	Downtime per month	Downtime per week	Downtime per day
99.9%	8.76 hours	43.8 minutes	10.1 minutes	1.44 minutes
99.99%	52.56 minutes	4.38 minutes	1.01 minutes	8.64 seconds

Fortune Cookie architectural topology in Microsoft Azure

You will notice that there are many Microsoft Azure products offered for free (https://azure.microsoft.com/en-us/free/). You will be using App Service, and Cosmos DB. App Service provides a server platform for deploying the Node.js webhook that you built in the previous chapter. Later, in the *Deploying a Node.js webhook* section, you will learn about many of the features provided by App Service. Cosmos DB will be used to store static fortune cookie quotes hardcoded in the code in the previous chapter so that the quotes can be dynamically returned using **structured query language (SQL)**.

The following diagram shows the Fortune Cookie architecture topology hosted in Microsoft Azure using App Service and Cosmos DB.

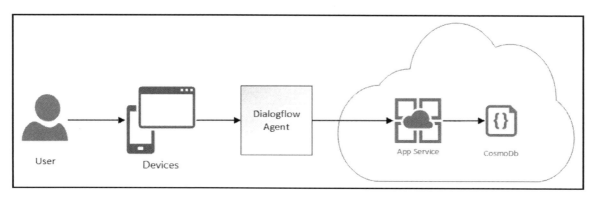

Fortune Cookie Architecture Topology in Microsoft Azure

Deploying a Fortune Cookie webhook to Microsoft Azure

Before you can begin deploying the Node.js webhook to Microsoft Azure, you will need to install various tools. Here are the steps you will need to follow to install and configure your computer:

1. Create a Microsoft Azure account. Go to `https://azure.microsoft.com/en-us/free/` and follow the instructions.
2. Install `https://nodejs.org/`. You will be using Node.js to locally debug and will test in Visual Studio Code.
3. Once Node.js is installed, check the Node.js version by typing `node -v` in the Node.js Command Prompt. I am using Version 8.9.4, but any more recent version will work.
4. Install the Azure CLI (`http://bit.ly/2w3J00u`). The Azure CLI is a command-line tool for managing the Microsoft Azure cloud platform.
5. In order to test your webhook, you will need to install Postman (`https://www.getpostman.com/`).
6. You will deploy your Node.js code using FTP. Download and install FileZilla (`https://filezilla-project.org/`).

Updating Fortune Cookie's Node.js webhook code

In the previous chapter, Node.js code was specifically written for Google Firebase's Cloud Function, which was integrated into Dialogflow. You need to modify the code slightly in order to make it work on the Node.js server:

1. Create a file called `server.js`.
2. Begin by declaring `require('express')`, which is a web-application framework for creating RESTful APIs that Dialogflow will be using. In the previous section, we relied on the Google Firebase framework to create RESTful APIs. Declare `require('body-parser')`, which will handle incoming requests as JSON data. Finally, declare `require('http')` to create an HTTP web server.

The following code declares the components needed by the Node.js express web server:

```
var express = require('express');
var bodyParser = require('body-parser');
var http = require('http');
```

3. Next, instantiate `express`, `body-parser`, and `http` components, and create an `http` server listening on port `8000`.

   The following code instantiates `express`, `body-parser`, and an `http` component, and then creates an HTTP server listening on port `8000`.

```
var app = express();
var server = http.createServer(app);
app.use(bodyParser.json());

var port = process.env.PORT || 8000;
server.listen(port, function () {
    console.log("Server is up and running...");
});
```

4. In the previous chapter, you relied on Google Firebase to intercept web requests from Dialogflow using `exports.dialogflowFirebaseFulfillment = firebase.https.onRequest`. In this chapter, you will use the Node.js express server to intercept calls from Dialogflow using `app.post('/fortuneCookie', function (req, res) {})`. Every other piece of code that was written in the previous chapter stays the same.

   The following code creates a POST method that Dialogflow will call to send a request to get the intents' fulfillments:

```
app.post('/fortuneCookie', function (req, res) {

    request = req;
    response = res;
    console.log('Fortune Cookie Request headers: ' +
JSON.stringify(request.headers));
    console.log('Fortune Cookie Request body: ' +
JSON.stringify(request.body));
    if (request.body.queryResult) {
      processV2Request();
    } else {
      console.log('Invalid Request');
      return response.status(400).end('Invalid Webhook Request');
    }
```

```
});
```

Testing a webhook locally

In this section, you will learn how to use Visual Studio Code to run Node.js code locally and then test it using Postman before deploying it to the actual Node.js server in Microsoft Azure App Service:

1. Open your Node.js prompt.
2. Run `npm init`, which will create a `package.json`. The `package.json` contains the dependency information for running your Node.js code.
3. Run `npm install express --save` and `npm install body-parser --save`. `express` and `body-parser` are the components required for the webhook you just created.
4. Edit `package.json` and add `"script": "./server.js"`. By default `server.js` will run.

   The following code shows the created `package.json` file:

   ```
   {
     "name": "fortuneCookie",
     "description": "",
     "version": "0.1.0",
     "author": "Henry Lee <henry@henrylee.link>",
     "dependencies": {
       "body-parser": "^1.9.0",
       "express": "^4.0.0",
       "jsonpath": "^0.2.0"
     },
     "script": "./server.js"
   }
   ```

5. Go to Visual Studio Code, click on the `server.js` file, and press *F5*. The Node.js HTTP server will be listening on port `8000`.
6. Click on line `18`, `request = req;`. You will be adding a breakpoint that gets triggered to stop the code from further executing when you post a method using Postman.

The following screenshot shows the breakpoint at line 18:

```
16 ⊟ app.post('/fortuneCookie', function (req, res) {
17
● 18        request = req;
19        response = res;
```

Line 18 breakpoint

7. Go to Postman and create a POST method to
   `http://localhost:8000/fortuneCookie`. In the `http` body, put `{ "queryResult": { "action": "input.welcome" } }`. Here, you are simulating what Dialogflow will be sending to your Node.js webhook.

The following screenshot shows Postman posting to a Node.js server running locally:

Postman posting to a local Node.js server

8. Go to Visual Studio Code editor and you will notice that the code execution stopped at line `18`, where the breakpoint is. If you hover over the `req` object, you will be able to see in detail the contents of the `req` object. Press *F5* to let the code execute.

The following screenshot shows the breakpoint at line 18 and the contents of the `req` object:

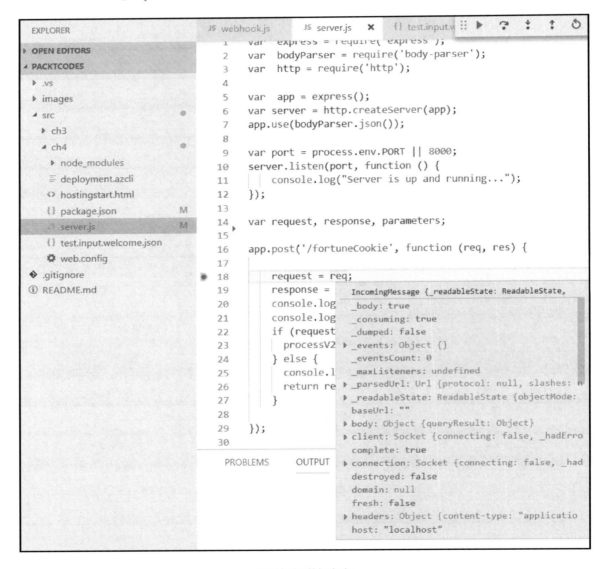

Visual Studio with breakpoint

9. Go to Postman and you will see the response received from the Node.js server running locally.

The following screenshot shows Postman receiving the response from the Node.js server running locally:

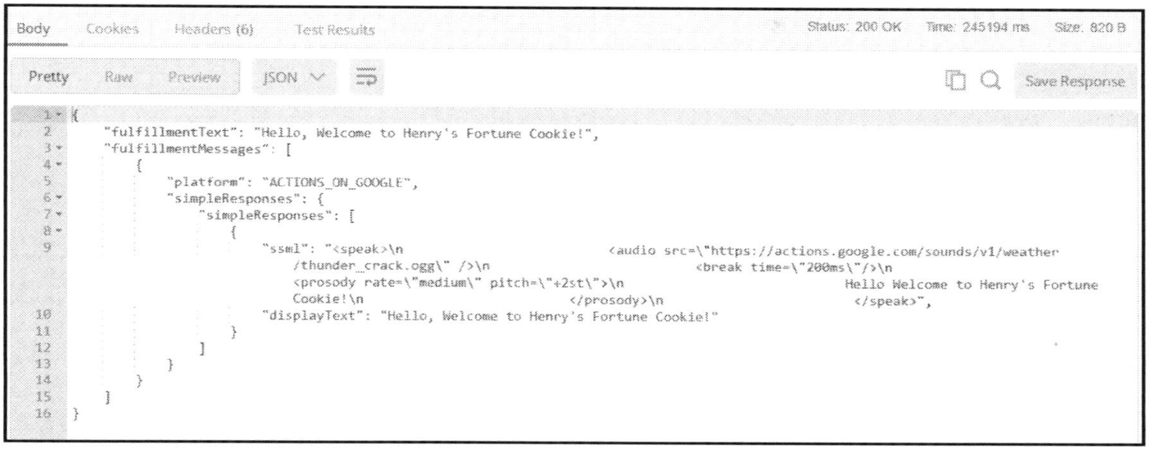

Postman receives the response from the Node.js server running locally

Creating a web.config to run Node.js in Microsoft Azure

Create a `web.config`, which will tell the Microsoft Azure web server what to do with `server.js`, which contains Node.js code, by adding `<add name="iisnode" path="server.js" verb="*" modules="iisnode"/>`. Also, you will redirect all requests to `server.js` by adding the URL rewrite rule with `<match url="/*" /> <action type="Rewrite" url="server.js"/>`.

The following code shows the complete `web.config` file, which will be deployed to the Node.js server:

```xml
<?xml version="1.0" encoding="utf-8"?>
  <configuration>
    <system.webServer>
      <handlers>
        <add name="iisnode" path="server.js" verb="*" modules="iisnode"/>
      </handlers>
      <rewrite>
        <rules>
            <rule name="DynamicContent">
                <match url="/*" />
```

```
            <action type="Rewrite" url="server.js"/>
          </rule>
      </rules>
      </rewrite>
  </system.webServer>
</configuration>
```

Creating Microsoft Azure App Service to host a Node.js webhook

Since you successfully tested your locally running Fortune Cookie webhook, you are ready to host the webhook on the Microsoft Azure App Service Node.js server:

1. Open Command Prompt, type `az login`, and follow the instructions on the screen.

2. Once you've logged in, type `az account list` to view a list of the accounts that you are managing. If you have multiple accounts, you will need to set the account you want to use using `az account set --s put-account-id`.

3. Create a resource group using `az group create --name HenryResourceGroup --location eastus`. Resource group is the logical name given to a container that contains multiple services. For example, let's say you created a resource group called `myWebApplication`, which contains the web server, the database, the file storage, and the virtual network. You can easily view all of the Microsoft Azure resources used by simply going to the `myWebApplication` resource group. You can also delete all the resources associated with creating `myWebApplication`.

4. Create a Microsoft Azure App Service Plan by using `az appservice plan create --name myAppServicePlan --resource-group HenryResourceGroup --sku FREE`. Think of an App Service plan as a server cluster that contains the collections of the servers. In your case, you will be creating a collection of Node.js servers that are highly available and redundant.

5. Create a Node.js web server using
   `az webapp create --name henryApp1234 --resource-group HenryResourceGroup --plan myAppServicePlan --runtime"NODE|8.1".`

6. Create a user that you will use to access the FTP site to deploy the code files with `az webapp deployment user set --user-name myusername --password mypassword`.

7. Let's view all the resources you have created so far. Log in to the Microsoft Azure portal (`https://portal.azure.com`).

8. Click on **Resource groups** on the right-hand menu and you will be able to see the resource that you just created.

The following image shows the **Resource groups**:

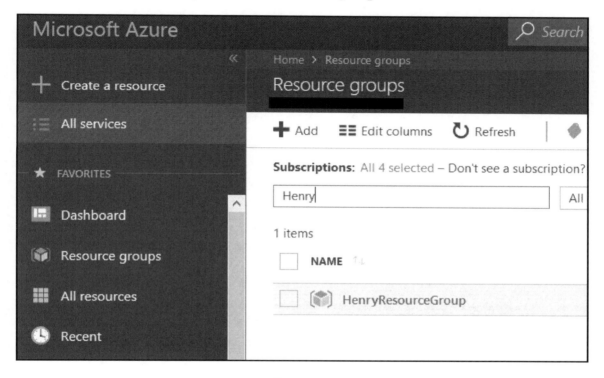

Resource groups

9. Click on the **HenryResourceGroup** and you will see the `henryApp1234` Node.js server created using the Azure CLI.

The following image shows the list of resources under **HenryResourceGroup**:

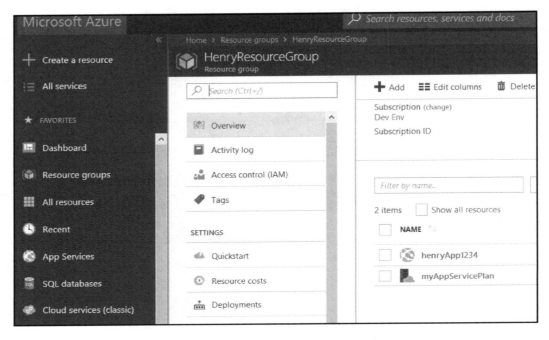

List of resources in the resource group

10. Click on `henryApp1234`. `henryApp1234` is the Node.js server.

The following screenshot shows the `henryApp1234` Node.js server information:

henryApp1234 Node.js server

Take a note of the following properties:

- **URL:** Dialogflow will use this URL to post requests in order to get fulfillment responses for the Fortune Cookie quotes
- **FTP deployment username:** The username will be used to log in to the FTP server for the deployment
- **FTP hostname:** The FTP site address, which you will need to connect to in order to deploy the webhook code

11. Open FileZilla and go to **File | Site manager**.
12. Add `New Site` and enter the **Host**, the username, the password, and select **Use explicit FTP over TLS if available**.

The following screenshot shows the FTP configuration for connecting to the Node.js server host in Microsoft Azure:

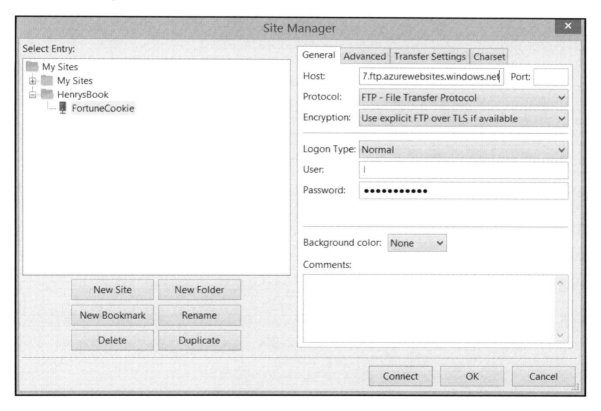

FTP site configuration connecting to Node.js server in Microsoft Azure

13. Click **Connect**. You will be deploying three files (`web.config`, `server.js`, and `package.json`) to `/site/wwwroot`.

The following screenshot shows the deployment of three files to the Node.js server via the FTP file manager:

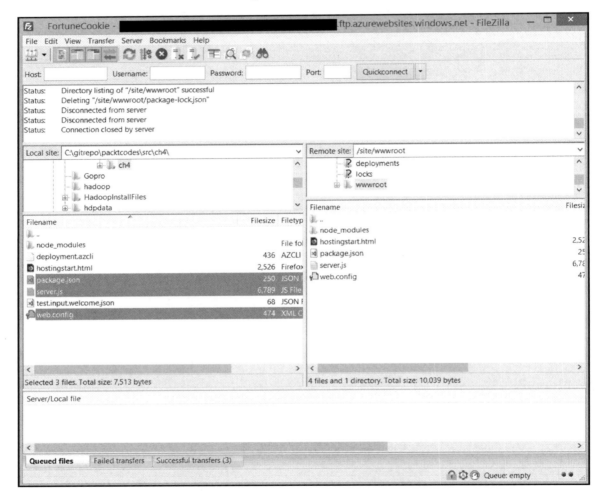

Deploying Node.js files to Microsoft Azure via FTP

14. You tested locally by pointing Postman to `http://localhost:8000/fortuneCookie`. Test with Postman by pointing the URL to `https://henryapp1234.azurewebsites.net/fortuneCookie`.

Configuring Dialogflow webhook

1. Log in to Dialogflow
2. Go to the **Fulfillment** section
3. Enable **Webhook** and enter the following URL from Microsoft Azure
   `https://henryapp1234.azurewebsites.net/fortuneCookie`

The following image shows the configured webhook pointing to the Microsoft Azure Node.js server that you deployed:

The text in this screenshot is not important. It shows how to enable webhook pointing to the Microsoft Azure Node.js server

Now you can use Google Assistant or the Dialogflow simulator to test, as shown in `Chapter 3`, *Building a Fortune Cookie Application*, and everything should work seamlessly!

Securing the Node.js webhook for Dialogflow

You will now make slight modifications to the Node.js code in order to secure the webhook. The one you deployed is not secure and anyone can access it.

1. Go to Dialogflow and to the **Fulfillment** section.
2. In the headers, add the key `mysecret` and the value `12345`.

The following screenshot shows the security header added to the webhook:

Webhook

Your web service will receive a POST request from Dialogflow in the form of the response to a user query service meets all the webhook requirements specific to the API version enabled in this agent.

Webhook example

URL*	https://henryapp1234.azurewebsites.net/fortuneCookie
BASIC AUTH	Enter username Enter password
HEADERS	mysecret 12345
	Enter key Enter value
	Enter key Enter value

⊕ Add header

Securing the webhook

3. Edit `server.js`. Add code that extracts the `mysecret` key using `let secret = req.get("mysecret")`. Then, check the value and see if it is equal to `12345`. If it is equal, process the request, and if not, return a 403 access denied response return `response.status(403).end('Access denied!')`.

The following code shows the modified code that secures the webhook:

```
app.post('/fortuneCookie', function (req, res) {
    let secret = req.get("mysecret");
    if(secret === "12345"){
      request = req;
      response = res;
      console.log('Fortune Cookie Request headers: ' +
JSON.stringify(request.headers));
      console.log('Fortune Cookie Request body: ' +
JSON.stringify(request.body));
        if (request.body.queryResult) {
          processV2Request();
        } else {
          console.log('Invalid Request');
          return response.status(400).end('Invalid Webhook Request');
```

```
        }
      }
      else {
         return response.status(403).end('Access denied!');
      }
});
```

4. Deploy the code to Microsoft Azure using FTP.
5. Test it using Postman. In Postman, you will need to add the `mysecret` key and value in the header section.

   The following image shows the headers in Postman when posting to a secure webhook:

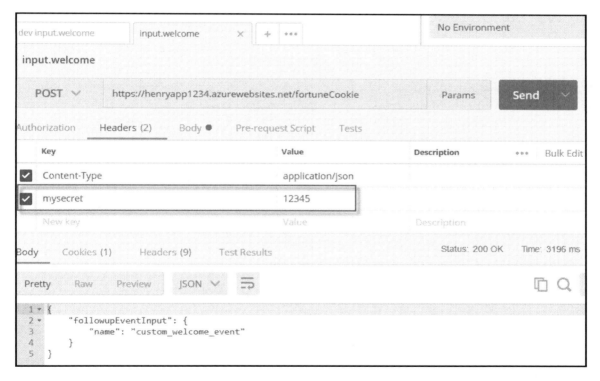

Postman posting to a secure webhook

6. Now test it with Google Assistant or the Dialogflow simulator.

That's it—you have now secured a webhook only your Dialogflow can access!

Storing Quotes in Cosmos DB

In the previous chapter, the Fortune Cookie quotes were part of the code file, and if you had to add a new quote, you would have to change the code file and redeploy the code. Redeploying the code in order to add a new quote is a maintenance nightmare. Typically, data is stored in a database because it allows you to insert new data without affecting the code. Having separation of concerns is an important architectural decision, where data concerns should be handled by the database and the code should be separate from the data. In this section, we will migrate the Fortune Cookie quotes out of the code and put them into Cosmos DB.

Why use Cosmos DB? The following are just some of the reasons:

- **NoSQL database**: There is no schema, making it easy to design the database based on JSON.
- **Highly available**: Service level agreement guarantees 99.99% uptime.
- **Distributed database**: The database can be globally distributed. So, if you are working from Korea, your application will point to Cosmos DB distributed in Korea to eliminate latency.
- **Multiple ways to query data**: In this chapter, you will learn how to use SQL-like language, as it is a very popular query language style. But Cosmos DB also supports other styles such as MongoDB, Graph, Casandra, and Table.
- **Speed**: Cosmos DB is very fast.
- **Scale**: Cosmos DB can scale to very large databases.
- **Low cost**: It is cheap to set up and maintain.

Creating Cosmos DB

Let's start by creating Cosmos DB and storing the fortune cookie quotes:

1. Log in to the Azure portal (`https://portal.azure.com`).
2. Click on the **+ Create a resource** button.
3. Search for Azure Cosmos DB and click on the **Create** button.
4. Use **ID** = `henrydb`, **API** = **SQL**, **Resource Group** = **HenryResourceGroup**, **Location** = **East US**.

The following screenshot shows the Azure Cosmos DB **Create** setting:

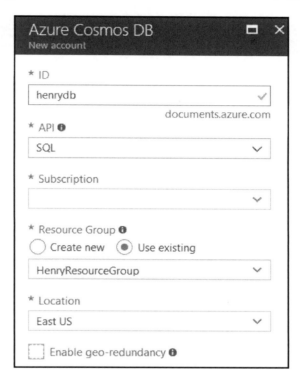

* ID

henrydb

documents.azure.com

* API

SQL

* Subscription

* Resource Group

◯ Create new   ◉ Use existing

HenryResourceGroup

* Location

East US

☐ Enable geo-redundancy

Cosmo DB Create setting

5. Now go to `henrydb` in Cosmos DB. You can always search your resources by going to **HenryResourceGroup**, in case you cannot find the resource that you are looking for.

6. In `henrydb`, click the **Add Collection** button.

7. Use **Database id** = `myDb`, **Collection id** = `myCollection`, **Storage Capacity** = **Fixed (10GB)**, **Throughput** = `400`. Here, I picked the cheapest setting.

The following image shows the Cosmos DB **Collection Create** setting:

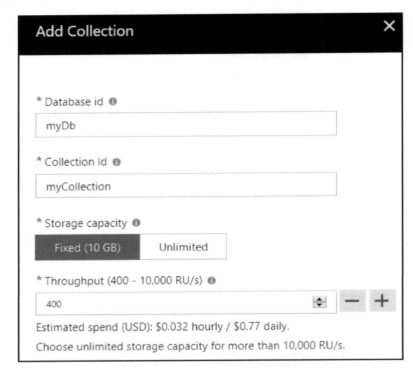

Cosmos DB create collection

Importing the Fortune Cookie quotes

You will now learn how to import a data file that contains the author quotes in JSON format to the Cosmos DB that you just created. This is a very useful technique that you can use if you have a large amount of data that you need to migrate onto a database:

1. Download and install the Microsoft Cosmos DB Data Migration Tool (`http://bit.ly/2C4Es0H`).
2. Log in to the Azure Portal and go to `henrydb` Cosmos DB.

3. On the menu, click on **Keys**. Here, you will find the URL, and the keys that are necessary in your code to create a connection string to connect to Cosmos DB. You will also use the same information in the Cosmos DB Data Migration tool.

The following image shows the Cosmos DB connection string information:

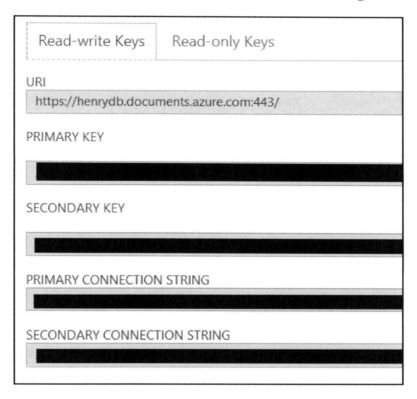

Cosmo DB Keys

4. Open the installed Cosmos DB Data Migration tool.
5. Choose the author.json file as the source that contains the author quotes. In the previous chapter, you already created this.
6. In the **Target Information** section, choose **Export to DocumentDB**, enter the connection string from step 3, and set **Collection** to myCollection. Hit **Next** and click **Import**.

The following screenshot shows the Cosmos DB Data Migration tool settings:

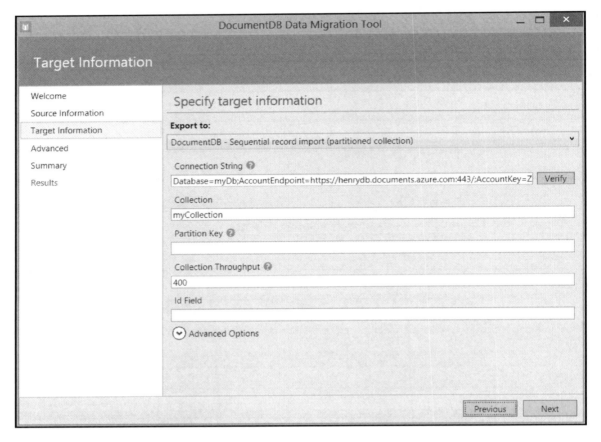

Cosmo DB Import JSON

7. Log in to the Azure Portal, go to `henrydb`, and click on **Data Explorer**. You will be able to see the imported `json` data.

The following screenshot shows the Cosmos DB Data Explorer, showing the imported `json` data:

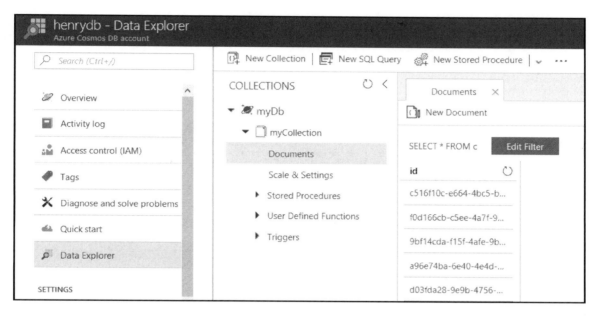

Cosmos DB Data Explorer

Updating the Node.js webhook to use Cosmos DB

Here, you will modify your code to use Cosmos DB to dynamically query data. You will remove the constant variable quotes that contain the author quotes.

1. Open Command Prompt and go to the directory where the `server.js` file is.
2. Type `npm install documentdb --save`. This will install the Cosmos DB component that you can use in the Node.js code to access Cosmos DB and query data. Also `--save` will save `documentdb` as dependencies in `package.json`.
3. Open `server.js` in Visual Studio Code.
4. Declare the Cosmos DB client using `var documentClient = require('documentdb').DocumentClient`.

5. Declare the Cosmos DB endpoint and primary key to create a Cosmos DB client: `var dbClient = new documentClient(endpoint, { "masterKey": primaryKey })`.

6. Declare `colLink`, which will be used to query Cosmos DB.

   The following code shows the declarations for querying CosmoDB:

   ```
   var documentClient = require('documentdb').DocumentClient
   var endpoint = "https://henrydb.documents.azure.com:443/";
   var primaryKey =
   "ZJBcmZppBpZB5nIfjUO1lvSmoLrvo6uzYGMoRaAcAayVZG0LG9HXTdjZhkvjE6OWFZ
   vowxFiNeRxBpZBWm1uLg==";
   var dbClient = new documentClient(endpoint, { "masterKey":
   primaryKey });
   var dbLink = 'dbs/myDb';
   var collLink = dbLink + '/colls/myCollection';
   ```

7. Remove `const quotes`. We will replace this by querying the quotes from Cosmos DB.

8. Create a `sendQuoteResponse` function. There are three functions that you need to incorporate into the Cosmos DB code: `sendQuote`, `sendQuoteWithFeeling`, and `sendAuthorQuote`. You will be refactoring the code, as all three of these functions will use Cosmos DB in very similar ways. You will create new function called `sendQuoteResponse`, which will basically receive the `query`, the `index` and the `functionName`. The `query` contains the SQL-like query syntax that will be sent to Cosmos DB to pull the result sets, the `index` will be used to select a specific result from the array of quotes, and finally, the `functionName` will be used for logging to make sure that, if something fails, you will know which function caused the error. Using `dbClient.queryDocuments(collLink, query).toArray(function (err, quotes)`, you will send the query request to Cosmos DB and then receive the result. When the query receives the result, it will send the response back to appropriate Dialogflow quote.

   The following code shows the `sendQuoteResponse`:

   ```
   function sendQuoteResponse(query, index, functionName) {
     dbClient.queryDocuments(collLink, query).toArray(function (err,
   quotes) {
       if(err)
         return response.status(400).end('Error while calling
   cosmoDB in ' + functionName);
       else {
         let responseJson = { fulfillmentText: quotes[index].quote
   };
   ```

```
          console.log(functionName + ":" +
JSON.stringify(responseJson));
          response.json(responseJson);
      }
    });
  }
```

9. **Modify** `sendQuote`, `sendQuoteWithFeeling`, **and** `sendAuthorQuote` **to use** `sendQuoteResponse`. **Previously,** `fulfilmentTexts` **were set with static quotes. In the new code, they are replaced with** `sendQuoteResponse` **but the query is built independently in each of the functions and sent to the** `sendQuoteResponse`. **The** `sendQuote` **function and the** `sendQuoteWithFeeling` **function creates the query** `let query = "SELECT * FROM c"`, **where the query selects all the quotes stored in Cosmos DB. On the other hand,** `sendAuthorQuote` **creates** `let query = "SELECT * FROM c where contains(lower(c.author), '" + parameters.Author.toLowerCase() + "')"`, **where the query filters the quotes by author name.**

   The following code shows the modified `sendQuote`, `sendQuoteWithFeeling`, and `sendAuthorQuote`:

```
function sendQuoteWithFeeling () {
  let responseJson, randomNumber;
  if(parameters.Feeling === "happy"){
    randomNumber = Math.floor(Math.random() * 5);
  }
  else {
    randomNumber = Math.floor(Math.random() * 4) + 5;
  }
  let query = "SELECT * FROM c";
  sendQuoteResponse(query, randomNumber, "sendQuoteWithFeeling");
}
function sendQuote () {
  let randomNumber = Math.floor(Math.random() * 9);
  let query = "SELECT * FROM c";
  sendQuoteResponse(query, randomNumber, "sendQuote");
}
function sendAuthorQuote () {
  let query = "SELECT * FROM c where contains(lower(c.author), '"
+ parameters.Author.toLowerCase() + "')";
  sendQuoteResponse(query, 0, "sendAuthorQuote");
}
```

10. Open Postman and test this locally, then deploy it to the Microsoft Azure Node.js server using FTP.

Installing a new component on Microsoft Node.js

The new modified code uses a Cosmos DB Node.js component called `documentdb`. The Node.js server that you previously created does not have a `documentdb` component. In this section, you will learn how to install a custom component on the server:

1. Go to the Azure portal and then navigate to `henryApp1234`, the Node.js server that you created.
2. On the menu of `henryApp1234`, click on **Console**.
3. In the **Console**, type `npm install documentdb -g`. This will install the missing component, allowing your code to run properly.

   The following screenshot shows the Microsoft App Service Node.js server **Console** where you can execute `npm` commands to install missing components:

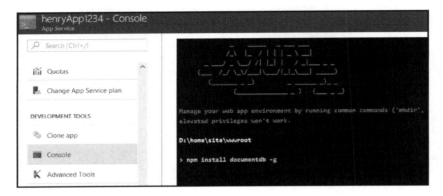

Microsoft Node.js server console

4. Using Postman, test the webhook and then test it using Google Assistant or the simulator.

Managing the Microsoft Azure Node.js service

Now you have successfully deployed your Node.js code, you will need to learn how to maintain it in Microsoft Azure. Microsoft Azure makes it very simple to maintain a Node.js service and also makes it very easy to scale out if your application happens to become very popular. Let's look at some of the menus that are in your `henryApp1234` Node.js service.

Creating a backup of the service

You never know when there could be a catastrophic failure in the virtual server that maintains your Node.js service. To prepare for that, it is best practice to create a backup of your server contents. When you go to `henryApp1234` in the Microsoft Azure portal, you will see **Backup** in the menu. Click on it and you can easily configure the **Backup service** setting by selecting the storage and configuring the time interval.

The following screenshot shows the **Backup Configuration** for App Service:

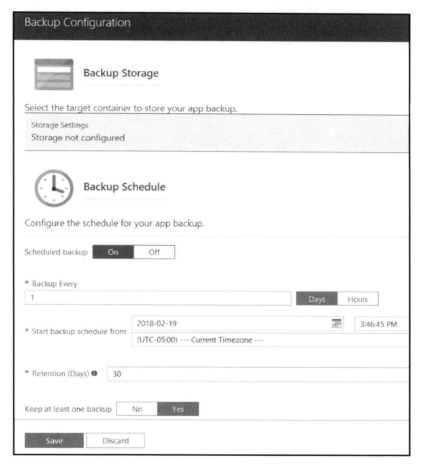

App Service backup

Scaling up or scaling out

If you create a popular voice application that millions of people will use, your Node.js server must scale up or scale out in order to meet the request demands coming from devices. Microsoft Azure App Service provides the ability to scale up and scale out very easily.

The following screenshot shows the Microsoft Azure App Service settings for `henryApp1234`:

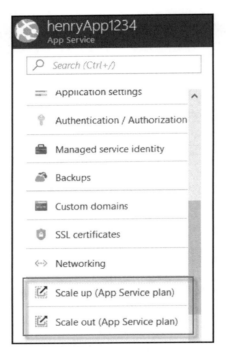

App Service settings

Scaling up is when you increase server capacity. For example, a typical server, when busy, will consume both the memories and the CPU cycles. When you click on the scale up setting in your `henryApp1234`, you will be presented with many options to choose from. Depending on what your Node.js service is doing, your needs will vary.

The following image shows server capacities according to their price:

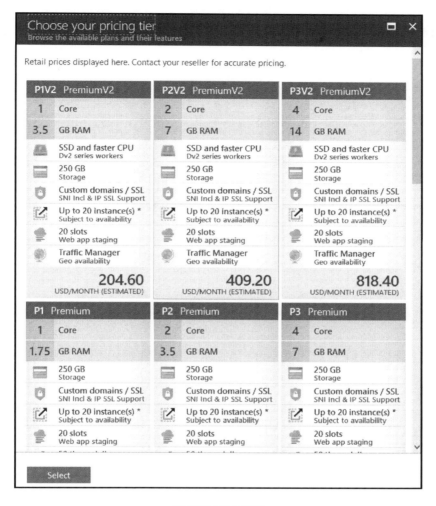

App Service scale-up options

Scaling up may not be enough to meet demand, so you will need to scale out as well. In scale-out architecture, you are basically creating multiple servers to fulfill request demands. In scale-out settings, you have the option to create an auto scale where you can create a rule based on CPU usage and allow Microsoft Azure to automatically create the new Node.js server by simply cloning the server you set up.

The following image shows scaling out settings based on a CPU percentage greater than 70%:

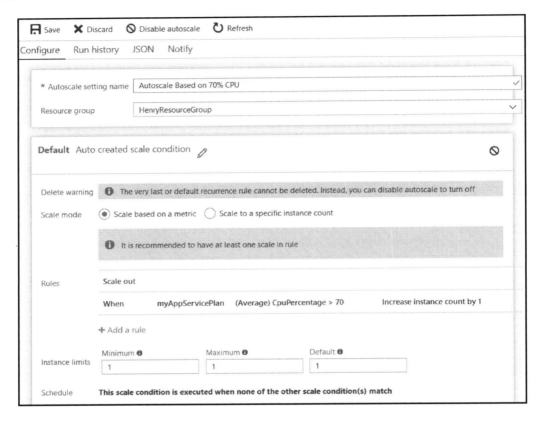

App Service autoscale

Managing Cosmos DB

Just like Microsoft Azure App Service for Node.js, you do not need to worry about backing up and scalability. Microsoft Azure provides an easy-to-use user interface to configure your Cosmos DB to handle much higher demand. Here, I am assuming that when you have greater demands for your database, it means that lots of users are using your application and that you are makings lots of money. This is the beauty of Microsoft Azure—that you start with free stuff and, if you are making money, you can increase your capacity and performance by simply configuring services to meet demand.

Scaling out Cosmos DB

When there is high demand for Cosmos DB, you will need to properly scale out. In Cosmos DB settings, there is a scale setting. Cosmos DB has a unit called **RU/s (request units per second)**, which is used to calculate cost and scalability. You can also think of RU/s as a number of transactions or requests per seconds. If many users are using the application, Dialogflow will send more concurrent requests to get the fulfillment. For example, if you have 1000 daily users, it is very likely that there will be 1 to 20 concurrent users, which means 1 to 20 RU/s. You can further estimate your Cosmos DB RU/s by going to Microsoft Request Units and the data storage calculator (`https://www.documentdb.com/capacityplanner#`).

The following screenshot shows the Cosmos DB scale setting:

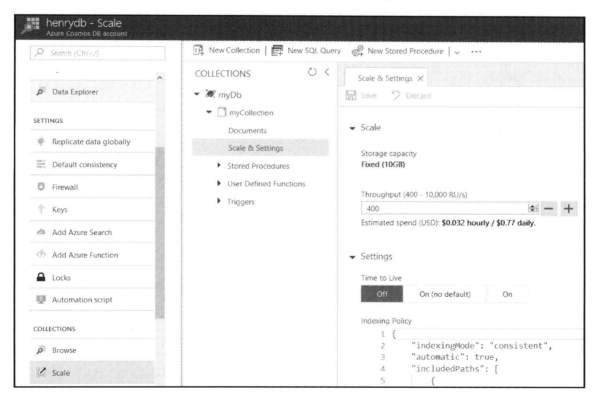

Cosmo DB scale setting

Geo-replicating Cosmos DB

Cosmos DB allows you to globally replicate your database. There are several reasons why this is needed. First, geo-replicating the database allows your application to query the database that is closest to the user to reduce the latency. For example, if the user is in Korea, you would not want your application to hit a database in the United States because there would be a huge delay trying to retrieve data in the Unites States from Korea. The second reason is backup and redundancy. Having replicated data means that if one of your regional databases goes down, you have a secondary database in another region. For example, let's say Cosmos DB in Korea suddenly goes down, but because the replicated database in the United States is up and functional, Korean users will retrieve data from the United States Cosmos DB. Korean users would experience some slowness in the application, but their applications would not crash. When the Korean Cosmos DB comes back online, the Korean users will retrieve data from the Korean Cosmos DB.

The following screenshot shows geo-replicating Cosmos DB:

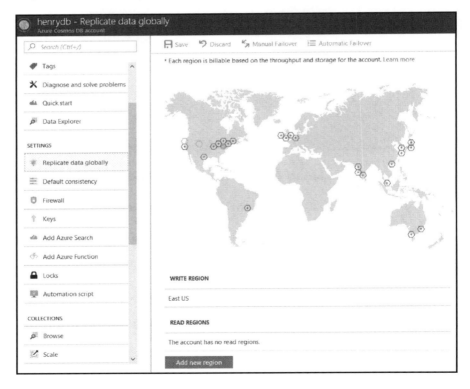

Cosmos DB geo-replication

In Cosmos DB, with the **Replicate data globally** setting, you can simply choose where you want to replicate your data to. When replicating data, the best practice is to replicate it in a similar region. For example, when dealing with United States users, consider choosing Central US, East US, and West US regions for the replication. Depending on your requirements, you might want to replicate to two regions or *n* number of regions.

 The more regions you replicate to, the higher the price of Cosmos DB. You can calculate the monthly price of Cosmos DB given to you by Microsoft. (http://bit.ly/2Gql3FK).

Creating end-to-end tests using the Dialogflow client SDK

In this section, you will learn how to use the Dialogflow client SDK (https://dialogflow.com/docs/sdks) to test the Fortune Cookie intents. Previously, you used two techniques to test your Dialogflow intents. First, you used the action simulator provided by Dialogflow. Then, you used Google Assistant from your phone. Writing Node.js code to create end-to-end tests using the Dialogflow client SDK is very useful for the following reasons:

- Programmatically written tests can be repeated and automated.
- It is faster to execute test code than manually performing mundane actions on a phone or the simulator.
- You can test as you create your Dialogflow intents, which will help you detect errors in the early stages of your development.
- If you make big changes to Dialogflow intents, your test will fail and will help you troubleshoot issues.
- Test scripts can be used as documentation for your voice user interface projects. For example, other developers will be able to understand your application simply by looking at the test scripts that you wrote.
- It saves money. Imagine having to test hundreds of intents manually. One way would be to hire a bunch of quality assurance people to carry out manual tests. However, if you have tested the scripts, you can programmatically execute hundreds of intents in a matter of minutes and it will eliminate the cost of hiring people.

Setting up the Dialogflow client SDK

In the Dialogflow version 1 API, you only need an authentication token to access the Dialogflow API. However, in version two, Google completely changed their approach by using the Google platform **Service Account** to authenticate the Dialogflow API.

1. Log in to Dialogflow
2. Click on the **FortuneCookie** agent setting
3. Click on the **Service Account** link

The following screenshot shows the `FortuneCookie` **Service Account**:

Fortune Cookie agent service account

Take note of the **Project ID** here, which you will be using in the *Creating test script using Dialogflow client SDK* section.

4. You will be directed to Google Cloud Platform. From the menu, go to **IAM & admin**, and then go to **Service accounts**.

   The following screenshot shows the Google Cloud Platform Service Accounts page:

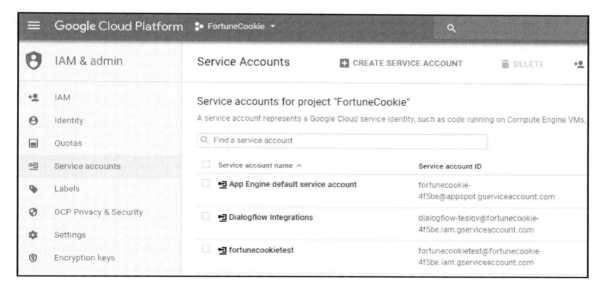

Google Cloud Platform Service Accounts

5. Click on **CREATE SERVICE ACCOUNT**. Enter the service account name as `fortunecookietest`. Choose the Dialogflow roles: **Dialogflow API Admin**, **Dialogflow API Client**, and **Dialogflow API Reader**. Choose **Furnish a new private key** with JSON as an option. Click **Create**.

The following image shows the settings for creating a service account:

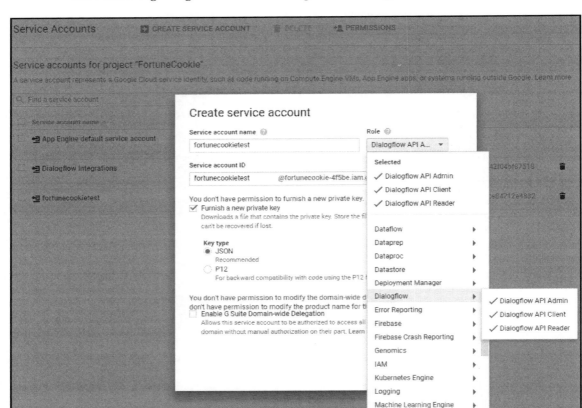

Google Cloud Platform Create service account

6. You will be asked to download a JSON file that contains the authentication key. You will need this key to set up your machine to access the FortuneCookie Dialogflow intents via the client SDK.

7. Install the Google Cloud SDK (http://bit.ly/2ukc8iA).

8. Start the Cloud SDK shell and run gcloud init. This will initialize your machine to be able to use Google Cloud Platform services.

9. Create a Windows environment variable, which sets the Google application credential file GOOGLE_APPLICATION_CREDENTIALS="Authentication JSON Key File Path". You downloaded this JSON key file in step 6.

The following screenshot shows the Windows variable environment setting for
GOOGLE_APPLICATION_CREDENTIALS.

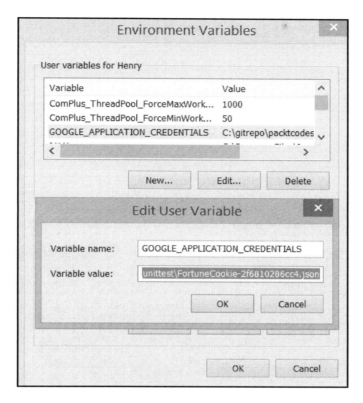

Google Cloud Platform Windows Environment Variables

10. Restart your computer.

Enabling the Dialogflow API for Fortune Cookie

In order to use the Dialogflow client SDK, you will need to enable the Dialogflow API for
the Fortune Cookie project. Since version 2, the Dialogflow API has started to utilize Google
Cloud Platform:

1. Log in to https://console.cloud.google.com. You should be using the same
   username that you use to log in to Dialogflow.
2. Select the FortuneCookie project.

The following screenshot shows the selected `FortuneCookie` project in Google Cloud Platform:

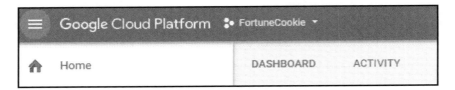

Google Cloud Platform selected project

3. In the menu, select **APIs & Services**.

The following screenshot shows the Google Cloud Platform's **APIs & Services** menu:

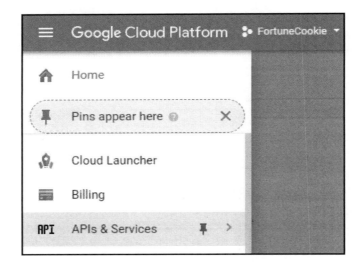

Google Cloud Platform APIs & Services Menu

4. Enable **Dialogflow API**. This will allow you to access the `FortuneCookie` Dialogflow agent using the Dialogflow client SDK.

The following screenshot shows the enabled Dialogflow API for the Dialogflow
`FortuneCookie` project:

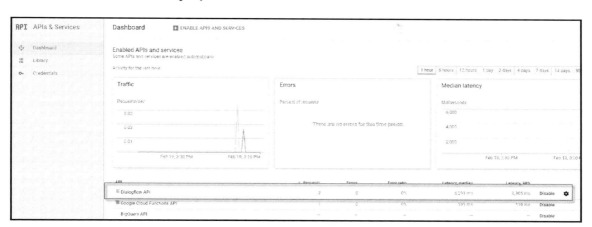

The text in this screenshot is not important. It indicate where to click, in order to enable the Dialogflow API

Creating a test script using the Dialogflow client SDK

In this section, you will create a test script to test `FortuneCookie` using the Dialogflow
client SDK in Node.js:

1. Open Command Prompt and type `npm install dialogflow --save`.
2. Create a file called `testscript.js`.
3. In `testscript.js`, you will begin by declaring the `projectId` you got in
   the *Setting up the Dialogflow client SDK* section. Then, declare `sessionId`, which
   identifies the session as your test session, and the `languageCode` as English.
4. Then, declare the Dialogflow `dialogflow =`
   `require('dialogflow')` component and create the
   Dialogflow `sessionClient.sessionPath(projectId, sessionId)` session,
   which you will use to trigger intents in `FortuneCookie`.

The following code shows the declared variables `projectId`, `sessionId`, and
`languageCode`, and uses them to create the Dialogflow session:

```
var projectId = 'fortunecookie-4f5be';
var sessionId = 'my-test-session-id';
```

```
var languageCode = 'en-US';

var dialogflow = require('dialogflow');
var sessionClient = new dialogflow.SessionsClient();
var sessionPath = sessionClient.sessionPath(projectId, sessionId);
```

5. Now you will create the `callFortuneCookie` function, which takes in a query that contains what the user will say. For example, a query could contain `give me a quote`. When `callFortuneCookie` is called, it will send the query to the Dialogflow agent and will receive a response.

   The following code shows the `callFortuneCookie` function:

```
function callFortuneCookie(query) {
  let request = {
    session: sessionPath,
    queryInput: { text: { text: query, languageCode: languageCode }
}
  };
  sessionClient
  .detectIntent(request)
  .then(responses => {
    console.log('Detected intent');
    let result = responses[0].queryResult;
    console.log(`  Query: ${result.queryText}`);
    console.log(`  Response: ${result.fulfillmentText}`);
    if (result.intent) {
      console.log(`  Intent: ${result.intent.displayName}`);
    } else {
      console.log(`  No intent matched.`);
    }
  })
  .catch(err => {
    console.error('ERROR:', err);
  });
}
```

First, the `callFortuneCookie` function will create a request object that sets the query and `languageCode` properties. Then, the `sessionClient.detectIntent` method is used to send the query. The Dialogflow session client will send the response, and the output will be printed to the console for you to see.

6. From Visual Studio Code, run the code by pressing *F5*.

The following screenshot shows the output when `testscript.js` is run:

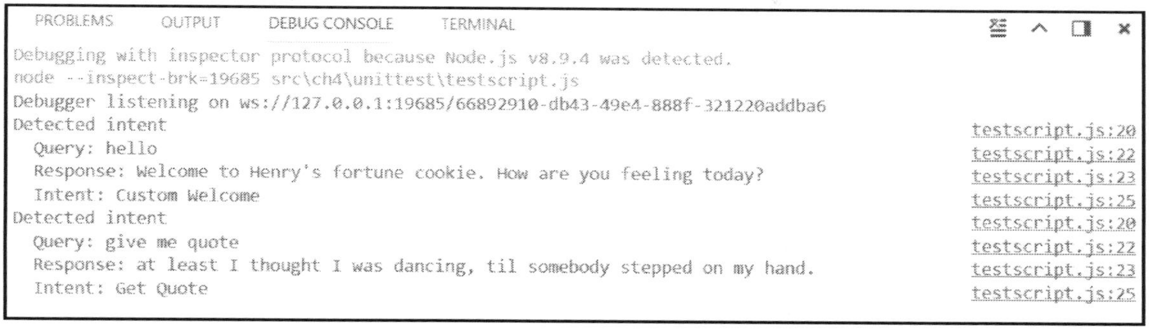

```
PROBLEMS    OUTPUT    DEBUG CONSOLE    TERMINAL
Debugging with inspector protocol because Node.js v8.9.4 was detected.
node --inspect-brk=19685 src\ch4\unittest\testscript.js
Debugger listening on ws://127.0.0.1:19685/66892910-db43-49e4-888f-321220addba6
Detected intent                                                              testscript.js:20
  Query: hello                                                               testscript.js:22
  Response: Welcome to Henry's fortune cookie. How are you feeling today?    testscript.js:23
  Intent: Custom Welcome                                                     testscript.js:25
Detected intent                                                              testscript.js:20
  Query: give me quote                                                       testscript.js:22
  Response: at least I thought I was dancing, til somebody stepped on my hand. testscript.js:23
  Intent: Get Quote                                                          testscript.js:25
```

Test script output

Summary

In this chapter, you learned how to deploy your Node.js fulfillment code to Microsoft Azure, which allows you to take advantage of a highly available and highly scalable platform, helping you not to worry about the complex network topology or complex server deployments. Now, you can simply focus on building your voice user interface projects and easily deploy middle-tier components to the Microsoft Azure cloud platform. You also learned how to persist your data in Microsoft NoSQL Cosmos DB, allowing you to create separation of concerns between your data and code so that you can dynamically update your data in the database without needing to update your code. Furthermore, we covered basic skills for managing Cosmos DB and the Node.js service in Microsoft Azure. Finally, you learned how to create an end-to-end test script in Node.js using the Dialogflow client SDK.

5
Deploying the Fortune Cookie App for Google Home

In `Chapter 3`, *Building a Fortune Cookie Application*, and `Chapter 4`, *Hosting, Securing, and Testing the Fortune Cookie in the Cloud*, you learned about developing and hosting the Fortune Cookie application. In this chapter, you will learn how to set up Google Home and deploy the Fortune Cookie application. You will also learn about features offered by Google Home that will assist your development. Finally, you will learn about the process involved in certifying an application for the Google Home marketplace.

In this chapter, you will learn about the following topics:

- Setting up Google Home
- Google Home's features
- Deploying an application to Google Home
- The Google Home marketplace application certification process

Setting up Google Home for the first time

In this section, I will be using a Google Home Mini to demonstrate setting up Google Home for the first time:

1. In the mobile marketplace (iOS or Android), download and install the Google Home application.
2. Log in to Google Home using the same Google account that you have been using to log in to Dialogflow.

3. Turn on the Google Home Mini and, in your Google Home application, you will be able to see the new device. The following screenshot shows the discovered device in the Google Home application:

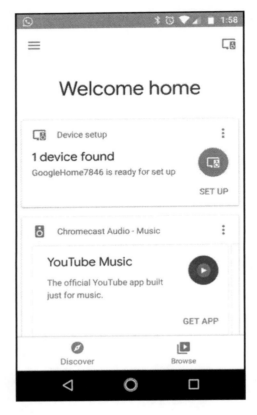

Google Home setup—device found

4. Click **Set up** and follow the directions you see on the screen. Finally, you will be asked to connect to the same Wi-Fi channel that your phone is connected to.

5. Once connected to Wi-Fi, you will set up the voice match. This is important, as you would not want anyone to use your Google Home. This is a great way to protect your device from being used by an unauthorized person, especially when you begin to connect your Google Home to other home devices such as lights, security cameras, and your garage.

The following screenshot shows the Google Home setup step for entering your voice as the only recognized source:

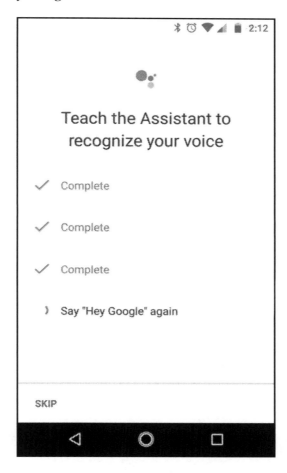

Google Home setup training voice

6. Next, set up your Google Home Mini's voice. I chose a female voice (**Voice 1**).

The following screenshot shows the Google Home setup for choosing the Assistant's voice:

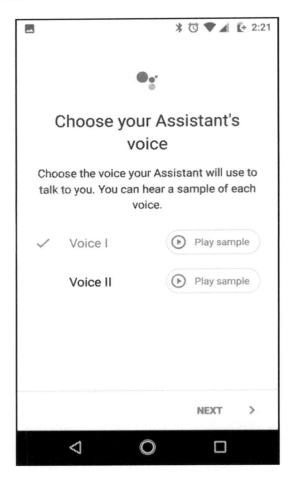

Google Home setup Assistant voice

7. In the next step, enter your home address so that Google can personalize your searches based on your home location.

8. In the following step, you can add multiple music applications. In my case, I use Spotify, so I added that. You can choose to add any of your favorite music services.

The following screenshot shows adding music services to a Google Home Mini:

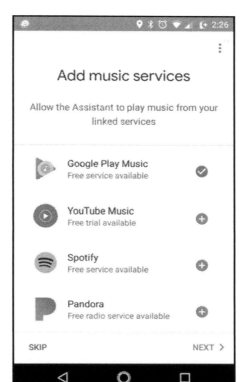

Google Home setup—adding music services

9. Once you are done, you will be directed to the Google Home welcome page, and you can test your Google Home Mini device by saying `Hello Google What time is it?`.

Notice that other family members can add the Google Home Mini by simply downloading the Google Home application. It's important to have your family members go through the same setup steps for the preceding Google Home Mini, adding their own voices. An important thing to note here is that, when adding Google Home devices, the user must be using the same Wi-Fi network as the Google Home device. Because you first have to log in to your personal Wi-Fi to add your voice, not everyone can access your Google Home devices without first logging into your Wi-Fi. Always take the security precaution of setting a strong Wi-Fi password.

Learning about Google Home's features

With a Google Home device, you can do many interesting things. First, you can use a Google Home device just like a typical search engine. Anything you would type to get a search result from Google, you can simply ask using your voice. Another thing I like to do is listen to music using Spotify, so you can link your favorite music to Google Home. If you have not done this, you can go to the Google Home application, go to the menu, select the music menu, and add your favorite music provider.

The following screenshot shows the Google Home application menu for adding a music provider:

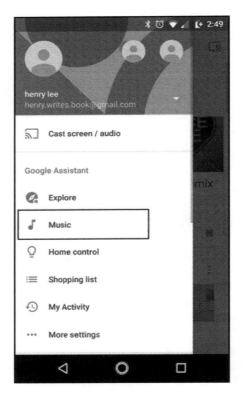

Google Home setup—music menu

Another feature that I use almost every day is the wake-up alarm by saying `Hey Google set my alarm every day at 8:30 am`. I also like to review my calendar events or create new events by saying `Hey Google what's my schedule like today?` or `Hey Google create haircut event at 5 pm today`.

Adding a home control device to Google Home

Personally, I use the Google Home device to control my lights at home and other home devices. As an example, let's learn how to set up an Insignia Wi-Fi smart plug (`http://bit.ly/2iPANZx`). The smart plug will allow you to control any device that is plugged in using voice commands:

1. Go and buy an Insignia Wi-Fi Smart Plug (`http://bit.ly/2iPANZx`).
2. Download the Insignia Connect application on your phone.
3. Start Insignia Connect and either create an account or sign in.

The following screenshot shows the Insignia Connect home screen:

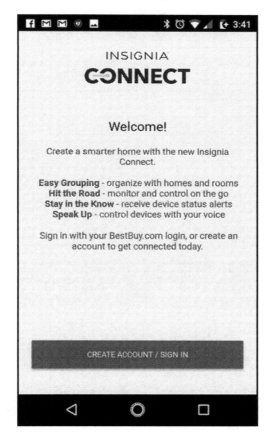

Insignia Connect setup home screen

4. Once you've logged in, click on the **Setup new device** button.
5. Select the device you purchased: Insignia smart plug.

The following screenshot shows adding a new device in the Insignia setup:

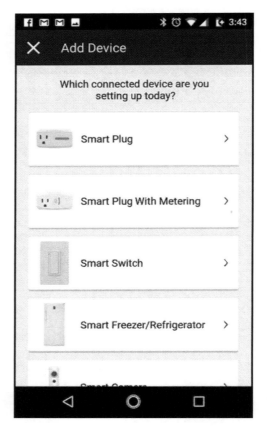

Insignia Connect setup—new device

6. Click **Continue** and your device will be found, and you will be asked to connect to Wi-Fi. Make sure that you use the same Wi-Fi you connected your Google Home device to and also connect your phone.
7. Once your Insignia smart plug is connected to Wi-Fi, its blinking green light will change to a solid green light.
8. Open your Google Home application. You will link your Insignia device to Google Home so that you can control it using your voice.

9. In the Google Home application, go to the menu and select **Home control**.

The following screenshot shows the Google Home application's **Home control** screen:

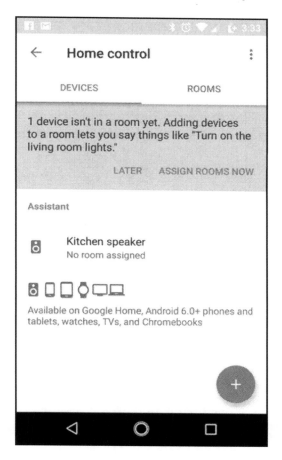

Google Home setup—home control

10. Click on the **+** button to add a new home control device.
11. Scroll to Insignia Connect and follow the instructions to sign in to Insignia Connect.

The following screenshot shows the Google Home setup step so that you can link to Insignia Connect devices:

Google Home setup—adding Insignia Connect

You can activate your lights by simply saying `Hey Google turn my lights on`.

You can create rooms in your Google Home and assign home devices to the appropriate rooms. Then, you can turn lights on and off by saying `Hey Google turn kitchen lights on`.

Deploying Fortune Cookie to Google Home

One of the biggest advantages of working with Dialogflow is that the Fortune Cookie that you built for Google Assistant can also work with Google Home with hardly any effort. Both Google Home and Google Assistant are integrated into Dialogflow, and the application will work on both devices. The only thing that's different about Google Home is that Google Home devices cannot display visual elements like phones can. This is the reason why whenever you create a response sent back to Dialogflow from your server, you always have to have the `displayText` for devices that do not support visual elements.

The following code recaps a typical fulfillment response that's sent back to Dialogflow from the server, which contains the SSML response for the audio response and `displayText` as a fallback response in case the device does not support the audio or visual response:

```
responseJson = {
        fulfillmentText: 'Hello, Welcome to Henry\'s Fortune Cookie!',
        fulfillmentMessages: [
          {
            platform: "ACTIONS_ON_GOOGLE",
            simpleResponses: {
              simpleResponses: [
                {
                  ssml: `<speak>
                         <audio
src="https://actions.google.com/sounds/v1/weather/thunder_crack.ogg" />
                         <break time="200ms"/>
                         <prosody rate="medium" pitch="+2st">
                           Hello Welcome to Henry's Fortune Cookie!
                         </prosody>
                       </speak>`,
                  displayText: "Hello, Welcome to Henry\'s Fortune Cookie!"
                }
              ]
            }
          }
        ]
      };
```

Certifying an application for the marketplace

In this section, you will configure Fortune Cookie in order to get it ready for the market certification process. In each configuration section, you will learn what to do and what not to do in order to avoid possible rejections in the marketplace certification process:

1. Before you begin, go to Actions on Google (`https://console.actions.google.com/`) and log in using the same account you use to log into Dialogflow. Once you've logged in, select the `FortuneCookie` project's overview. You will need to configure three sections: **App information**, **Location targeting**, and **Surface capabilities**.

   The following screenshot shows the Google Home certification configuration section for `FortuneCookie`:

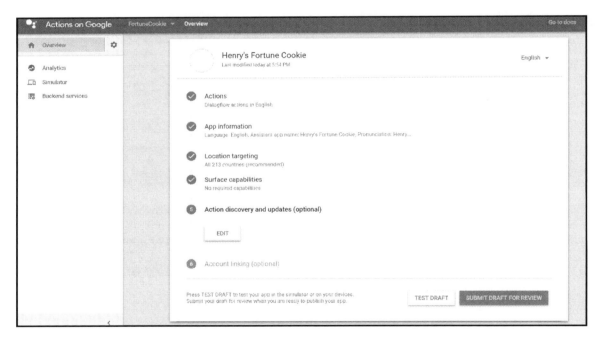

Google Home certification

   The **App information** section consists of six sections that need to be configured: **Assistant app name**, **Details**, **Images**, **Contact details**, **Privacy and consent**, and **Additional information**.

The following screenshot shows the **App information** section:

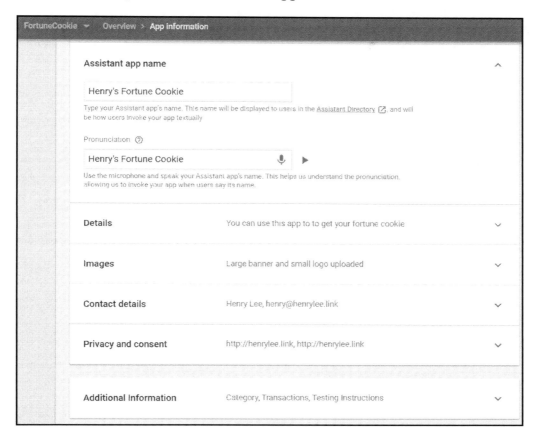

Google Home certification app information

2. In **Assistant app name**, put `Henry's Fortune Cookie`, or whatever you prefer to call your application. In the **Pronunciation** section, put `Henry's Fortune Cookie` as well. You can play this to make sure that your application name can be easily pronounced.

The following screenshot shows the Assistant app name section for the `FortuneCookie` application:

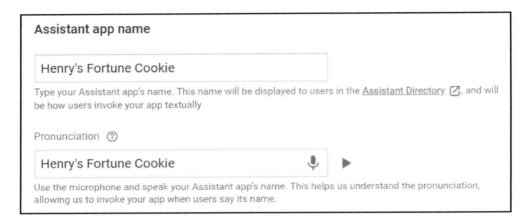

Google Home Certification Assistant app name

It's important to note here that the assistant name you choose should not use any names that are branded. For example, you cannot use single words such as Google, Yahoo, or Microsoft. If you decide to use a single word, then the word must be branded and you must prove to Google that the word you are using is legally branded. To do this, you need to go to **Actions** on Google, head to the menu, **Overview | Project Settings**, and go to the **BRAND VERIFICATION** section. In the **BRAND VERIFICATION** section, you need to submit either a website link or an Android marketplace application to say that you actually own the brand name.

The following screenshot shows the **BRAND VERIFICATION** section:

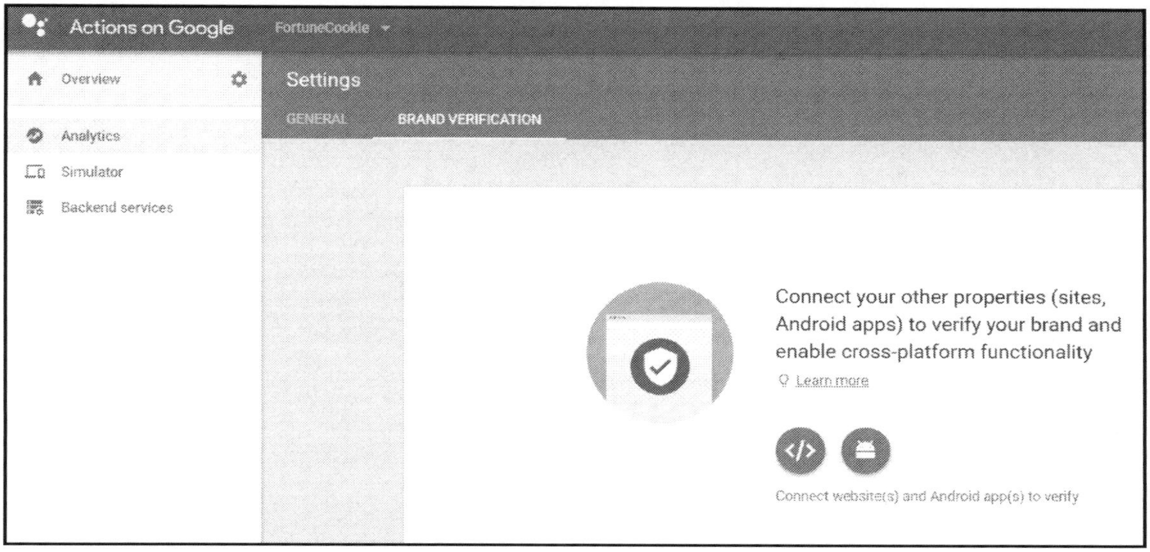

Google Home Certification BRAND VERIFICATION

3. Go to the **Details** section. Add the text **"to get your fortune cookie"** to the assistant app introduction section. This is a quick introductory phrase that will be used by the Google Home device to introduce your application, so make it short and concise.

4. Choose **Female 1** as the assistant voice. Here, you can choose whichever voice you prefer. Click the **Check match user's language** setting, which will be important if you are targeting multiple languages. You want to make sure that the Google Home voice uses the user's native language.

5. Add Short and Full descriptions of the application, which will be displayed on the Google Home marketplace.

6. In the **Sample invocations** section, add an example of how to invoke the `FortuneCookie` **application by adding** `Ok Google Ask Henry's Fortune Cookie to Give me a Quote`.

The following screenshot shows the FortuneCookie Details section:

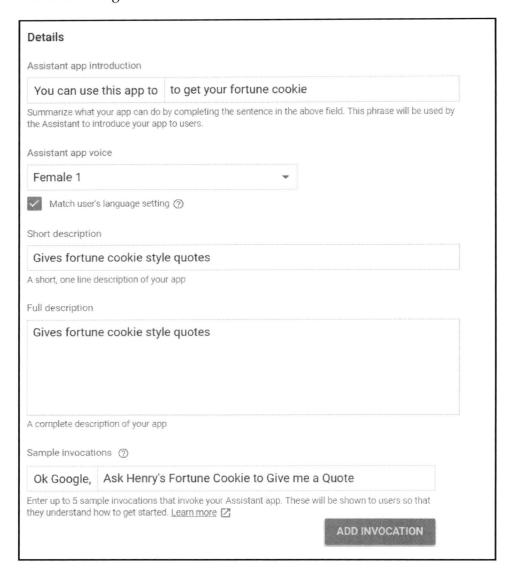

Google Home Certification Details

Notice that, as you are testing your FortuneCookie application, Google is smart enough to suggest multiple invocations that you can add.

The following screenshot shows the invocations suggested by Google:

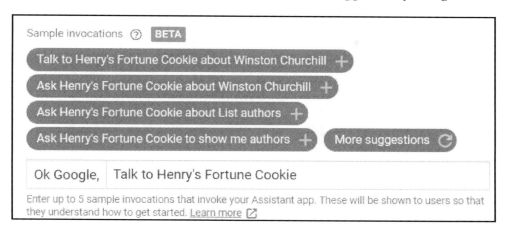

Google Home Certification Sample invocations

7. Go to the **Images** section and add large banner images (1,920 by 1,080) and a small logo (192 by 192) in PNG format.

The following screenshot shows the **Images** section:

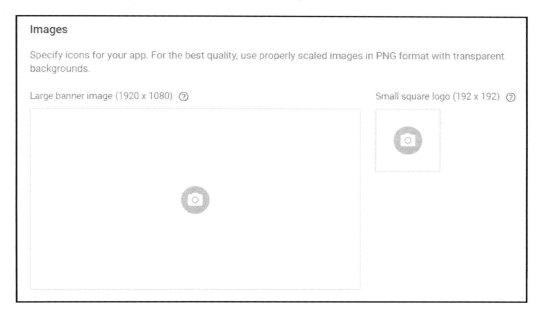

Google Home Certification Images

8. In the **Contact details** section, add your email address and developer name.

9. In the **Privacy and consent** section, add a link to the **Privacy policy** and a link to the terms of service. A general privacy statement and the general terms service cannot be used. For example, if your application is `FortuneCookie`, your privacy statement and terms of service statement must explicitly spell out your application's name, otherwise Google will reject the application submission.

10. Go to **Location targeting**. Here, you can choose where you want your application to be deployed.

11. Go to the **Surface capabilities** section. For `FortuneCookie`, you need to say `Yes` to `Does your Assistant app require audio output?` and no to `Does your Assistant app require a screen output?`

12. Click on **Submit draft** for it to be reviewed.

You have successfully submitted your application for the review process, and when your application successfully passes the certification process, it will be available to everyone using Google Home!

Learning about general guidelines

As a general guideline, the following types of voice applications will not be allowed:

- Applications with sexual content
- Applications that endanger children
- Applications that promote violence
- Applications that bully and harass
- Applications that deal with illegal activities
- Applications that promote gambling activities

Here are some other market certification rejection reasons that I have encountered:

- If an application requires the user to log in to proceed, you will need to provide a demo account for the Google tester to test your application, otherwise your application will be rejected.
- If your fulfillment server does not return a response within five seconds, the voice application will crash without any kind of error.
- You cannot use a single word as the name of an application, for example, `Ok Google talk to Henry`, unless `Henry` is trademarked. You have to submit legal documents to Google to prove that `Henry` is trademarked.

Summary

In this chapter, you learned a lot about using Google Home, such as how to create a schedule, how to listen to music, and searching in Google using your voice. You also learned how to integrate home appliances such as the smart plug, and then how to integrate them with Google Home, enabling you to turn lights on and off using your voice. Finally, you learned about the Google Home certification process by deploying `FortuneCookie`, which you built in an earlier chapter.

In the next chapter, you will learn how to build a voice user interface application for Amazon Echo devices using the Alexa Skills Kit (ASK).

6
Building a Cooking Application Using Alexa

In this chapter, you will learn how to create voice user interfaces using the **Alexa Skills Kit (ASK)**, which is necessary to deploy an application to an Amazon Echo device. In order to learn about programming in ASK, you will create a cooking application that teaches the user how to cook a dish step by step. First, you will set up an Amazon Echo and then familiarize yourself with the ASK software development kit. Once comfortable with ASK, you will utilize intents, utterances, and slots in ASK to create the conversations necessary for the cooking application. Then, using Node.js, you will create a Webhook that will provide recipe ideas. Next, you will learn how to debug and test conversations and then deploy Henry's Kitchen to Amazon Echo for further testing. Finally, you will finish this chapter by learning how to back up the Alexa skill you have created so that you can restore the skill if things go wrong.

In this chapter, we will cover the following topics:

- An introduction to the ASK SDK
- The ASK development setup
- Learning about intents, utterances, and slots
- Implementing a Node.js Webhook to serve Alexa skills
- Learning how to set up an Amazon Echo
- Programming, debugging, and testing in the ASK
- Deploying and testing using Amazon Echo
- Backing up an Alexa skill

Introducing the ASK

In 2014, Amazon introduced voice interaction capabilities such as setting an alarm, playing music, streaming podcasts, playing audio books, and providing traffic and weather reports through Amazon Echo devices. In order to make Amazon Echo extensible through third-party applications, the ASK was introduced as a software developer kit. The ASK processes natural language spoken to Amazon Echo devices. Just as Dialogflow processes the speech of users received from Google Home devices into machine-understandable code, the ASK will do the exact same thing for Amazon Echo devices. By 2017, Alexa had grown to having over 5,000 employees working on it and the adoption of Alexa continues to grow, grabbing 70% of the market share (`https://bit.ly/2Nj7tY6`) alongside Google Home.

There are three ways to build with the ASK:

- Using graphical user interfaces by logging in to the Amazon Alexa console (`https://developer.amazon.com/alexa/console/ask`)
- Using the ASK JSON schema file and uploading it to the Amazon Alexa console (`https://amzn.to/2vooE6j`)
- Using the ASK **command-line interface (CLI)** (`https://amzn.to/2H8zfbd`)

In this chapter, you will learn the first two of these, using the Alexa console and the JSON schema file. The third option is useful if you are thinking of creating the automation process to build and deploy to the ASK. You will find it very useful to use the graphical interfaces to build with the ASK because, later, it will help you to visually validate the ASK that you have built using the JSON schema or the ASK CLI.

Amazon Alexa was inspired by *Star Trek*, in which crew members spoke to the starship Enterprise computer system in order to perform their daily routines. Do you remember Captain Picard requesting *"Tea. Earl Gray. Hot"*?

Building a Henry's Kitchen Alexa skill

In this chapter, you will build a cooking application called Henry's Kitchen and learn how to create voice user interfaces using the ASK for Amazon Echo devices. Using Henry's Kitchen, your users will be able to make the following statements:

- I want to cook a vegetarian burger
- I want to make a pizza

After receiving the request from the user, Henry's Kitchen will consume the REST API from a third party called **Spoonacular** (https://spoonacular.com/food-api) and then use the result received from Spoonacular, which will recommend the types of dishes the user can cook and send them back to Alexa. Finally, Alexa will send the answer back to the user via an Amazon Echo device.

In summary, here are the steps that describe the workflow:

1. The user sends a request to the Amazon Echo.
2. The Amazon Echo sends the request to the Henry's Kitchen Alexa skill.
3. Alexa decodes the request into an intent and sends the request to the web service endpoint Node.js server hosted in Microsoft Azure.
4. The web service endpoint Node.js server calls a third-party REST API, Spoonacular.
5. Spoonacular sends food recommendations to the Node.js server.
6. The web service endpoint Node.js server responds to Alexa with the result.
7. Alexa sends the response to the Amazon Echo.
8. The Amazon Echo responds to the user.

The following flowchart shows the architectural diagram of Henry's Kitchen:

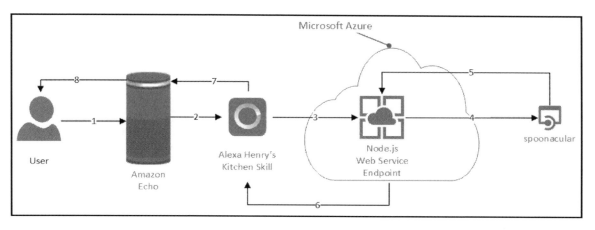

Henry's Kitchen architecture

Setting up the ASK development environment

Before you begin, let's set up your development environment:

1. Install the Node.js editor Visual Studio Code (`https://code.visualstudio.com/`).
2. Install Node.js (`https://nodejs.org`).
3. Once Node.js is installed, check the Node.js version by typing in Node.js. Command Prompt `node -v`. I am using version 8.9.4 but any more recent versions will work.
4. Create an Amazon developer account (`https://developer.amazon.com/alexa`).
5. Create a Microsoft Azure account. Go to `https://azure.microsoft.com/en-us/free/` and follow the instructions.
6. Install the Azure CLI (`http://bit.ly/2w3J00u`). The Azure CLI is a command-line tool for managing the Microsoft Azure cloud platform.
7. In order to test your Webhook, you will need to install Postman (`https://www.getpostman.com/`).
8. You will deploy your Node.js code using the FTP. Download and install FileZilla (`https://filezilla-project.org/`).

Creating an Alexa skill

Creating an Alexa skill is analogous to creating a mobile application. In this section, you will create your first skill, called Henry's Kitchen:

1. Open your Chrome browser and go to `https://developer.amazon.com/alexa/console/ask`.
2. Click on the **Create skill** button.
3. In the **Skill Name** box, type in `Cooking`.
4. Choose **Custom** model and click on the **Create Skill** button.

The following screenshot shows the steps taken to choose a model when creating an Alexa skill:

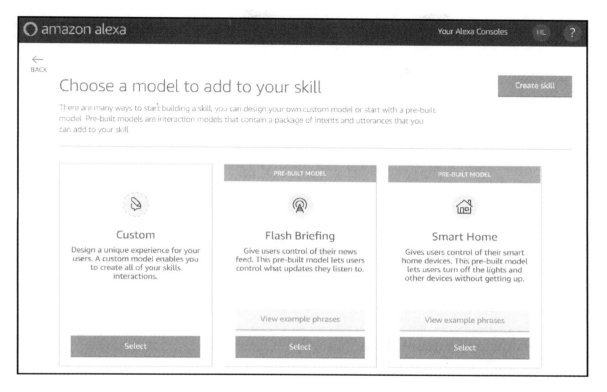

The ASK console - choose a model

5. After a few seconds, your first skill, called `Cooking`, will be created and you will land on the ASK console's landing page.

The following screenshot shows the ASK console landing page after you have finished creating the skill:

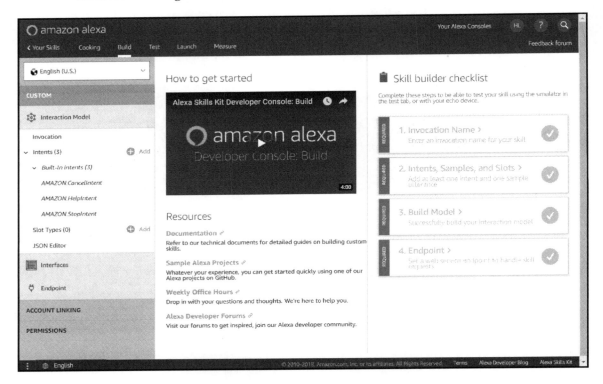

The ASK console landing page

You have successfully created your first skill. In the following sections, you will create slots, intents, and utterances for Henry's Kitchen.

Creating wake up words

In order for the user to use your skills, you need to create wake up words that will allow Alexa to send user sayings to your skill. For example, you want your user to make a request to Henry's Kitchen by saying `Alexa ask Henry's Kitchen I want to cook burger` and Henry's Kitchen will be the wake up phrase to trigger your application on Amazon Echo devices:

1. Open your Chrome browser and go to the Alexa Skills console (`https://developer.amazon.com/alexa/console/ask`).

    The following screenshot shows the Alexa console, which lists the skills that you have created:

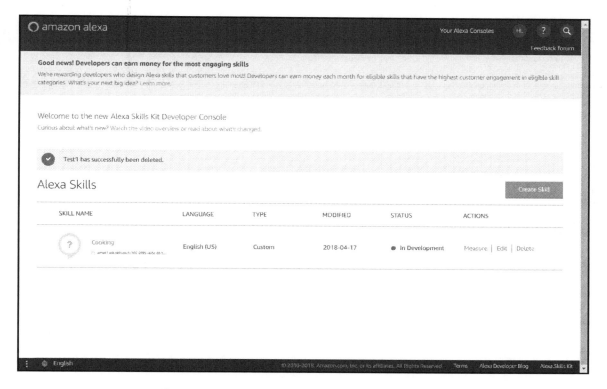

The text in this screenshot is not important. It shows you the skills that you have created

2. You will notice the **Cooking** skill that you just created. Click on the **Cooking** skill.

3. On the menu on the left, click on **Invocation**.

The following screenshot shows how to create an invocation for the skill:

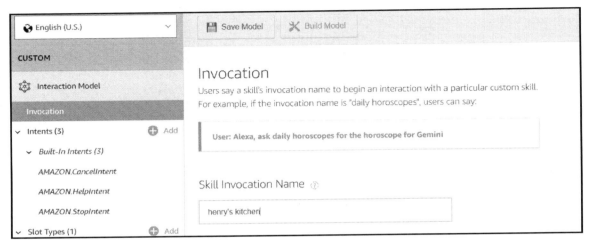

ASK Console - Create Invocation

4. Type in `henry's kitchen` in lowercase, as uppercase is not allowed for the skill invocation name.
5. Click on the **Save Model** button at the top.

Building slots

You can think of slots as specific types within a category. For example, when the user wants a cooking idea, they can give general food types such as pizza, burger, pasta, or brown rice, or can say 'I want to cook a burger, or, I want to cook a pizza'. Slots can be used to create variations of what the user will say so you have to create multiple variations of what the user will say in order to create an intent:

1. Open your Chrome browser and go to the Alexa skills console (`https://developer.amazon.com/alexa/console/ask`).
2. You will notice the `Cooking` skill that you just created. Click on the `Cooking` skill.
3. On your Alexa Skill console, there is menu on the left-hand side called **Slot Type(0) +Add**. Click the **Add** button.

4. Create a custom slot type named `Foods`.

The following screenshot shows how to create a custom slot:

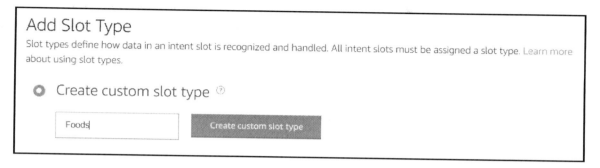

ASK Console - Create custom slot type

5. Enter `Fish`, `Pizza`, and `Burger` as slot types.

The following screenshot shows the entered types for the slot:

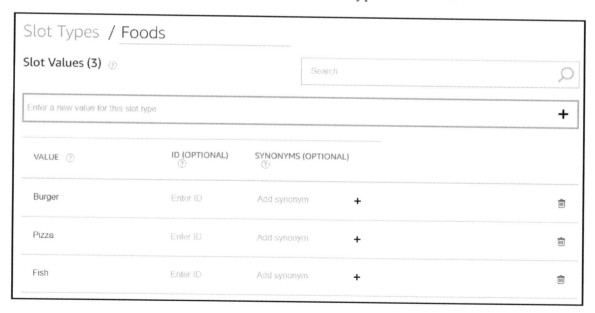

ASK Console - enter slot types

6. Click the **Save Model** button at the top of the page.

You have created a food slot so that you can create intents that can capture when the user says they want to cook food: `Alexa ask Henry's Kitchen I want to cook Burger`. Let's add a bit more complexity by adding a `DietTypes` slot, which will allow the user to ask `Alexa ask Henry's Kitchen I want to cook vegetarian burger`. Follow the preceding steps 1 through 6 to create a `DietTypes` slot that contains: `pescetarian`, `vegetarian`, and `vegan`.

The following screenshot shows the `DietTypes` slots after following steps 1 through 6 by replacing `Foods` with `DietTypes` and using the slot types `pescetarian`, `vegetarian`, and `vegan`:

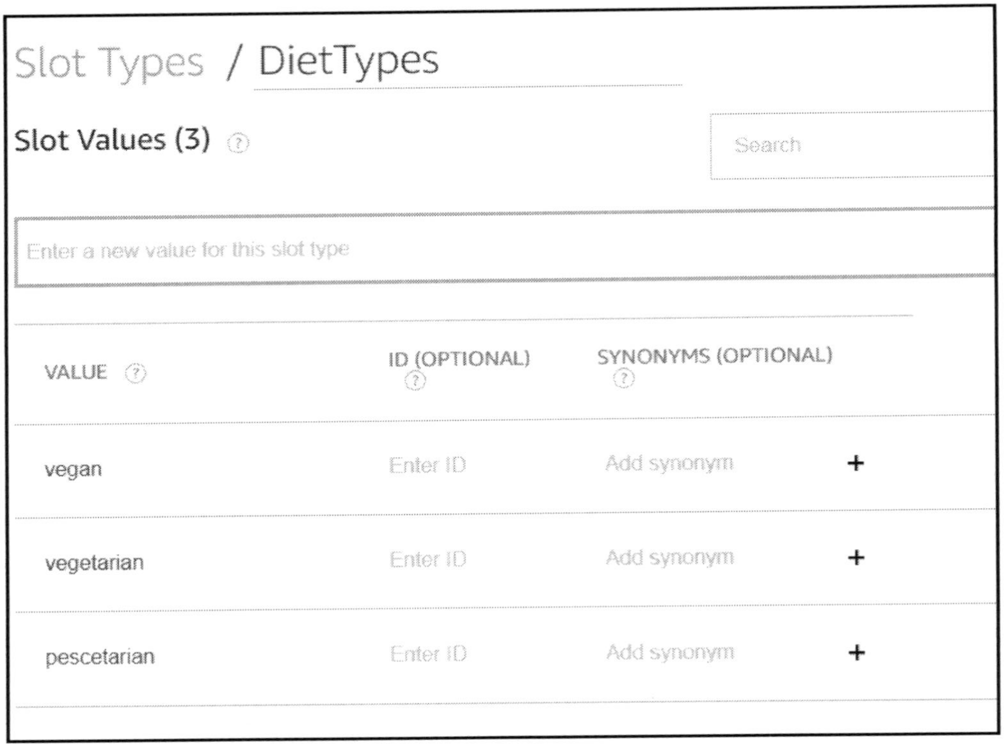

ASK Console Create DietTypes Slot

Building intents

In the ASK, intents are like identifiers that the ASK will identify when it receives user commands from Amazon Echo devices. Being able to translate the user's spoken language into a specific intent that the backend server can use to process and send a response to the Amazon Echo device is important. For example, when the user asks `Alex ask Henry's Kitchen I want to cook vegetarian burger`, the ASK will identify and send the matching intent to the backend server. In the backend server, you can use the identified intent to go and find various vegetarian burgers and suggest them to the user:

1. Open your Chrome browser and go to the Alexa Skills console (`https://developer.amazon.com/alexa/console/ask`).

2. You will notice the `Cooking` skill that you just created. Click on the **Cooking** skill.

3. On your Alexa Skill console, there is menu on the left-hand side called **Intents(3) +Add**. Click the **Add** button.

4. Type in `GetCookingIntent` and click on the **Create custom intent** button, as shown in the following screenshot:

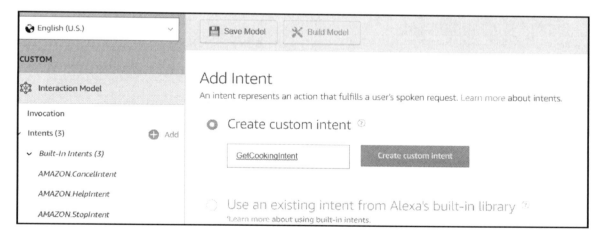

ASK console create GetCookingIntent

In the next section, you will learn how to add utterances to `GetCookingIntent`.

Building utterances

Utterances are like templates that match the speech pattern of what the user says. When the user's speech pattern matches any one of the utterances defined in the intent, the intent information will be sent back to the backend server. For example, when you create an utterance using the `Foods` and `DietTypes` slots that you created in the previous section, such as `I want to cook {DietTypes} {Foods}`, the ASK will match speech patterns such as, `I want to cook a vegetarian burger`, `I want to cook a vegetarian pizza`, or any combination of `DietTypes` and `Foods`.

1. Open your Chrome browser and go to the Alexa Skills console (`https://developer.amazon.com/alexa/console/ask`).
2. You will notice the `Cooking` skill that you just created. Click on the **Cooking** skill.
3. On the left-hand menu, click on **GetCookingIntent**, which you created in the previous section.
4. In the utterance textbox, add the following utterances one by one, as follows:
   - `I want to cook {DietTypes} {Foods}`
   - `I want to make {DietTypes} {Foods}`
   - `I want to make {Foods}`
   - `I want to cook {Foods}`

The following screenshot shows the utterances for **GetCookingIntent** using **DietTypes** and **Foods**:

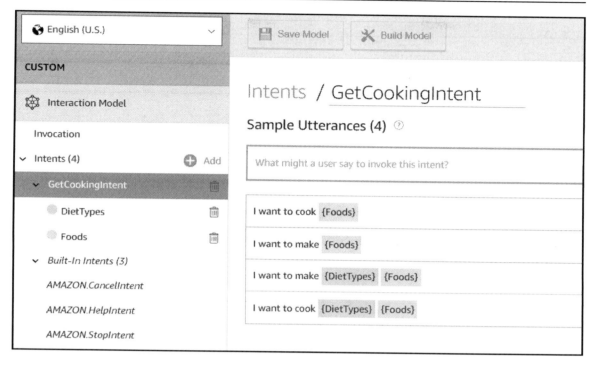

ASK console – Create utterances for GetCookingIntent

5. Notice that, in the utterance, you can reference the slots using brackets: **{DietTypes}** and **{Foods}**. On the left-hand menu, under **GetCookingIntent**, you will see **DietTypes** and **Foods**. Click on **DietTypes** and associate it to the **DietTypes** slot found in the dropdown on the right.

The following screenshot shows associating `DietTypes` defined in the `GetCookingIntent` utterances with the `DietTypes` slot:

ASK Console Associate DietTypes Slot in GetCookingIntent

6. Click on **Foods** on the left-hand menu under **GetCookingIntent** and associate `Foods` to the `Foods` slot found on the dropdown on the right.

The following screenshot shows associating `Foods` defined in the `GetCookingIntent` utterances with the **Foods** slot.

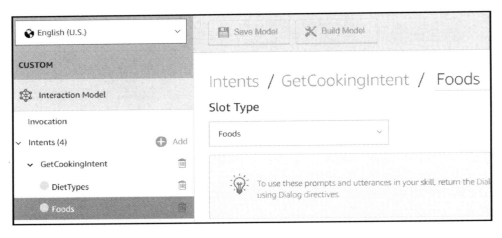

ASK Console Associate Foods Slot in GetCookingIntent

7. Click on the **Save Model** button at the top.

In the next section, you will create your own endpoint in order to receive requests from Alexa in order to fulfill intents.

Creating a web service endpoint to handle skill requests

In the previous sections, you created a Henry's Kitchen skill that sends the recipe ideas. The Node.js server endpoint will fulfill Henry's Kitchen skill requests by querying a third-party service called Spoonacular (https://spoonacular.com/food-api). Spoonacular will provide food recommendations to the endpoint service to construct the response that will be sent back to the user.

Here are the steps necessary to create Node.js code for the endpoint web service:

1. Open Visual Studio Code.
2. You are going to write some Node.js codes to handle Alexa skill requests. Before you begin, create three files:
   - server.js: This is the Node.js server's entrypoint to execute the server code.
   - package.json: This contains the Node.js dependencies required to execute server.js. When you type npm install on the Node.js Command Prompt where package.json is, all of the Node.js dependencies will be installed.
   - web.config: This is the configuration file to run Node.js code in the Microsoft Azure App Service hosting environment.
3. In web.config, enter the following configuration settings. Notice that <add name="iisnode" path="server.js" verb="*" modules="iisnode"/> and <action type="Rewrite" url="server.js"/> will force all requests to be served by server.js.

   The following code shows the configuration settings to host Node.js server code in Microsoft Azure App Service:

   ```xml
   <?xml version="1.0" encoding="utf-8"?>
   <configuration>
     <system.webServer>
       <handlers>
         <add name="iisnode" path="server.js" verb="*"
   modules="iisnode"/>
   ```

```xml
      </handlers>
      <rewrite>
        <rules>
            <rule name="DynamicContent">
                <match url="/*" />
                <action type="Rewrite" url="server.js"/>
            </rule>
        </rules>
      </rewrite>
    </system.webServer>
  </configuration>
```

4. In `package.json`, you will need to define the name, description, version, and author of the Node.js server application. You will also define dependencies and, in the script property, you will specify the entrypoint of the Node.js server application. Notice the dependencies that you will be using—here are their purposes:

   - `alexa-verifier-middleware`: In order to protect your endpoint, Alexa requires you to check all incoming requests from Alexa through a series of steps. This helper module simplifies a complex security check in order to communicate with Alexa.

   - `body-parser`: This is the Node.js module that parses and formats the incoming HTTP request body into a JSON object so that the request body can be easily accessed throughout the Node.js code.

   - `express`: This is the Node.js HTTP web server component for creating a REST API .

   - `unirest`: This is the helper module for calling a third-party REST API such as Spoonacular.

The following code shows the `package.json` for the Node.js server application:

```json
{
  "name": "cookingapp",
  "description": "endpoint to handle henry's kitchen alexa skill
requests",
  "version": "0.1.0",
  "author": "Henry Lee <henry@henrylee.link>",
  "dependencies": {
    "alexa-verifier-middleware": "^1.0.1",
    "body-parser": "^1.18.2",
    "express": "^4.16.3",
    "unirest": "^0.5.1"
  },
  "script": "./server.js"
```

```
}
```

5. Open the `server.js` file in Visual Studio Code.

6. Declare all of the necessary components that will be used in Node.js code to create the Henry's Kitchen web service: `express`, `body-parser`, `http`, `alexa-verifier-middleware`, and `unitrest`.

   The following code shows the declarations of the components necessary for creating the Henry's Kitchen endpoint service in Node.js:

   ```
   var express = require('express');
   var bodyParser = require('body-parser');
   var http = require('http');
   var verifier = require('alexa-verifier-middleware');
   var unirest = require('unirest');
   ```

7. Create an Express server to create the REST API and then set up the router paths. Notice that creating the router paths is equivalent to creating REST API endpoints. The base URL is given to you by the Azure hosting, for example `https://myhenrytestapp.azurewebsites.net`, and if you are debugging locally it would be `http://localhost:8000`. So, in the code, when you define the Alexa path as `app.use("/alexa", alexaRouter)`, you can consume this endpoint using `https://myhenrytestapp.azurewebsites.net/alexa`. Also, you will be applying the Alexa `verifier` so that any incoming requests to `/alexa` will go through `alexa-verifier-middleware`. Finally, add `bodyparser` to the `alexaRouter.use(bodyParser.json())` router so that all incoming requests will be automatically converted into JSON objects.

   The following code defines the Alexa path `/alexa` using the router and applying the Alexa `verifier` and `bodyparser`:

   ```
   var app = express();
   var alexaRouter = express.Router();
   app.use("/alexa", alexaRouter);
   alexaRouter.use(verifier)
   alexaRouter.use(bodyParser.json());
   ```

8. Create the `/ping` path so that, when deployed to the server, going to `https://myhenrytestapp.azurewebsites.net/ping`, or when debugging locally, going to `http://localhost:8000/ping`, you will see **Welcome to Cooking Service**. This is a very useful way to check whether the deployment of your service to the server started and is working properly.

The following code shows the `/ping` path:

```
app.use("/ping", function (req, res, next) {
    res.send('Welcome to Cooking Service');
});
```

9. Create an HTTP server and bind it to the Express server in order to create a REST API.

The following code binds the Express server to the HTTP server in order to create the REST API:

```
var server = http.createServer(app);
var port = process.env.PORT || 8000;
server.listen(port, function () {
    console.log("Server is up and running...");
});
```

10. Under the `/alexa` path, you will create another path called `/cookingApi`. This way, you can now host multiple Alexa skill endpoints because, in step 6, you applied a verifier to the `/alexa` path so that any incoming requests going through `/alexa` will go through the Alexa verifier security check. For example, `https://myhenrytestapp.azurewebsites.net/alexa/cookingApi` is under the `/alexa` path so the Alexa security `verifier` will handle the security handshake with Alexa requests.

In order to parse the JSON object, you will need to be familiar with the Alexa request format (`https://amzn.to/2fVsObs`). One of the most important things to look for is `req.body.request.type`. The following are descriptions of the types that you will be looking for:

- `LaunchRequest`: When the user first starts your Alexa skill, Alexa will send the request. This is where you will put the welcome message of your voice application.
- `IntentRequest`: Alexa receives and converts user requests into matching intents based on the utterances. You can find out the name of the intent by looking at `req.body.request.intent.name`. This will allow you to handle specific intents in your server code.
- `SessionEndedRequest`: This intent type will be triggered when the user exits by saying `exit`, if the user does not respond for a long time, and if an error occurs. One thing to note here is that you might want to track the duration of the user's activity in your voice application by tracking `LaunchRequest` and `SessionEndedRequest`.

The following code shows the /cookingApi path handling multiple intent types: LaunchRequest, IntentRequest, and SessionEndedRequest:

```
alexaRouter.post('/cookingApi', function (req, res) {
    if (req.body.request.type === 'LaunchRequest') {
        res.json({
            "version": "1.0",
            "response": {
              "shouldEndSession": true,
              "outputSpeech": {
                "type": "PlainText",
                "text": "Welcome to Henry's Cooking App"
              }
            }
        });
    }
    else if (req.body.request.type === 'IntentRequest' &&
            req.body.request.intent.name === 'GetCookingIntent') {
        BuildGetCookingInstruction(req, res);
    }
    else if (req.body.request.type === 'SessionEndedRequest') {
        console.log('Session ended', req.body.request.reason);
    }
});
```

Notice in LaunchRequest you are building the welcome response to the user. You can find out more about the Alexa response format at https://amzn.to/2hZ4tpa. First, you define the version set as 1.0, which is the version of the response. In the near future, Alexa might upgrade the response version as Amazon improves its services. Then, there is the response object containing shouldEndSession set to true, which will end the session after serving the response. If you set this to true, you will need to engage the user with a follow-up intent. This advanced topic will be covered in the next chapter. Finally, there's outputSpeech which contains a PlainText type and a text property that contains the response that you want the user to hear from the Amazon Echo device.

The following code shows the Alexa response object sending a welcome message to the user:

```
res.json({
    "version": "1.0",
    "response": {
      "shouldEndSession": true,
      "outputSpeech": {
        "type": "PlainText",
```

```
            "text": "Welcome to Henry's Cooking App"
      }
   }
});
```

11. Create the `BuildGetCookingInstruction` function, which will handle the `GetCookingInstructionIntent` request. First, build a base URL to call the Spoonacular REST API, called `Get Search Recipes` (https://bit.ly/2JBnhDP).

    The following code shows building a base URL to call `Get Search Recipes` at Spoonacular:

    ```
    var url =
    'https://spoonacular-recipe-food-nutrition-v1.p.mashape.com/recipes
    /search?';
        url += 'number=3&offset=0&instructionsRequired=true';
    ```

    Notice that the base URL contains `number=3`, which is the number of results returned and `instructionsRequired=true` will return food search results that contain cooking instructions:

12. `Get Search Recipes` takes two parameters: `query` and `diet`. When Alexa sends the request with `GetCookingInstructionIntent`, there will either be a captured `Foods` slot in `request.intent.slots.Foods.value` or a `DietTypes` slot in `request.intent.slots.DietTypes.value`. You can build the Spoonacular `Get Search Recipes` URL by setting `url +=` `` `&query=${foodName}` `` and `url +=` `` `&diet=${dietTypes}` ``.

    The following code shows setting query and diet parameters for `Get Search Recipes`:

    ```
    var request = req.body.request;
        if(request.intent.slots.Foods.value) {
            var foodName = request.intent.slots.Foods.value;
            url += `&query=${foodName}`;
        }
        if(request.intent.slots.DietTypes.value) {
            var dietTypes = request.slots.intent.DietTypes.value;
            url += `&diet=${dietTypes}`;
        }
    ```

13. After constructing the Spoonacular `Get Search Recipes` URL, you can make a REST API GET request. In order to use Spoonacular, you will need the key that you received when you signed up for the free service. Set the **X-Mashape-Key** header with the API key and the **X-Mashape-Host** header. The Spoonacular `Get Search Recipes` will return three results, which you can loop through the results and construct a response text using the recipe names:

```
unirest.get(url)
        .header("X-Mashape-Key", "Enter your own key here")
        .header("X-Mashape-Host", "spoonacular-recipe-food-
nutrition-v1.p.mashape.com")
        .end(function (result) {
            var dishTitle = '';
            for(i=0; i < result.body.results.length; i++) {
                dishTitle += result.body.results[i].title + ', ';
            }
            var responseText = `I found following dishes that you
can cook ${dishTitle}`;
            res.json({
                "version": "1.0",
                "response": {
                    "shouldEndSession": true,
                    "outputSpeech": {
                    "type": "PlainText",
                    "text": responseText
                    }
                }
            });
        });
```

Deploying and debugging the web service endpoint

In `Chapter 4`, *Hosting, Securing, and Testing Fortune Cookie in the Cloud*, you learned how to deploy the Fortune Cookie Webhook (Node.js server tier) to Microsoft Azure. You will follow the exact same steps to create a Microsoft Azure App Service to host the Henry's Kitchen web service endpoint. When you have successfully created your Microsoft Azure App Service to host the Henry's Kitchen endpoint, you should have a web service address similar to `https://myhenrytestapp.azurewebsites.net`.

Configuring and testing the endpoint in the Alexa console

Once you are done deploying the endpoint Node.js service to the Microsoft Azure App Service, you will need to set it up in the Alexa `Cooking` skill:

1. Using your Chrome browser, log in to the Alexa console.
2. Go to the `Cooking` skill.
3. Go to the **Endpoint** screen by clicking on the menu on the left.
4. Choose **HTTPS**. Then, enter `https://myhenrytestapp.azurewebsites.net/alexa/cookingApi` in the **Default Region** textbox and choose **My development endpoint is a sub-domain of a domain that has wildcard certificate from a certificate authority** from the dropdown found below the **Default Region** textbox.

The following screenshot shows configuring the endpoint for the skill so that the request can be custom handled by the Node.js cooking service you created:

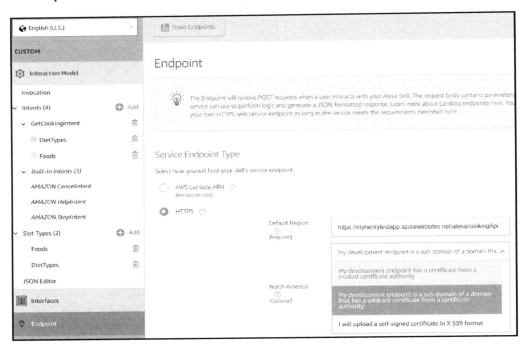

The text in this screenshot is not important. It shows you how to enable Endpoint for Alexa

5. Click on the **Save Endpoints** button.
6. Click **Build** from the top menu and you will notice that the skill builder checklist is totally green:
   1. You have created an invocation name: `henry's kitchen`
   2. You have created `GetCookingIntent`, `Foods`, and `DietTypes` slots.
   3. You have built a model.
   4. You have configured the endpoint.

The following screenshot features the Alexa **Build** screen, showing a successfully built skill that is ready to be tested:

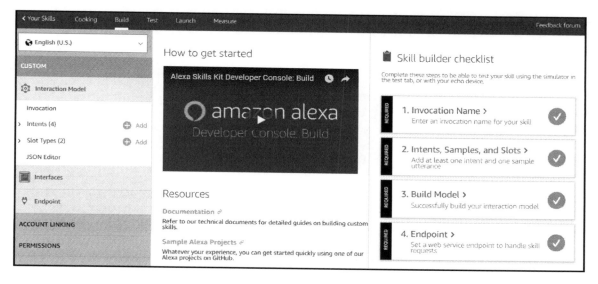

Alexa console Build screen

7. Click on the **Test** menu at the top. Enable the **Test is enabled for this skill** radio button at the top.
8. In the Alexa Simulator textbox, enter one of your utterances: `alexa ask henry's kitchen I want to cook burger`. Notice here that you must start with the wake up words `alexa ask` and then use the cooking skill's invocation name `henry's kitchen`, before adding the utterance `I want to cook burger` to trigger the intent.

The following screenshot shows the Alexa Simulator:

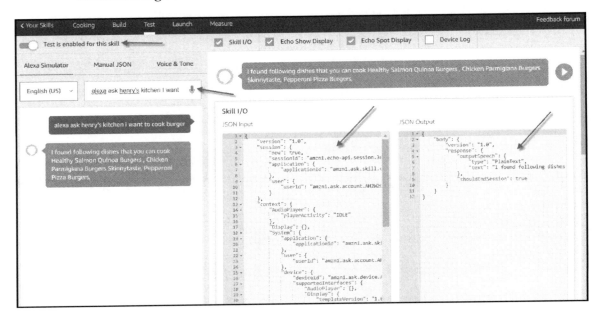

The text in this screenshot is not important. It shows how to enable the debugging mode in Alexa Simulator

9. Notice in the preceding screenshot that the simulator has output the response. On the right-hand side, you will see the JSON input and the output. The JSON input is necessary for you to debug locally in the following section. Copy the JSON input and save it somewhere else so that you can use it later.

Debugging the endpoint locally

In the previous section, you configured the endpoint in the Alexa Cooking skill and managed to test it using the Alexa console. In this section, you will run the endpoint service locally in order to be able to troubleshoot any issues you might come across. Testing locally, you can step through the code and debug issues, which will be very useful:

1. Open Visual Studio Code.
2. Open the server.js file where you wrote the endpoint code.
3. Comment out line 10 //alexaRouter.use(verifier). When running and debugging locally, you need to bypass Alexa's security middleware, and by doing so you can debug using the JSON input from step 9.

4. Hit *F5* to start debugging the `server.js` locally. The endpoint is running on `http://localhost:8000`.

5. Open Postman.

6. Create a GET Ping service. In the **enter request URL** textbox, type in `{{url}}/ping`.

The following image shows the HTTP GET ping:

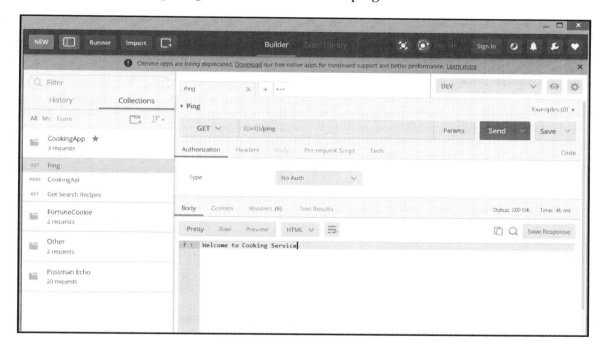

Postman HTTP GET ping

7. `{{url}}` is the variable that changes for DEV and PROD. In DEV, it will use `http://localhost:8000`, and in PROD, it will use`https://myhenrytestapp.azurewebsites.net`. Open **Manage Environments**.

The following image shows the **Manage Environments** menu:

Manage Environments

8. Once the **Manage Environments** window opens, you can create DEV and PROD with the url variable with http://localhost:8000 for DEV and https://myhenrytestapp.azurewebsites.net for PROD.

The following image shows the creation of the url environment variable:

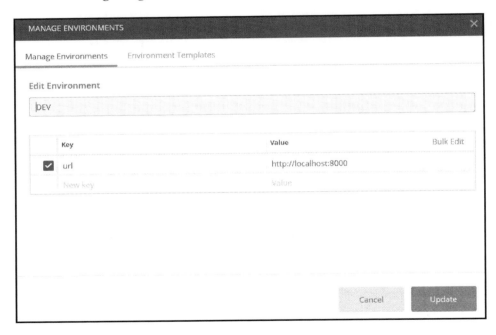

Postman – Manage Environments

9. Once the environment variable is set up, you can select DEV and click **Send**, and you will see **Welcome to Cooking Service**. This is a great way to quickly test whether the service is running properly.

10. In Postman, create an HTTP POST for the cooking API. Use the {{url}}/alexa/cookingApi URL and make sure you select DEV.

The following screenshot shows Postman for the HTTP POST cooking API that handles Alexa GetCookingIntent:

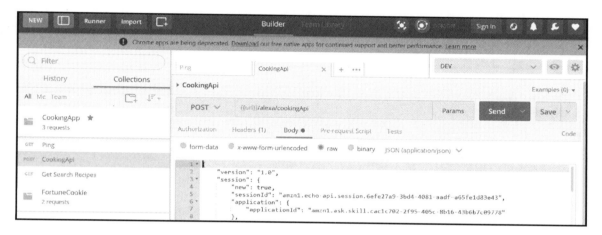

Postman HTTP POST cooking API.

11. In the body, paste the JSON input that you acquired when you were testing in the Alexa console in step 9 of the preceding *Configuring and testing the endpoint in the Alexa console* section.

12. Go to Visual Studio Code and add a breakpoint at line 63. This is where the endpoint will receive the request from Postman with the input JSON and send the food search query to the Spoonacular web service to get food recommendations. You will be able to see the response being constructed.

13. Go back to Postman and click the **Send** button, and then go back to Visual Studio Code and you will see that the code execution has stopped at line 63. You can hit *F10* to step through the code. When the code executes, you can go back to Postman and you will be able to see the response.

The following screenshot shows debugging the Spoonacular search by recipes API call:

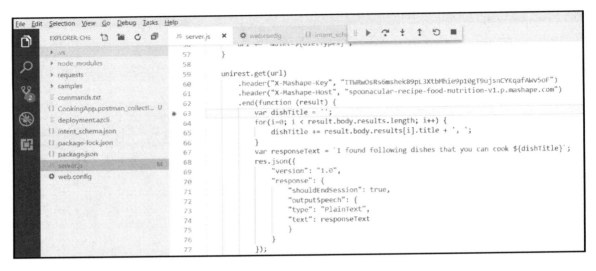

Debugging in Visual Studio Code line 63

The following code shows the response received from the local endpoint web service after submitting the request from Postman:

```
{
    "version": "1.0",
    "response": {
        "shouldEndSession": true,
        "outputSpeech": {
            "type": "PlainText",
            "text": "I found following dishes that you can cook Healthy
Salmon Quinoa Burgers , Chicken Parmigiana Burgers Skinnytaste, Pepperoni
Pizza Burgers, "
        }
    }
}
```

Working with Amazon Echo

In Chapter 5, *Deploying the Fortune Cookie App to the Google Home*, you learned about Google Home devices, which listen for the wake words OK Google and respond to user requests. Similarly, Amazon Echo devices listen to the wake word Alexa and respond to user requests, providing relevant answers. Amazon Echo and Google Home compete in the voice-controlled device space and both provide marketplaces for developers to submit voice user interface applications that handle specific tasks. For Google Home, you learned to build the FAQ chatbot and the Fortune Cookie. In this chapter, you will build a cooking application that helps the user learn how to cook. The concepts you will learn range from building Alexa skills using the ASK for the Amazon Echo analogues to building intents using Dialogflow for Google Home. If you are thinking of monetizing your voice user interface application, you will need to focus on building for both platforms: Google Home and Amazon Echo.

Setting up and testing in Amazon Echo

Let's set up your Alexa Echo for the first time. For the setup instructions, I will be using an Amazon Echo Dot.

1. Using your browser, navigate to https://alexa.amazon.com. You can also download the Amazon Alexa application from your mobile device. For these instructions, I will be using Amazon Alexa on an Android phone.

The following screenshot shows the Amazon Alexa application from the Android marketplace:

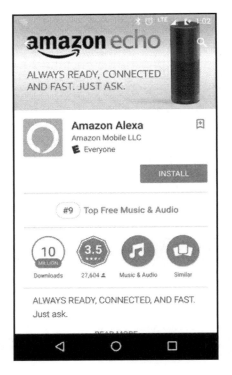

Amazon Alexa Android application

2. Sign in to your Amazon Alexa application using your Amazon developer account that you used to create the skill.
3. Click on the **Settings** button located at the bottom right and then click on the **BEGIN SETUP** button.
4. On the **Choose a device to setup** page, select your device. On the **Choose language** page, click **Continue** after choosing your language.

The following screenshot shows the **Choose a device to setup** page during the Amazon Echo setup:

Amazon Echo Setup - Choose Device Setup

5. On **Begin Echo Dot setup** click the **Connect to WiFi** button.

6. On the **Wait for the orange light ring** page, if you do not see the orange ring going around your Amazon Echo, hold the action button on your Amazon Echo for five seconds and then click **Continue**.

The following photo shows the action button on the Amazon Echo Dot:

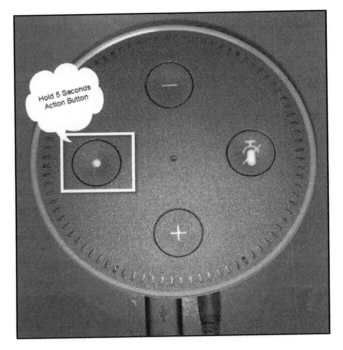

Amazon Echo Setup - Reset

7. You will be asked to manually connect to the Echo Dot via Wi-Fi on your phone. On Wi-Fi, select **Amazon-XXX**.

The following screenshot shows the **Manually connect to Echo Dot** page during the setup:

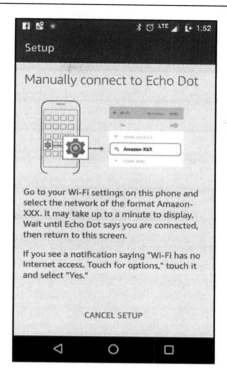

Amazon Echo setup - Manually connect to Echo Dot

8. Once connected to Amazon-XXX Wi-Fi, Amazon Alexa will ask you to select the Wi-Fi that your Amazon Echo Dot should connect to. That's it! You have successfully connected your Amazon Echo to Wi-Fi. As a quick test, ask `Alexa what's today's weather like` and Alexa should provide you with today's weather.

9. Since you logged in using the developer Amazon account that you used to set up your Alexa skill, your Cooking App skill will be ready to use on your Echo Dot. Simply ask Alexa, `Alexa ask henry's kitchen I want to cook burger` and Alexa will send a request to your custom web service endpoint and respond to you.

Viewing history in Amazon Echo

When you are working with a device, it is sometimes difficult to troubleshoot, especially when you do not know whether the device received your request. Whenever you speak, Amazon keeps track of all the voices that the Amazon Echo device receives. In this section, you will learn how to view the device logs. Also, you might want to clear these logs permanently, as having these logs might cause some privacy concerns:

1. Open Amazon Alexa on your mobile device and sign in using your Amazon account.
2. Open up a menu and go to **Settings**.
3. Click on **History**.

   The following screenshot shows the Amazon Alexa mobile application's **History** setting in the **Settings** menu:

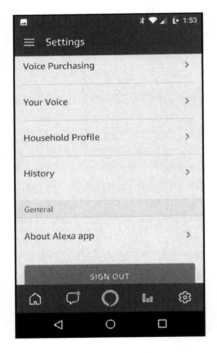

Amazon Alexa mobile application History menu

4. You will be able to view all the voice recordings that Amazon received through the Amazon Echo device.

The following image shows the history of the voice recordings sent to your Amazon Echo device:

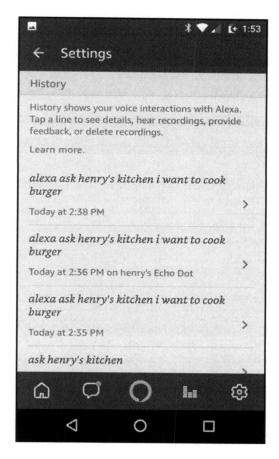

History of voice recordings

5. Click on one of the recordings and you will be able to delete it.

The following screenshot shows deleting a voice recording:

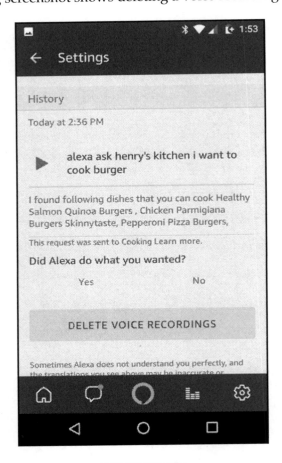

Deleting a voice recording

6. In step 5, you can delete one recording at a time but you might want to completely remove all recordings. To do this, open a browser and go to https://www.amazon.com/mycd. You will see your Amazon Echo device under the **Devices** tab.

The following screenshot shows the list of devices in Amazon device management:

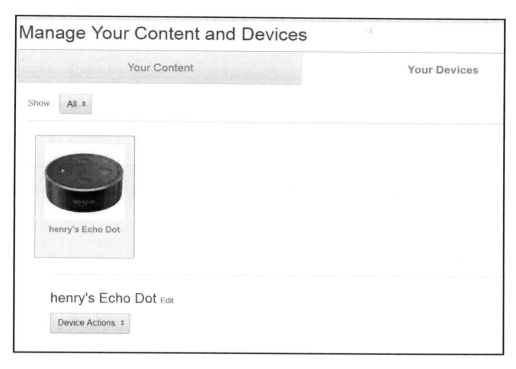

Manage Your Content and Devices

| Your Content | Your Devices |

Show : All ⬍

henry's Echo Dot

henry's Echo Dot Edit

Device Actions ⬍

Manage Amazon device

7. Notice that there is a **Device Actions** dropdown. Select **Manage voice recordings**.
8. Windows will pop up with a **Delete** button, allowing you to clear all voice recordings made by the device.

The following image shows managing voice recordings, where you can delete all of the recordings made by the device:

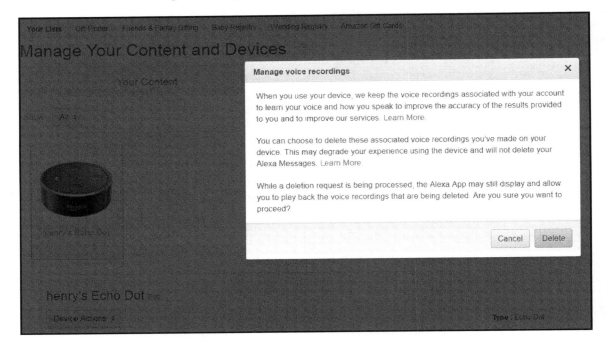

Manage voice recordings

Backing up the Alexa skill

In this section, you will learn how to back up the Alexa Cooking App skill you built. Everything you have built so far in the ASK can be exported to JSON, and later, you can restore the JSON to recreate an Alexa skill.

1. Log in to the Alexa console using the browser.
2. Once you log in, go to Cooking App Skill.
3. On the left-hand menu, there is a **JSON Editor**.

The following screenshot shows the **JSON Editor** menu:

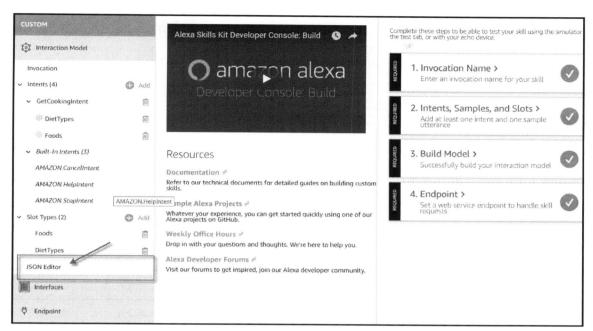

JSON Editor menu in the Alexa console

4. On the right-hand side, you will see the JSON that describes the schema definition of the Alexa skill you built. Note that there is not a direct way to export the file from the web, so you would need to copy and paste the JSON into the file.

The following screenshot shows the JSON schema of the Alexa skill you built:

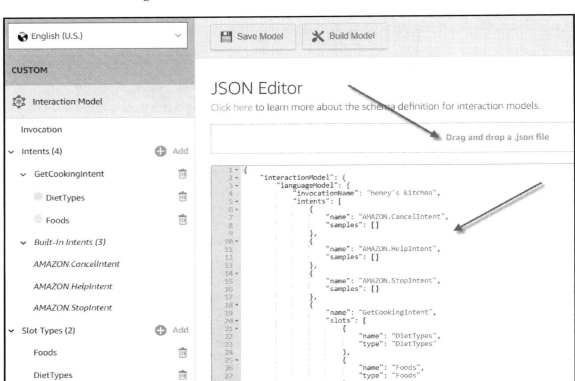

Alexa skill JSON schema

Note that if you need to re-import the Alexa JSON schema, you come back to the same screen and simply drag and drop the JSON schema file you saved in step 2. Then, you can click on **Save** and build the model. It is also important to note here that the Alexa skill JSON schema does not contain endpoint configuration. You must refer to the *Configuring and testing the endpoint in the Alexa console* section to reconfigure the endpoint web service.

Summary

In this chapter, you learned how to create an Alexa skill called Henry's Kitchen, which takes food types from the user and recommends cooking ideas. In order to get those cooking ideas, you created a Node.js endpoint web service that queries the Spoonacular third-party REST API to get cooking recipes. During the voice application development process, you have mastered intents, slots, and utterances using the Alexa console. Also using Node.js, you have learned how to create a web service that can take requests from Alexa and respond to Alexa. Then, you went through the process of debugging the web service endpoint using the Alexa JSON input locally. You managed to deploy the web service endpoint to the Microsoft Azure cloud in order to test using an Amazon Echo device. Finally, you managed to back up the entire Alexa skill you created so that you can restore it, if need be. In the next chapter, we will take basic concepts from this chapter and delve into more advanced topics, such as sessions and creating conversations in order to handle more advanced inquiries from the user.

7
Using Advanced Alexa Features for the Cooking App

In this chapter, you will continue to enhance the cooking application created in the previous chapter. First, you will add logging capability to the Node.js server, which will write logs to Microsoft Azure Blob storage. You will be able to observe the incoming requests and outgoing responses and if there are critical errors, you will be able to easily troubleshoot them by downloading the log. Then, you will be introduced to advanced topics, in order to build more of a conversational **voice user interface** (VUI) that will help engage the users of the cooking application. In order to build a conversational VUI, you will learn to manage application state. Also, you will build dialog models in order collect missing slot values and then check with the user what those collected slot values are. Furthermore, in this chapter, you will learn to uniquely identify the users requesting your cooking skill, in order to save the context for later use. Finally, the chapter ends by teaching you how to submit the cooking application to the Amazon marketplace.

The following topics will be covered in this chapter.

- Logging application events
- Creating dialog interfaces
- Using built-in intents
- Managing dialog states
- Amazon marketplace certification process

Logging application events and data

Until now, you have managed to log application events and data using `console.log`. But logging to the Visual Studio Code console is only useful when you are debugging locally on your machine. In production, you need an easy way to view the log when an error occurs. This chapter deals with more complex scenarios and requires a solid logging strategy in order to capture the requests and responses going into and out of the web service endpoint. You will take advantage of Microsoft Azure Blob storage to log application event data. Microsoft Azure Blob storage offers many compelling advantages:

- It is cheap. Microsoft Azure Blob will cost you $0.002 GB/month (`https://bit.ly/2dLTE51`), which is virtually free as you will be using no more than 1-2 GB for a small application per month.
- It is reliable. You do not have to manage expensive storage array infrastructure.
- It has built-in backups. Typically, if you are working with the filesystem, you tend to back up files in case of corruption, but Microsoft Azure provides a cheap backup solution if you need one.
- It is available from anywhere. Since it is in the cloud, the file storage can be accessed securely from anywhere using the access key.
- It is simple to use. I have worked with overly complex solutions in the past, and nothing beats a simple solution that does the job well.

Setting up an Azure Blob storage

First, let's create Microsoft Blob storage so you can wire up the logging code to write to the blob file.

1. Open your browser FireFox or Chrome.
2. Log into the Microsoft Azure Portal (`https://portal.azure.com`) using the Microsoft account that you created.

3. Once logged in on the menu, left-click on **All services** and type `storage` in the **All services** textbox on the right. You will see the **Storage accounts** menu is listed. Click on the **Storage accounts** menu.

The following screenshot shows the **Storage accounts** menu found in Microsoft Azure service offerings:

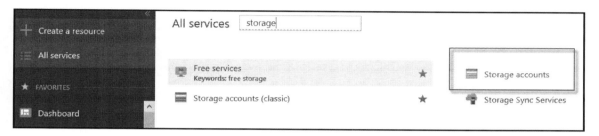

Storage accounts in Microsoft Azure

4. Click **Add** at the top. The **Create Storage accounts** window will slide out to the right.

5. Fill in the boxes with the following information and use the rest of the default settings. **Name** = `henrytestlog`, **Account kind** = **Blob storage**, **Replication** = **Locally-redundant storage (LRS)**, for **Subscription** choose your own subscription, which should be set by default, and for **Resource Group** choose existing and select `HenryResourceGroup`. Click **Create**. Notice here that in the previous chapter, you created resource group called `HenryResourceGroup` to deploy the web service endpoint. Any Microsoft Azure resources that you create for this cooking application will be associated to `HenryResourceGroup`. The replication strategy for the Blob is LRS, which means that the files are not geographically replicated across multiple states. You would want to use **Geo-redundant storage (GRS)** if you are dealing with critical files you can't afford to lose. For simple logging files, you would want to stick to LRS.

The following screenshot shows the **Create storage account** setting:

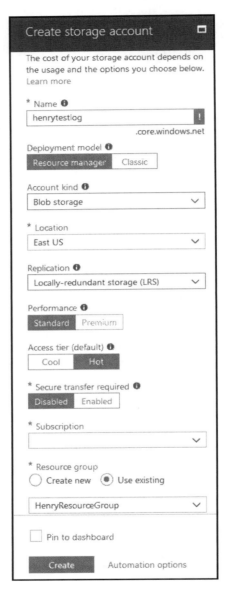

Create storage account settings

6. Step 5 will take a few minutes to create the `henrytestlog` storage. When finished, go to the storage accounts resource, following step 1. You will see the list of storage accounts. At the top, you will see an empty textbox to search or filter the long list. Type `henry` and you will see `henrytestlog`. Click on **henrytestlog**.

The following screenshot shows the filtered list of storage accounts for `henrytestlog`:

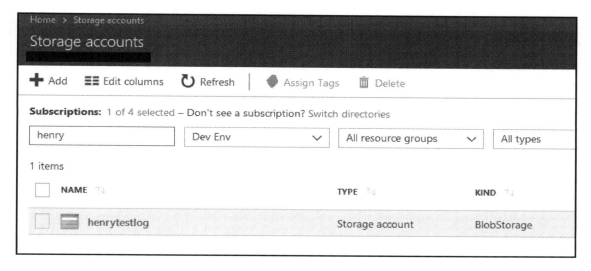

Filtered list of storage accounts

7. Notice a new window will slide to the right. Choose the **Access keys** settings.
8. Here, take note of **Storage account name** and **key1**. You will need these later to configure the Node.js logging component that you will be using.

The following screenshot shows the **Access keys** setting for the storage account:

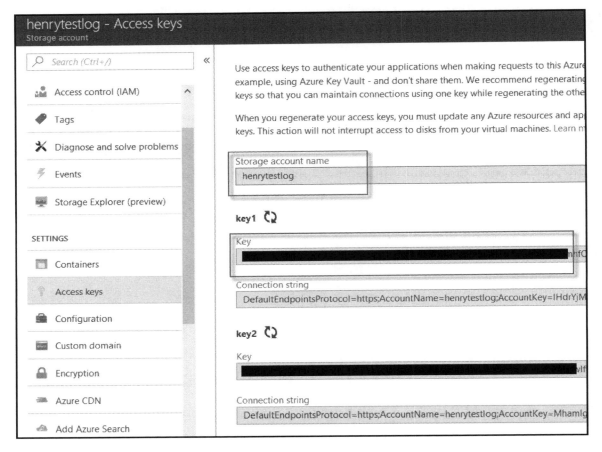

The text in this screenshot is not important. It shows a storage account key to access Microsoft Azure storage created by you.

9. In the left menu, go to **Containers**. When the new window slides out in the top menu, click **+Container**.

10. Type in the **Name** as `applog` and choose **Public access level** as **Private (no anonymous access)**. Choosing access level private will require a key to access the storage. You saw the access keys in step 8.

The following screenshot shows the creation of a container for the Blob storage:

Creating a container in the Blob storage

11. Once created, you will see the container you just created in the **Containers** section. The following screenshot shows the container created:

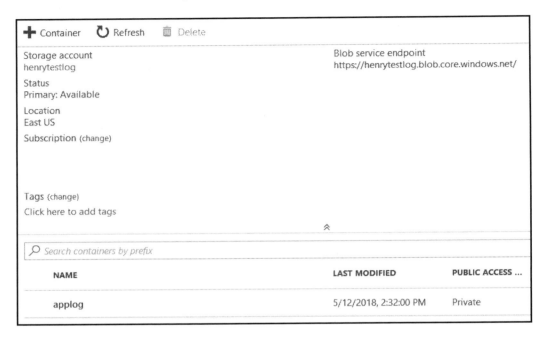

Created container

You successfully created the Blob storage called `henrytestlog`, and inside the Blob you created a container called `applog`. In the following section, you will utilize this `applog` container and create a logging file inside of the `applog` container.

Setting up application logging in the cooking application

In this section, you will take code from the previous chapter and add logging using the Node.js component called **Winston** (`https://github.com/winstonjs/winston`) and the Microsoft Azure Blob transport for Winston called Winston Azure Blob transport (`https://bit.ly/2GdwWhG`), which extends the Winston component to be able to log in to Microsoft Azure Blob storage:

1. Open Visual Studio Code.

2. Go to **File** | **Open Folder** and to your working directory where you have code from `Chapter 6`, *Building a Cooking Application Using Alexa*. There should be three files: `server.js` contains the Node.js code for the web service endpoint, `package.json` describes the dependency components used in Node.js, and `web.config` contains configuration settings in order to deploy Node.js to the Microsoft Azure App Service.

3. In Visual Studio Code, go to the Terminal. If you do not see the Terminal, go to **View** | **Toggle Panel**.

The following screenshot shows the Terminal in VS Code where Node.js commands can be typed and executed:

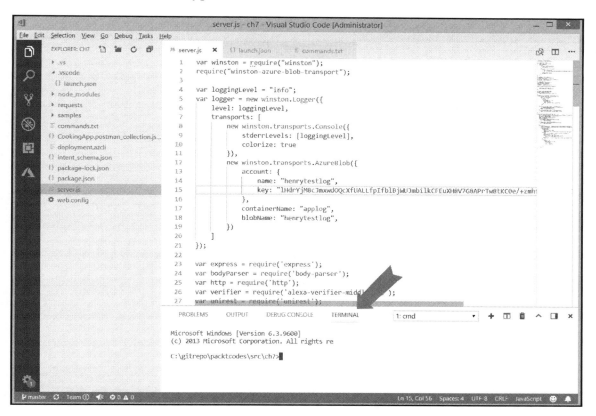

Visual Studio Code Terminal Window

4. Type `npm install --save winston` and when finished, type another command, `npm install --save winston-azure-blob-transport`. The Winston Node.js logging component will be used to log in to the Microsoft Azure Blob storage that you created in the previous section.

5. Open `package.json` and verify that the Winston components are added.

The following code shows the `package.json` that contains the Node.js application dependencies:

```
{
  "name": "cookingapp",
  "description": "endpoint to handle henry's kitchen alexa skill
requests",
  "version": "0.1.0",
  "author": "Henry Lee <henry@henrylee.link>",
  "dependencies": {
    "alexa-verifier-middleware": "^1.0.1",
    "body-parser": "^1.18.2",
    "express": "^4.16.3",
    "unirest": "^0.5.1",
    "winston": "^2.4.2",
    "winston-azure-blob-transport": "^0.2.7"
  },
  "script": "./server.js"
}
```

6. In the menu, go to **View** | **Debug** or the icon on the left that looks like a crossed out bug.

7. Click on the setting icon that looks like a gear, which will open the `launch.json` file. `launch.json` controls the application debugging behavior when you start your Node.js application in Visual Studio Code.

The following screenshot shows opening the `launch.json` file:

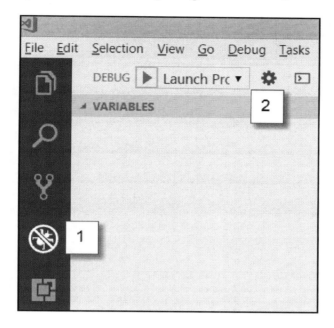

Opening launch.json for Visual Studio Code

8. In the `launch.json` file, add `"console": "integratedTerminal"` and save the file. With this setting, the Node.js application will run in the integrated Terminal where you typically execute Node.js `npm` commands. The Winston logging component will be logging to the integrated terminal. Also, create an `env` property and add `ISDEBUG` set to `true`. The `process.env.ISDEBUG` variable is true when the code is running in Visual Studio Code and you can use the variable to enable and disable lines of the code.

The following JSON contains the `launch.json` settings:

```
{
  "version": "0.2.0",
  "configurations": [
    {
      "type": "node",
      "request": "launch",
      "name": "Launch Program",
      "program": "${workspaceFolder}/server.js",
      "console": "integratedTerminal",
      "env": {
```

```
            "ISDEBUG": "true"
        }
      }
    ]
  }
```

9. Open the `server.js` file.

10. At the top, add the Winston logging component so you can use it in the code. Declare `winston` and `winston-azure-blob-transport`, and instantiate `winston.Logger` with the level set to info. Then, add transports to `winston.Logger`. First, add `winston.transports.Console` with `stderrLevels` set to logging level `info` and `colorize` set to true. Second, add `winston.transports.AzureBlob` and add the Azure Blob configuration setting that you got when you set it up in the previous section, found under the **Access Keys** section in Azure Blob. You would need to set `account.name` to `henrytestlog`, `account.key` to the Azure Blob account key, `containerName` to `applog`, and `blobName` to `henrytestlog`.

The following code shows how to configure the Winston console and Azure Blob loggers:

```
var winston = require("winston");
require("winston-azure-blob-transport");
var loggingLevel = "info";
var logger = new winston.Logger({
    level: loggingLevel,
    transports: [
        new winston.transports.Console({
            stderrLevels: [loggingLevel],
            colorize: true
        }),
        new winston.transports.AzureBlob({
            account: {
                name: "henrytestlog",
                key: "Put your key you got from Azure blob Access
Key"
            },
            containerName: "applog",
            blobName: "henrytestlog",
        })
    ]
});
```

There are six logging levels, in order of severity, with the first one being the most severe: `error`, `warn`, `info`, `verbose`, `debug`, and `silly`. If you set the logging level to the info the severity of info will log info, warn and error . Depending on the type of logging you need, you might need to set the logging level to debug when you are in development mode, but you might want to change debug to info or error in production.

11. Let's add some logging to the ping service and to when the application starts. To the ping service, add `logger.info("ping service.")`. Where the application starts, you will notice there is a line code that logs to `console.log("Server is up and running...")`. Replace `console.log` with `logger.info("Server is up and running...")`. From here on, you will not be using `console.log`, but instead use a custom logging solution that logs to Azure Blob using `logger.info`.

    The following code shows adding and replacing console logging with the Winston logger:

    ```
    app.use("/alexa", alexaRouter);
    if(!process.env.ISDEBUG) {
        logger.info("Setup Alexa verifier.");
        alexaRouter.use(verifier);
    }

    alexaRouter.use(bodyParser.json());
    app.use("/ping", function (req, res, next) {
        logger.info("ping service.");
        res.send('Welcome to Cooking Service');
    });

    var server = http.createServer(app);
    var port = process.env.PORT || 8000;
    server.listen(port, function () {
        logger.info("Server is up and running...");
    });
    ```

12. Press *F5* or in the menu, at the top, go to **Debug | Start Debugging**.

13. Open Postman. In the previous chapter, you configured various service calls, including the Ping service. Set the environment to DEV, choose the **Ping service**, and press **Send**.

14. Come back to Visual Studio Code and you will see, in the Terminal, the info logs that you added in the previous steps.

The following screenshot shows the info logs in Visual Studio Code:

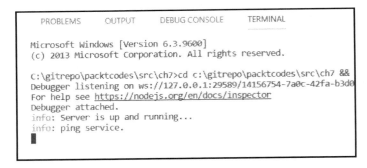

Logging to the Terminal

15. Using the browser, log in to Microsoft Azure portal (`https://portal.azure.com`).

16. Go to the `henrytestlog` Azure Blob storage and then go to the **Container** section. You will see the `applog` container in the list.

The following screenshot shows the `applog` container in the list:

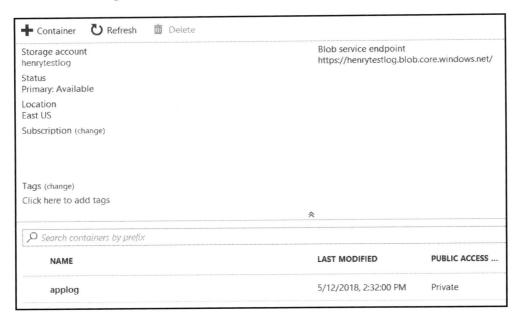

Shows applog container

17. Click on applog.

18. You should see the henrytestlog file in the applog container.

The following screenshot shows the henrytestlog file in the applog container:

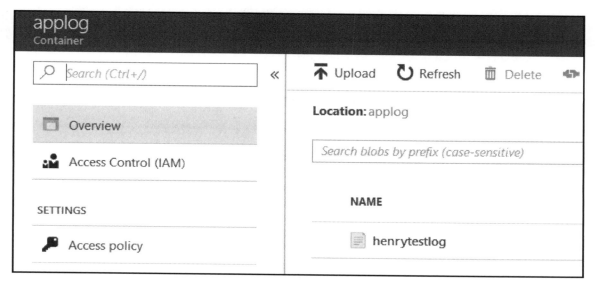

Container with the logging file inside

19. Click on the henrytestlog file and then click on **Download,** and you should be able to see the logs that you saw in the Visual Studio Code Terminal.

The following screenshot shows downloading the log file from the container:

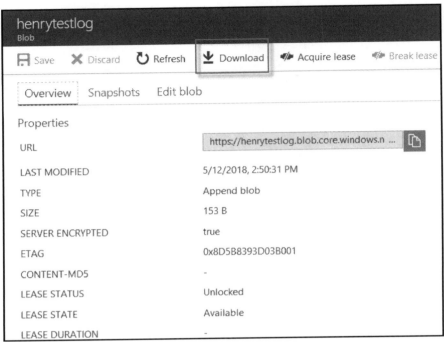

Downloading the applog file

In the following sections, you will be utilizing the logger throughout the code in order to log events, data, and exceptions to help troubleshoot issues you might run into in production.

About dialog interfaces

In this section, you will improve the previous chapter's Cooking application by adding Alexa's dialog features. Notice that the `GetCookingIntent` you created in previous chapter contains `DietTypes` and `Foods` slots. If the user does not provide all the required fields, you will not be able to complete the search query for finding dishes. In order to make sure the user gives you all the required information, you will be using `Dialog.Directive`. There are four dialog directives:

- `Dialog.Delegate`: Alexa automatically handles conversations, which helps gather the information required for the intents based on the dialog model created in the skill builder. The slots and intents can have prompts to ask the user for the required information, then the utterances will be defined in the slots and the intents to match the user's responses to the specific required values, and finally confirmation will be defined for the slots and the intents to confirm with the user that the provided values are indeed correct. This is the most commonly used directive for creating the conversation to gather the required fields.

- `Dialog.ElicitSlot`: It is very similar to `Dialog.Delegate`, but instead of a predefined dialog model, `Dialog.ElicitSlot` is manually created during the conversation in the code.

- `Dialog.ConfirmSlot`: This can be used to tell Alexa to ask the user for a yes or no answer. Depending on the how the user answers, `confirmationStatus` can be either `CONFIRMED` or `DENIED`. This is useful whenever you need specific confirmation that the slot value the user selected is indeed what the user wants.

- `Dialog.ConfirmIntent`: Once the user has provided all the required slot values for the intent, you can ask the user one last time if the selected slot values are what the user wants. Be careful with this directive as it can get very annoying for the user, especially if there are many slots defined for the intents because `Dialog.ConfirmIntent` will repeat all the slot values chosen by the user and confirm that their values are correct.

Building GetCookingIntent dialog models

For `GetCookingIntent`, you will build the dialog model using the skill builder in the Alexa console. The `GetCookingIntent` dialog model will ask the user for `DietTypes` and `Foods` slots if they are not provided. If the user provides a `DietTypes` slot value, you will create another dialog that asks the user if the provided value is correct. In this section, you are not create the conversations, but rather one-off models that interact with the user at a specific point in the conversation. In the following sections, you will learn to stitch all this together, which will allow the user to experience the conversational flow. In summary, the following models will be created:

- `DietTypes` is a required slot dialog to gather missing `DietTypes` slot values
- `DietTypes` is a confirmation to check with the user that the selected `DietTypes` slot value is correct
- `Foods` is a required slot dialog to gather missing `Foods` slot values

Here are the steps you can follow to create dialog models for the `DietTypes` and `Foods` slots:

1. Open the browser and log in to `https://developer.amazon.com/alexa/console/ask`.
2. Choose `Cooking` skill from the list.
3. On the dashboard, expand `GetCookingIntent` on the left side and select `DietTypes`.
4. Enable the **Is this slot required to fulfill the intent?** option.
5. Enter in **Slot Filling | Alexa speech prompts**: `do you have any dietary requirement like vegan, vegetarian or pescetarian?` Whenever `GetCookingIntent` does not receive the `DietTypes` slot value from the user, you can prompt the user to provide the missing `DietTypes`.
6. Add the following utterances that will capture the `DietTypes` slot value from the user's responses: `yes I am {DietTypes}`, `{DietTypes}`, and `I am {DietTypes}`.
7. Enable **Does this slot require confirmation?**
8. Enter in **Slot Confirmation | Alexa speech prompts**: `You said you are {DietTypes}?` Once the `DietTypes` slot value is extracted successfully, you can confirm with the user the value is what he or she provided.

The following screenshot shows configuring **Slot Filling** and **Slot Confirmation** for the `DietTypes` slot:

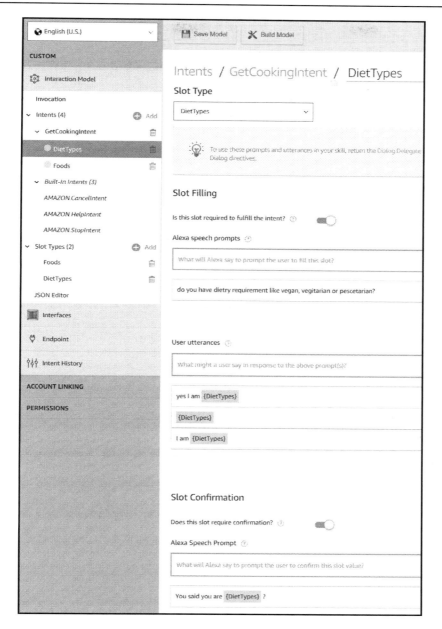

Configuring Slot Filling and Slot Confirmation for DietTypes

9. Under `GetCookingIntent,` **click on** `Foods.`

10. Enable **Is this slot required to fulfill the intent?**

11. Enter in **Slot Filling | Alexa speech prompts**: `What kind of food would you like to cook?`. Whenever `GetCookingIntent` does not receive a `Foods` slot value from the user, you can prompt the user to provide the missing `Foods`.

12. Add the following utterances that will capture the `Foods` slot value from the user responses: `I want to make {Foods}` and `I want to cook {Foods}`.

The following screenshot shows configuring **Slot Filling** for the `Foods` slot:

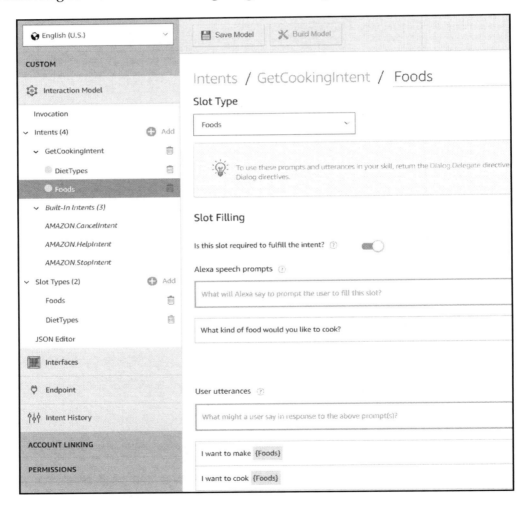

Configuring Slot Filling for the Foods slot

You have successfully configured the dialog models prompting the user to extract missing DietTypes and Foods slots.

Handling the GetCookingIntent dialog model in code

In the previous section, you created a dialog model using Alexa console's skill builder and in this section, you will process the dialogs coming from Alexa. Whenever Alexa matches GetCookingIntent, there are important properties that get set whenever the intent begins to initiate a conversation. The GetCookingIntent, when received from the Node.js server the request object, will contain dialogState set to one of STARTED, IN_PROGRESS, and COMPLETED because GetCookingIntent has the dialog models that you created in the previous section. Also, if confirmation is required for the slot given by the user, there will be a status property called confirmationStatus set to either NONE, DENIED, or CONFIRMED.

When a creating conversational flow, you will need to pay attention to the dialogState and confirmationStatus properties properly to handle the responses, so that Alexa can deliver an appropriate response to the user to acquire missing slots or confirm fulfilled slots. First, when the user does not specify DietTypes or Foods, dialogState will be set to STARTED in the request object. When responding to the STARTED state, you need to include Dialog.Delegate in directives with the updatedIntent object. If dialogState is in IN_PROGRESS, you would need to send Dialog.Delegate without updatedIntent. If dialogState is in the COMPLETED state, you will notice that all the DietTypes and Foods slots contain values that you can use to get the result from the Spoonacular search API.

The following screenshot shows the `GetCookingIntent` dialog flow:

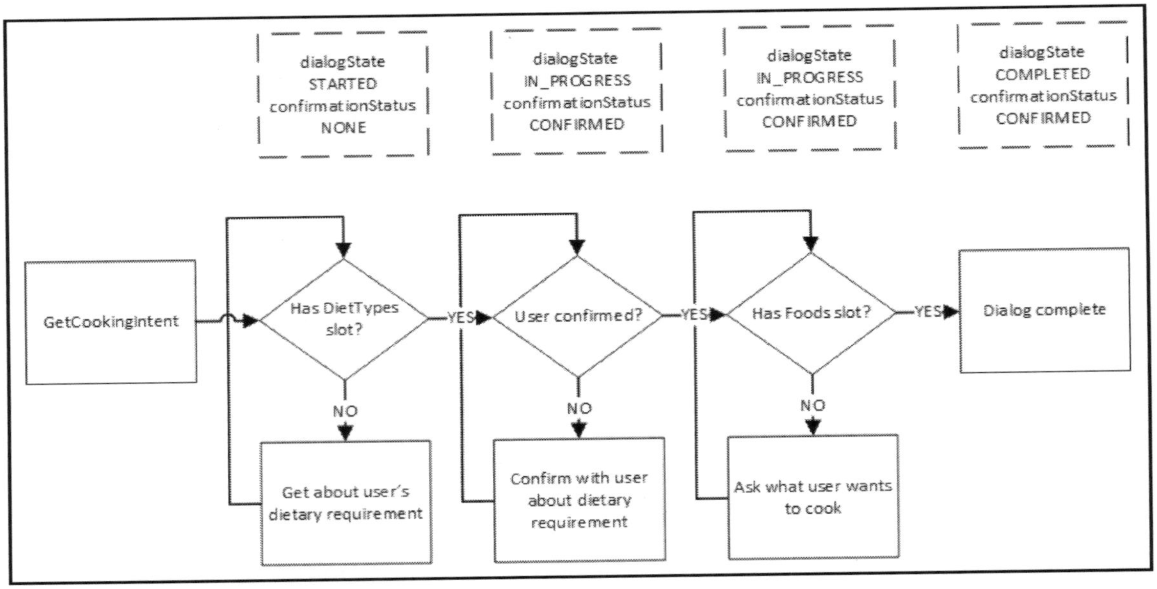

GetCookingIntent dialog model

Here are the detailed steps for writing the code to handle the conversational flow using the dialogue models that you created in the previous section:

1. Open Visual Studio Code.
2. Go to **File | Open Folder** and to the the `Chapter 7` code that you started to create for logging in the previous section: **Setting Up Application Logging in Cooking Application**.
3. Go to the `server.js` file.
4. You will create a function called `StartCookingInstructionDialog` that will manage the dialog flow for `GetCookingIntent`. Begin with adding some logging, `logger.info(`${request.intent.name} ${request.dialogState}`)`, to track `dialogState`. Then, you will handle `request.dialogState == 'STARTED'`. You will set `shouldEndSession` to `false`, and then add `Dialog.Delegate` to `directives` with `updatedIntent`, which contains slot values. In `updatedIntent`, you will be adding the slot values and names that are involved in the conversation, which are `DietTypes` and `Foods`.

5. When `dialogState` is not `COMPLETED`, you know that the conversation is currently in progress and as long as the `dialogState` does not change to `COMPLETED`, you would need to send `Dialog.Delegate` in `directives` without `updatedIntent`. Finally, when the dialog completes, you can resume handling `GetCookingIntent`. `StartCookingInstructionDialog` will maintain the conversational flow until `COMPLETE dialogState` is received and `return false` only when the conversation is over, which will trigger `BuildGetCookingInstruction` in the entry point to the `cookingApi` POST method.

The following code handles the `STARTED`, `IN_PROGRESS`, and `COMPLETED` dialog states:

```
function StartCookingInstructionDialog(req, res) {
    var request = req.body.request;
    logger.info(`StartCookingInstructionDialog
${request.intent.name} ${request.dialogState}`);
    if(request.dialogState == 'STARTED'){
        res.json({
            "version": "1.0",
            "response": {
                "shouldEndSession": false,
                "directives": [
                    {
                        "type": "Dialog.Delegate",
                        "updatedIntent":{
                          "name": "GetCookingIntent",
                          "slots":{
                            "DietTypes": {
                                "name": "DietTypes",
                                "value":
request.intent.slots.DietTypes.value
                                              ?
                      request.intent.slots.DietTypes.value
                                              : ""
                            },
                            "Foods": {
                                "name": "Foods",
                                "value":
request.intent.slots.Foods.value
                                              ?
request.intent.slots.Foods.value
                                              : ""
                            }
                        }
                    }
```

```
                }
            ]
        },
    });
} else if (request.dialogState != 'COMPLETED'){
    res.json({
        "version": "1.0",
        "response": {
            "shouldEndSession": false,
            "directives": [
                {
                    "type": "Dialog.Delegate"
                }
            ]
        }
    });
} else {
    return false;
}
return true;
};
```

6. Modify the code that handles the `cookingApi` POST method. In the `cookingApi` POST method, there is a section that gets executed when `req.body.request.type === 'IntentRequest' && req.body.request.intent.name === 'GetCookingIntent'`. Here, you will be checking `StartCookingInstructionDialog`, which will return false if the conversation is completed; if not, it will return true. When the conversation is over, you can safely execute `BuildGetCookingInstruction`. At the beginning of the function, you will add `logger.info(JSON.stringify(req.body, null, '\t'))`, which will log all incoming requests from Alexa. Finally, add `try-catch` around the entire code, which will handle and log errors if there are any exceptions while executing any lines of code.

The following code utilizes `StartCookingInstructionDialog` in the `cookingApi` POST method:

```
alexaRouter.post('/cookingApi', function (req, res) {
    try{
        logger.info(JSON.stringify(req.body, null, '\t'));
        if (req.body.request.type === 'LaunchRequest') {
            logger.info("LaunchRequest");
            res.json({
                "version": "1.0",
                "response": {
                    "shouldEndSession": true,
```

```
                    "outputSpeech": {
                        "type": "PlainText",
                        "text": "Welcome to Henry's Cooking App"
                    }
                }
            });
        }
        else if (req.body.request.type === 'IntentRequest' &&
                req.body.request.intent.name ===
'GetCookingIntent') {
            if (!StartCookingInstructionDialog(req, res))
                BuildGetCookingInstruction(req, res);
        }
        else if (req.body.request.type === 'SessionEndedRequest') {
            logger.error('Session ended', req.body.request.reason);
            if(req.body.request.reason=='ERROR')
                logger.error(JSON.stringify(req.body.request, null,
'\t'));
        }
    } catch(e){
        logger.error(e);
    }
});
```

7. In `BuildGetCookingInstruction`, you will be putting various bits of logging code. In the beginning of the function, add `logger.info("BuildGetCookingInstruction")` so we know this method is being called. Then, in `unirest.end` check whether the `result.error` is empty; if it's not empty, it means there is an error, so log the error with `logger.error('Error processing spoonacular.')`, `logger.error('Error processing spoonacular.')`, and `logger.error('Error processing spoonacular.')`. If the call is successful, the result received from Spoonacular will be logged with `logger.info(result.body.results)`. Finally, the response that will be sent to Alexa will be logged using `logger.info(JSON.stringify(responseToAlexa, null, '\t'))`.

The following code is for `BuildGetCookingInstruction`:

```
function BuildGetCookingInstruction(req, res) {
    var url =
'https://spoonacular-recipe-food-nutrition-v1.p.mashape.com/recipes
/search?';
    url += 'number=3&offset=0&instructionsRequired=true';
    var request = req.body.request;
    logger.info("BuildGetCookingInstruction");
```

```
        if(request.intent.slots.Foods.value) {
            var foodName = request.intent.slots.Foods.value;
            url += `&query=${foodName}`;
        }
        if(request.intent.slots.DietTypes.value) {
            var dietTypes = request.intent.slots.DietTypes.value;
            url += `&diet=${dietTypes}`;
        }


    unirest.get(url)
        .header("X-Mashape-Key",
"TTWRwOsRs6mshek89pL3XtbMhie9p10gT9ujsnCYKqafAWv5oF")
        .header("X-Mashape-Host", "spoonacular-recipe-food-
nutrition-v1.p.mashape.com")
        .end(function (result) {
            var responseText = "";
            if(result.error){
                logger.error('Error processing spoonacular.');
                logger.error(result.body);
                logger.error(result.error);
                responseText = `I am sorry there was an issue
processing your request.`;
            } else {
                logger.info("Successfully received results from
spoonacular.");
                logger.info(result.body.results);
                var dishTitle = '';
                for(i=0; i < result.body.results.length; i++) {
                    dishTitle += result.body.results[i].title + ',
';
                }
                responseText = `I found following dishes that you
can cook ${dishTitle}`;
            }
            var responseToAlexa = {
                "version": "1.0",
                "response": {
                    "shouldEndSession": false,
                    "outputSpeech": {
                        "type": "PlainText",
                        "text": responseText
                    }
                }
            };
            logger.info(JSON.stringify(responseToAlexa, null,
'\t'));
            res.json(responseToAlexa);
        });
```

```
};
```

Deploying and testing the GetCookingIntent dialog model

In the previous section, you completed the code for handling the dialog model of `GetCookingIntent`. In this section, you will deploy the code to the Microsoft Azure App Service and test it using the Alexa simulator on the website.

1. Open the browser and go to Microsoft Azure Portal (`https://portal.azure.com`).

2. Follow the instruction described in `Chapter 4`, *Creating Microsoft Azure App Services to Host Node.js webhook,* and set up and deploy Node.js application to the Microsoft Azure App Service. You will be using FTP to deploy the following files: `server.js`, `web.config`, and `package.json`.

 In `Chapter 4`, *Hosting, Securing, Testing Fortune Cookie in Cloud,* you had to install the Node.js components express and body-parser on the Microsoft Azure App Service server using the console. Remember to install additional components that are new in this chapter by executing the commands `npm install winston`, `npm install winston-azure-blob-transport`, and `npm install alexa-verifier-middleware` from the server console. If you face any issues, consider copying the entire `node_modules` from your local directory that contains all the dependency modules to the server using FTP.

3. Open the browser and log in to `https://developer.amazon.com/alexa/console/ask`.

4. Choose the `Cooking` skill from the list.

5. Go to **Test**.

6. From the simulator type or say `alexa ask henry's kitchen I want to cook burger`.

7. Observe the JSON input in `Skill I/O` window. You will notice that the `request.dialogState` is set to `STARTED` and `request.intent.slots.DietTypes.value` is missing, while `request.intent.slots.Foods.value` is set to `burger`. Because `request.intent.slots.DietTypes.value` is missing, Alexa will want to initiate a conversation and will be sending a request to the server to ask what action Alexa should be taking. When the server receives this request, you have already written the code to send `Dialog.Delegate` in directives with `updatedIntent`.

The following JSON shows the request object that shows `STARTED dialogState`:

```
"request": {
    "type": "IntentRequest",
    "requestId": "amzn1.echo-
api.request.9b4d7463-1bed-49df-95ac-733068904dff",
    "timestamp": "2018-05-25T20:56:11Z",
    "locale": "en-US",
    "intent": {
        "name": "GetCookingIntent",
        "confirmationStatus": "NONE",
        "slots": {
            "DietTypes": {
                "name": "DietTypes",
                "confirmationStatus": "NONE"
            },
            "Foods": {
                "name": "Foods",
                "value": "burger",
                "resolutions": {
                    "resolutionsPerAuthority": [
                        {
                            "authority": "amzn1.er-authority.echo-
sdk.amzn1.ask.skill.cac1c702-2f95-
405c-8b16-43b6b7c09778.Foods",
                            "status": {
                                "code": "ER_SUCCESS_MATCH"
                            },
                            "values": [
                                {
                                    "value": {
                                        "name": "Burger",
                                        "id":
"496451f3d45d2f22ba6695e53b3a2e12"
                                    }
                                }
```

```
                    ]
                }
            ]
        },
        "confirmationStatus": "NONE"
    }
}
},
"dialogState": "STARTED"
}
```

The following is the response to the `dialogState` STARTED sent from the server to Alexa:

```
{
    "body": {
        "version": "1.0",
        "response": {
            "directives": [
                {
                    "type": "Dialog.Delegate",
                    "updatedIntent": {
                        "name": "GetCookingIntent",
                        "slots": {
                            "DietTypes": {
                                "name": "DietTypes",
                                "value": ""
                            },
                            "Foods": {
                                "name": "Foods",
                                "value": "burger"
                            }
                        }
                    }
                }
            ],
            "shouldEndSession": false
        }
    }
}
```

8. Type or say `i am vegetarian`. Notice that `dialogState` is changed to `IN_PROGRESS` and the missing `request.intent.slots.DietTypes.value` is now filled with `vegetarian`. But, notice that `request.intent.slots.DietTypes.confirmationStatus` is NONE, and because we enabled in our dialog model to confirm the user response for the `DietTypes` slot, the conversational flow is not over until `request.intent.slots.DietTypes.confirmationStatus` is set to CONFIRMED. In the JSON output, notice that `Dialog.Delegate` in directives does not contain `updatedIntent`.

   The following JSON output shows the response sent from the web endpoint server in response to the `IN_PROGRESS` status:

   ```json
   {
       "body": {
           "version": "1.0",
           "response": {
               "directives": [
                   {
                       "type": "Dialog.Delegate"
                   }
               ],
               "shouldEndSession": false
           }
       }
   }
   ```

9. Type or say `yes`. Notice that the JSON input did not change because the session ended, and any activity regarding the `dialogState` COMPLETED is processed in the server. In order to see more details of the log when the COMPLETED status is sent, you would need to go to the log in the Microsoft Azure Blob storage and look into `henrytestlog`.

10. Go to Microsoft Azure portal and download `henrytestlog` from the Blob storage in order to track down the COMPLETED status interactions.

11. After the first entry shows `dialogState` set to COMPLETED, next logging entry shows where `BuildGetCookingInstruction` function is called, and then the Spoonacular search API is called and the server receives the result, which is logged as the fourth entry. Finally, the server creates a response and sends it to Alexa.

The following log entries show the capture activities when the COMPLETED dialogState **is sent to the server:**

```
[info] - 2018-05-25T22:08:10.511Z - StartCookingInstructionDialog
GetCookingIntent COMPLETED
[info] - 2018-05-25T22:08:10.511Z - BuildGetCookingInstruction
[info] - 2018-05-25T22:08:11.027Z - Successfully received results from
spoonacular.
[info] - 2018-05-25T22:08:11.027Z -  - [ { id: 777569,
    title: 'Mediterranean Quinoa Burgers',
    readyInMinutes: 45,
    servings: 6,
    image: 'mediterranean-quinoa-burgers-777569.jpg',
    imageUrls: [ 'mediterranean-quinoa-burgers-777569.jpg' ] },
  { id: 758521,
    title: 'Black Bean-Quinoa Burgers',
    readyInMinutes: 45,
    servings: 8,
    image: 'black-bean-quinoa-burgers-758521.jpg',
    imageUrls: [ 'black-bean-quinoa-burgers-758521.jpg' ] },
  { id: 728903,
    title: 'Super Food Black Bean Vegan Burgers',
    readyInMinutes: 50,
    servings: 6,
    image: 'super-food-black-bean-vegan-burgers-728903.jpg',
    imageUrls: [ 'super-food-black-bean-vegan-burgers-728903.jpg' ] } ]
[info] - 2018-05-25T22:08:11.027Z - {
    "version": "1.0",
    "response": {
        "shouldEndSession": false,
        "outputSpeech": {
            "type": "PlainText",
            "text": "I found following dishes that you can cook
Mediterranean Quinoa Burgers, Black Bean-
                                Quinoa Burgers, Super Food Black
Bean Vegan Burgers, "
        }
    }
}
```

Working with built-in Intents

Building an intent to capture user requests can be a complex task because the task requires you to build utterances and slots. Luckily, Alexa provides built-in intents that you can utilize without having to do lots of upfront work. You can find many of the built-in intents at `https://amzn.to/2xgf3j8`. In this section, you will take advantage of `AMAZON.HelpIntent`, which gets triggered when the user says `alexa ask henry's kitchen help me`. From the server, you will be able to capture the help intent by filtering the request for `req.body.request.type === 'IntentRequest' && req.body.request.intent.name === 'AMAZON.HelpIntent'`. You can further enhance the help intent by adding your own utterances from the Alexa skill builder console.

1. Open a browser and go to the Alex skill builder console at `https://developer.amazon.com/alexa/console/ask`.
2. Click on the `Cooking` skill.
3. When you expand **Intents**, there should be **Built-In Intents** and you will find `AMAZON.HelpIntent`. If you do not find `AMAZON.HelpIntent`, click on **+Add** next to **Intents**.
4. Choose **Use an existing Intent** from Alexa's built-in library and in the search box, enter `Help`.
5. Click on the **Add** button to add `AMAZON.HelpIntent`.

The following screenshot shows adding AMAZON.HelpIntent:

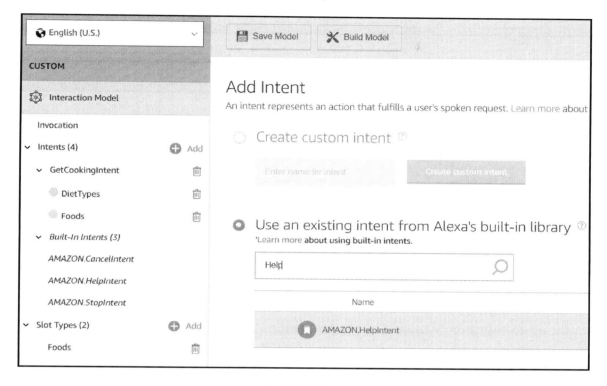

Adding AMAZON.HelpIntent

6. Click **Intents | Build-In Intents |** AMAZON.HelpIntent.
7. Under **Sample Utterances**, add: I need help, help me, how do I use this.

The following screenshot shows adding utterances to the AMAZON.HelpIntent:

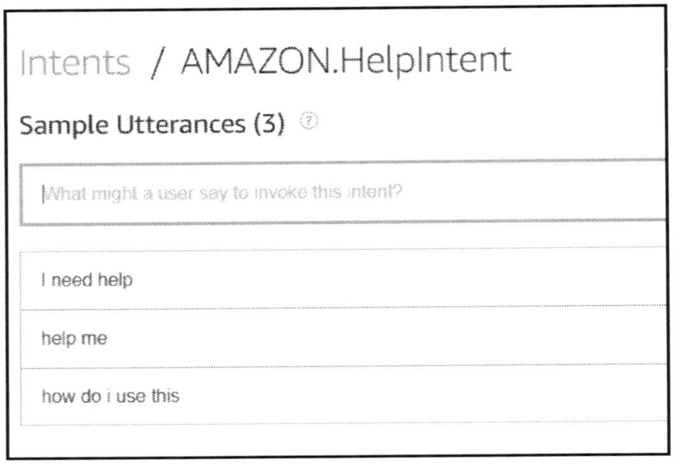

Intents / AMAZON.HelpIntent

Sample Utterances (3) ⑦

> What might a user say to invoke this intent?

I need help

help me

how do i use this

Adding AMAZON.HelpIntent utterances

8. Click **Save Model** and then **Build Model**.
9. Open Visual Studio Code.
10. Go to **File | Open Folder**, then to the the the Chapter 7 code that you have been working on.
11. Click the server.js file.
12. In the alexaRouter.post('/cookingApi' POST method, you will looking for an incoming help intent where req.body.request.type === 'IntentRequest' && req.body.request.intent.name === 'AMAZON.HelpIntent' and then execute BuildHelpIntentResponse.

    The following code checks for AMAZON.HelpIntent and executes BuildHelpIntentResponse:

    ```
    else if (req.body.request.type === 'IntentRequest' &&
        req.body.request.intent.name === 'AMAZON.HelpIntent') {
        BuildHelpIntentResponse(req, res);
    }
    ```

13. Add a BuildHelpIntentResponse function that will respond to the Alexa with You can say alexa ask henry's kitchen I want to cook burger.

The following shows the `BuildHelpIntentResponse` function:

```
function BuildHelpIntentResponse(req, res) {
    logger.info('BuildHelpIntentResponse');
    res.json({
        "version": "1.0",
        "response": {
            "shouldEndSession": true,
            "outputSpeech": {
                "type": "PlainText",
                "text": "You can say alexa ask henry's kitchen I want to
cook burger."
            }
        }
    });
};
```

After deploying `server.js`, you can test it using the Alexa simulator from the browser. You can initiate `AMAZON.HelpIntent` by saying `alexa ask henry's kitchen help me`, and you will see the response returned from the server. You can also verify all this by looking at the log.

The following shows the response to `AMAZON.HelpIntent` from the server:

```
{
    "body": {
        "version": "1.0",
        "response": {
            "outputSpeech": {
                "type": "PlainText",
                "text": "You can say alexa ask henry's kitchen I want to
cook burger."
            },
            "shouldEndSession": false
        }
    }
}
```

About dialog states

During the conversation, you need to understand the previous context in order to fulfill a new request from the user. For example, when the user says `alexa ask henry's kitchen get more recipes`, you realize that the user is asking for more recipes based on previously provided `Foods` and `DietTypes` slots. In order to fulfill this context-based request, you need to store the data from previous conversations. To achieve this, you will be using the Redis key value pair in memory caching database. Redis is easy to use and very popular in the open source community for storing simple data, and Redis will be perfect for storing and retrieving the application dialog states.

Here is the conversational flow while managing states on a Redis server:

1. `GetCookingIntent` completes first time.
2. Store the `DietTypes` and `Foods` slots, and offset the value to Redis using `userId`. The offset starts at `0` and time to expire is set to 2 minutes. The `userId` is passed on every request as part of the session object and it is unique. You can use `userId` as the key for Redis to store data. The time to expire value set on the data will automatically expire the data after two minutes if the value is not used. If the data is used, the timer will reset.
3. The user asks for more recipes and triggers `GetMoreRecipesIntent`.
4. Check Redis using `userId`. If the user has previously triggered `GetCookingIntent`, retrieve the `DietTypes` and `Foods` slot values and offset. Increase the offset by three. Save the new data back to Redis.
5. If the data does not exist, create a response telling the user how to ask for recipes. Otherwise, call Spoonacular using the retrieved data and upon a successful call, create a response and send it back to Alexa.

Coding the state management

You learned a state management strategy in the previous section. In this section, you will be applying state management to the existing code. Open the browser and log in to `https://developer.amazon.com/alexa/console/ask`:

1. Add a new intent and call the intent `GetMoreRecipesIntent`.
2. For `GetMoreRecipesIntent`, add the following utterances: `i want more recipes` and `get more recipes`.
3. Save the model and then build the it.
4. From the browser, log in to the Microsoft Azure portal (`https://portal.azure.com`).
5. From **All Services**, filter Redis and choose **Redis Caches**.

   The following screenshot shows the Redis Cache from the list of services in Microsoft Azure:

Redis Caches

6. Click on the **+Add** button to add a new **Redis Cache**.
7. Put the DNS name as `henrytest`; in the subscription, choose your **Microsoft Azure subscription**; for the resource group, choose the existing `HenryResourceGroup`; set **Location** as **East US 2**, or select whichever region you are close to (west or central); and set **Pricing tier** as **Basic C0 (250 MB)**.

The following screenshot shows the **Redis Cache** settings:

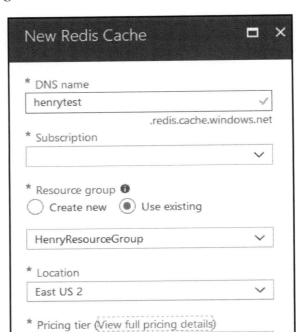

Creating Redis Cache

8. Click **Create** and wait for the **Redis Cache** to be created, and you will be able to see henrytest Redis in the list to select.
9. Click on **henrytest Redis cache**.
10. Click on **Access Keys** from the left menu.
11. Save the server address and the port which is typically 6380 found in the **Primary** key connection string. You will be using this value when you create the Redis client in code in later steps.

The following screenshot shows the **Redis Access Keys**:

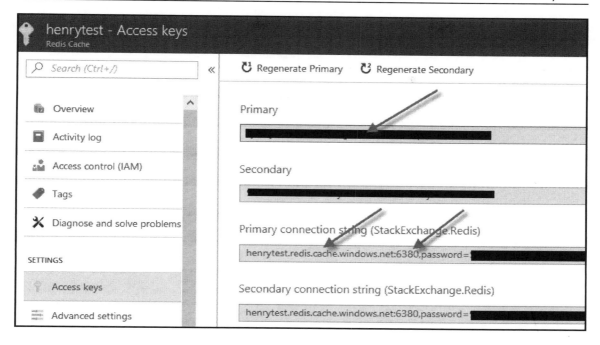

Redis access keys

12. Open Visual Studio Code.

13. Go to **File** | **Open Folder**, then to the `Chapter 7` code that you have been working on.

14. You will be using a new Node.js component called `redis`. Install the new component by typing this in the Node.js Terminal where your `Chapter 7` `server.js` is located: `npm install redis`.

15. Open `server.js`.

16. At the very top, declare Redis: `var redis = require("redis")`.

17. Add the Redis password `var redisAuth = ' password to connect to redis'`, Redis address `var rediHost = 'henrytest.redis.cache.windows.net'`, and Redis port `var redisPort = 6380`. You should be able to get these values from step 11.

The following code shows the Redis connection information:

```
var redis = require("redis");
var redisAuth = 'password to connect to redis';
var rediHost = 'henrytest.redis.cache.windows.net';
var redisPort = 6380;
```

18. In the `cookingApi` POST method, add a condition that checks for `req.body.request.type === 'IntentRequest' && req.body.request.intent.name === 'GetMoreRecipesIntent'` and executes `GetOffset(req, res, false)`.

    The following code shows executing the `GetOffset` function when `GetMoreRcipesIntent` is triggered:

    ```
    else if (req.body.request.type === 'IntentRequest' &&
        req.body.request.intent.name === 'GetMoreRecipesIntent') {
        GetOffset(req, res, false);
    }
    ```

19. `GetOffset` gets called by `GetCookingIntent` if the user triggers `GetCookingIntent` for the first time; `GetOffset` will save the `DietTypes` and `Foods` slot values and offset. If `GetOffset` is called by `GetMoreRecipesIntent`, previously saved `DietTypes` and `Foods` slot values and the offset are retrieved from Redis. After retrieving the state values from Redis, the offset will be incremented by 3 and state values will be passed to the `BuildGetCookingInstruction` method. If the state value is not found in Redis because the state value has expired, a response is created to ask the user for recipes for food. Notice here that the state value is saved or retrieved using `session.user.userId`, which is unique and can be used as the identifier of the request user.

    The following shows the `GetOffset` function code:

    ```
    function GetOffset(req, res, saveFromRequest) {
        logger.info('GetOffset');
        var client = redis.createClient(rediPort, rediHost,
            { auth_pass: redisAuth, tls: { servername: rediHost } });
        var request = req.body.request;
        var session = req.body.session;
        var timeInSeconds = 60 * 2;
        if (save) {
            var queryObject = {
                offset: 0,
                foodName: request.intent.slots.Foods.value,
                dietTypes: request.intent.slots.DietTypes.value
            };
            client.set(session.user.userId,
    JSON.stringify(queryObject), 'EX',
            timeInSeconds);
        }
        else {
    ```

```
client.get(session.user.userId, function (error, result) {
    if (error) {
        logger.error(error);
    } else if (result) {
        var queryObject = JSON.parse(result);
        queryObject.offset = queryObject.offset + 3;
        client.set(session.user.userId,
            JSON.stringify(queryObject), 'EX',
timeInSeconds);
        BuildGetCookingInstruction(req, res, queryObject);
    } else {
        logger.info('GetOffset: queryObject is not found or
        expired.');
        res.json({
            "version": "1.0",
            "response": {
                "shouldEndSession": true,
                "outputSpeech": {
                    "type": "PlainText",
                    "text": "You can say alexa ask henry's
kitchen I

                    want to cook burger to get
                    the list of recipes."
                }
            }
        });
    }
});
    }
};
```

20. In `BuildGetCookingInstruction`, you will change the logic to build the Spoonacular `url` variable to search for the recipes based on the value retrieved from Redis. First, you will add the offset value to the `url` found in `queryObject`, and if the `queryObject` does not exist, a default value of 0 will be used: `var offset = queryObject ? queryObject.offset : 0; url += `&offset=${offset}`;`. Similarly, `DietTypes` and `Foods` will be constructed from `queryObject` or using a request object containing the slot values. The key point to take away here is that the empty `queryObject` means `GetCookingIntent` is called the first time, and the slot values and the offset will be saved the first time into Redis, in anticipation that the user might trigger `GetMoreRecipesIntent`.

The following code shows constructing the Spoonacular search URL:

```
var offset = queryObject ? queryObject.offset : 0;
url += `&offset=${offset}`;

if (queryObject || request.intent.slots.Foods.value) {
    var foodName = queryObject ? queryObject.foodName :
request.intent.slots.Foods.value;
    url += `&query=${foodName}`;
}
if (queryObject || request.intent.slots.DietTypes.value) {
    var dietTypes = queryObject ? queryObject.dietTypes :
request.intent.slots.DietTypes.value;
    url += `&diet=${dietTypes}`;
}
```

21. After receiving the result from Spoonacular, you need to check whether the call to Spoonacular was based on the previous state saved or the first time call by checking whether `queryObject` is empty. The `queryObject` argument is passed from the `GetOffset` function only after retrieving the state values from Redis. `GetOffset` is responsible for saving and retrieving the state from Redis. If `queryObject` is empty, you would need to save the state values found in the request object by calling `GetOffset` with `savedFromRequest` set to `true` and passing the `req` and `res` objects before sending the response to Alexa.

The following code shows calling `GetOffset` in order to save the `DietTypes` and `Foods` slot values the very first time:

```
logger.info('BuildGetCookingInstruction Saving queryObject');
if (!queryObject) {
    GetOffset(req, res, true);
}
```

Submitting cooking app to Amazon marketplace

In order to submit your app to the Amazon marketplace and get it approved, your voice application must abide by their policies. Here is a quick list of subjects you would need to consider:

- **Violation of trademarks and branding**: Respect intellectual property and do not infringe upon others' copyright. Consider before using any resource whether there are any legal implications. For example, you would not want to use images from other companies or use trademarked voices as part of your application.
- **Child directed**: Your voice application should not sell products to, or collect data from, children.
- **Health**: Collecting and exposing personal health information is not allowed.
- **Purchasing and selling products**: In order to sell products, your voice application must utilize Amazon In-Skill purchasing (`https://amzn.to/2GTwYM9`).
- **Advertising**: Voice applications that stream audio or sell products are allowed to play advertising audio, but Amazon has the right to reject and ban voice applications if they are found to be inappropriate.
- **Pornography**: Any pornographic or sexual applications will not be allowed.
- **Violence**: Any topics that deal with violence are not allowed.
- **Religion, ethnicity, and culture**: Any inappropriate topics dealing with religion, ethnicity, and culture are not allowed, for example, voice applications that voice support for Nazis or the KKK will not be allowed.
- **Contact emergency services**: It is prohibited to create an application that contacts services such as 911 or other emergency products and services.
- **Content**: The voice application is not allowed to promote any illegal content, for example, promoting the downloading of pirated movies and music. Also, any content dealing with terrorism or illegal drugs will not be allowed.

Now you know about the policies for submitting a voice application, you can send your voice application to the marketplace. Here are the steps:

1. Open a browser and go to the Alexa skill builder console at `https://developer.amazon.com/alexa/console/ask`.
2. Click on the `Cooking` skill.

3. In the top menu, click on **Launch**. The Amazon market place submission process is divided into four sections: **Store preview, Privacy and Compliance, Availability**, and **Submission**.

4. In **English (US) Store Preview section**, enter the following information:
   - **Public Name** : Henry's Kitchen
   - **One Sentence Description** : Gives cooking ideas based on the food and ingredients
   - **Detailed Description** : Need ideas about cooking recipes based on the ingredients? Ask Henry's Kitchen what you would like to cook
   - **Example Phrases** : **1.** Alexa, open henry's kitchen, **2.** I want to cook burger
   - **Category** : Cooking & Recipes
   - **Key Words** : cooking, recipes
   - **Privacy Policy URL** : http://www.henrylee.link/
   - **Terms of Use URL** : http://www.henrylee.link/

5. Click **Save and continue** to **Privacy & Compliance**:
   - **Does this skill allow users to make purchases or spend real money?**: No
   - **Does this Alexa skill collect users' personal information**: No
   - **Is this skill directed to or does it target children under the age of 13?**: No
   - **Does this skill contain advertising?**: No
   - **Export Compliance**: Click on the checkbox to accept the term
   - **Testing Instructions**: Use the Amazon Echo device to test and say Alexa ask Henry's Kitchen I want to cook burger

6. Click **Save and continue** to **Availability**.
   - **Who should have access to this skill?**: Public
   - **Where would you like this skill to be available?**: In all countries and regions where Amazon distributes skills
   - **Beta Test**: If you would like to ask others to beta test your voice application, you can add their email addresses; up to 500 are allowed

7. Click **Save and continue** and go to the submission page.

8. If you correctly filled in all the required fields, you will be allowed to submit. Click **Submit for review**.

Summary

Continuing from `Chapter 6`, *Building a Cooking Application Using Alexa*, you applied advanced topics, such as creating dialog models to collect missing slots, and applied them to the Henry's Kitchen app. Also, you learned to manage and save application state to Microsoft Azure Redis in order to handle more complex conversation flows. The chapter also introduced more comprehensive logging, which allows the Node.js server handling Alexa requests to log events and data to Microsoft Azure Blob storage. You learned to download the logs and review them to understand the voice application flows and interaction between Alexa and the server. Finally, after understanding the submission policy, the application was submitted to the marketplace.

In the next chapter, you will utilize and slightly modify the same server code, and learn to convert an Alexa skill to a Google Dialogflow intent.

8
Migrating the Alexa Cooking Application to Google Home

Today, Amazon and Google voice assistant devices are the most popular among consumers. In order to increase your voice application's adoption, you would need to deploy your voice application to both Amazon Echo and Google Home devices. Unfortunately, Amazon and Google use their own proprietary voice technologies and it takes some work to make your voice application work across both platforms. In Chapter 6, *Building a Cooking Application Using Alexa* and Chapter 7, *Using Advanced Alexa Features for the Cooking App,* you learned about Alexa Skills Kit for Amazon Echo devices and in Chapter 5, *Deploying the Fortune Cookie App to Google Home,* Chapter 6, *Building a Cooking Application Using Alexa,* and Chapter 7, *Using Advanced Alexa Features for the Cooking App,* you learned about Dialogflow for Google Home devices. In this chapter, you will learn important techniques to migrate your Amazon Alexa Skills Kit to Google's Dialogflow. Also, the web service endpoint that you created in Chapter 6, *Building a Cooking Application Using Alexa* and Chapter 7, *Using Advanced Alexa Features for the Cooking App* for Alexa requests will be modified to handle Google's Dialogflow requests as well.

The goal of this chapter is to help you create a voice application for the Amazon and Google platforms with minimal modification, emphasizing the reusability of the code in order to create consistent user experiences and save development time.

The following topics are covered this chapter:

- Comparing Alexa skill and Dialogflow agent
- Converting slots to entities
- Converting intents
- Converting slot fillings to required parameters
- Handling conversation states
- Converting Alexa web service endpoints to Dialogflow webhooks

Comparing an Alexa Skills Kit and Dialogflow agent

Alexa Skills Kit and Dialogflow serve as development platforms for creating voice applications for Amazon and Google devices such as the Amazon Echo and the Google Home, respectively. The techniques used to create the voice interfaces on both platforms are very similar, and converting from one platform to the other is not very difficult. In this section, each of the components from Alexa and Dialogflow will be presented, with high-level comparisons between them that will help you understand and migrate Alexa skill to Dialogflow agent.

Comparing an Alexa Skill to a Dialogflow agent

Alexa Skill and Dialogflow agent are natural language processing modules that manages the conversation flow. You can think of the Alexa Skill or the Dialogflow agent as the voice application that you are going to create. Once you are finished creating your voice application, you will deploy the Alexa Skill to Amazon Echo devices and Dialogflow agent to Google Home devices.

Comparing intent

Both Alexa and Dialogflow use the term intent. The intent will help identify what the user says and converted them to the specific actions. From the backend server, the code will map the intent to a specific task. In Alexa, you define sample utterances, whereas in Dialogflow you define training phrases for the intent.

Comparing slots to entities

The slots or the entities are used in the intent to extract the parameters from the user request. For example, if the user says `I love a dog`, you can create either slots or entities called `Animals` that contains `dog` and `cat`, which will help identify and extract the animal `dog` from the user saying. In Alexa, you use slots in the intent as follows: `I love {Animals}`. In Dialogflow, you use this: `I love @Animals:Animal`.

Sometimes, when the user says something and maps to the intent, you might want to make sure that the user provides a specific value in order to take an action on the intent. In Alexa, you can use a technique called slot filling, and in Dialogflow you can make the entities required. Both Alexa and Dialogflow's approaches are very similar, and are to ensure that the user provides the required slots or entities during the conversation.

Both platforms provide built-in slots or entities. For example, following compares Alexa built-in slots to Dialogflow built-in entities:

- `AMAZON.Date` - `@sys.date`: Capture dates during a conversation with a user
- `AMAZON.Number` - `@sys.number`: Identify and capture any kind of number from the user's speech
- `AMAZON.PhoneNumber` - `@sys.phone-number`: Identify phone numbers from user requests
- `AMAZON.Country` - `@sys.geo-country`: Can capture country names, such as Korea or United States

These are some of the common examples that you might end up using. You can find more built-in slots for Alexa at `https://amzn.to/2luqdrJ` and built-in entities for Dialogflow at `https://bit.ly/2MmaAOe`.

Converting the Henry's Kitchen Alexa Skill to Dialogflow

In the previous section, you learned about similarities and differences between the Alexa skill and Dialogflow agent. In this section, you will be converting the previously built Henry's Kitchen Skill from Alexa into Dialogflow Agent. Before you begin, make sure that you have created Dialogflow account. You can find more detailed information in `Chapter 2`, *Build a FAQs Chat Bot*, and `Chapter 3`, *Build a Fortune Cookie Application*, regarding Dialogflow.

Creating the agent

Dialogflow agent is similar to Alexa Skill. Dialogflow agent will contain your conversational flows:

1. Open Firefox or Chrome.
2. Go to `https://console.dialogflow.com` and log in to Dialogflow.
3. Click the down arrow in the top-left corner, next to the Gear icon, and select **Create new agent**.

   The following screenshot shows the **Create new agent** menu:

Create new agent menu

4. Enter `HenrysKitchen` as an agent name and use all the defaults. You may change the default time zone to match your own time zone.

The following screenshot shows creating the agent:

Creating the agent

5. Click the **Create** button.

Converting slots to entities

HenrysKitchen **contains two slots,** Foods **and** DietTypes. **Slots and entities are the exact same concept and no extra migration effort is needed.**

1. Open Firefox or Chrome.
2. Go to https://console.dialogflow.com and log in to the Dialogflow.
3. If HenrysKitchen is not selected, click the down arrow in the top-left corner, and you should see the HenrysKitchen agent.
4. In the left menu, click on the plus (**+**) next to the **Entities**.
5. Enter Foods as the entity name.
6. Next to the **SAVE** button, you will see three dots. Click on these three dots and select **Switch to raw mode**. This will allow you to copy and paste the JSON that will create the Foods entity.

The following screenshot shows the three-dot menu that contains **Switch to raw mode**:

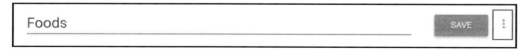

Menu containing Switch to raw mode

7. Copy and paste the JSON that contains the arrays of values and synonyms. The values and synonyms are `Burger`, `Pizza`, and `Fish`.

The following JSON represents the `Foods` entity in Dialogflow:

```
[
    { "value": "Burger", "synonyms": [ "Burger" ] },
    { "value": "Pizza", "synonyms": [ "Pizza" ] },
    { "value": "Fish", "synonyms": [ "Fish" ] },
    { "value": "", "synonyms": [] }
]
```

8. Click **Save**.
9. Create another entity called `DietTypes`. Follow steps 4 through 8, but using the `DietTypes` JSON. The values and synonyms are `vegan`, `vegetarian`, and `pescetarian`.

The following JSON represents the `DietTypes` entity in Dialogflow:

```
[
    { "value": "vegan", "synonyms": ["vegan"] },
    { "value": "vegetarian", "synonyms": ["vegetarian"] },
    { "value": "pescetarian", "synonyms": ["pescetarian"] },
    { "value": "", "synonyms": [] }
]
```

Converting Alexa intents to Dialogflow intents

Alexa and Dialogflow take a similar approach to creating the intents. The intents will contain slots or entities in order to create a templatized conversation, so that multiple variations of user utterances will by captured. In Alexa, the intent contains various utterances, which are called training phrases in Dialogflow.

1. Open Firefox or Chrome.
2. Go to `https://console.dialogflow.com` and log in to the Dialogflow.
3. If **HenrysKitchen** is not selected, click the down arrow in the top-left corner, and you should see the `HenrysKitchen` agent.
4. In the left menu, click on the plus (**+**) next to **Intents** to add new intent.
5. Enter `GetCookingIntent` as the intent name.

6. In the training phrases section, enter
   `I want to cook @DietTypes:DietTypes @Foods:Foods,` and `I want to make @DietTypes:DietTypes @Foods:Foods`. Before entering the phrases, make sure to click on the double quote sign ("), which will toggle to @. The @ sign means that the entered phrase is templatized using the entities.

The following screenshot shows entering the `GetCookingIntent` phrases:

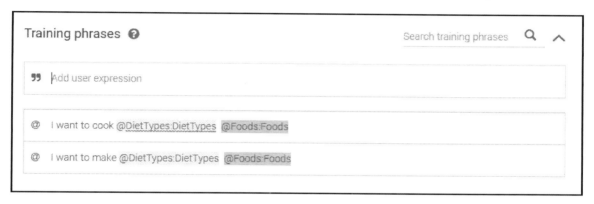

GetCookingIntent training phrases

7. In the **Action and parameters** section, enter `input.cooking` as the action name. This is the identifier that you will be looking for in the webhook code to identify the intent.

8. In Alexa, the slot filling concept was introduced, where Alexa asks the user for missing slot values. You will see two values in **Actions and parameters**: `DietTypes` and `Foods`. Click REQUIRED check boxes.

9. Click **Define prompts** link on **prompts** column found on `DietTypes` row. When the popup appears, enter `do you have dietary requirement like vegan, vegetarian or pescetarian?` and then close it.

10. Click **Define prompts** link on **prompts** column found on `Foods` row. When the popup appears, enter `What kind of food would you like to cook?` and then close it.

The following screenshot shows the completed **Action and parameters** section for `GetCookingIntent`:

GetCookingIntent action and parameters

11. In the **Fulfillment** section, **Enable webhook call for this intent**.

The following screenshot shows the enabled webhook call for the intent:

Enabled webhook for the intent

12. Click **Save**.
13. Create another new intent called `GetMoreRecipesIntent`.

The following screenshot shows `GetMoreRecipesIntent`:

GetMoreRecipesIntent

14. For the training phrases of `GetMoreRecipesIntent,` **enter** `get more recipes` and `I want more recipes.`

The following screenshot shows the `GetMoreRecipesIntent` **training phrases:**

GetMoreRecipesIntent training phrases

15. In the **Action and parameters** section, enter `input.more` as the action name.

The following screenshot shows the `GetMoreRecipesIntent` action and parameters:

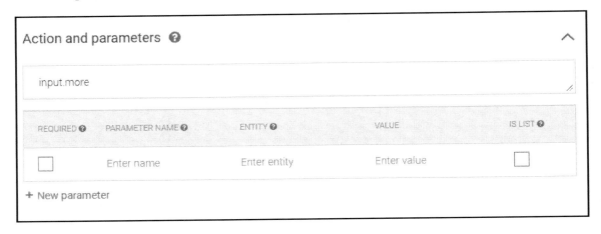

GetMoreRecipesIntent action and parameters

16. In the **Fulfillment** section, enable **Enable webhook call for this intent**.
17. Click **SAVE**.
18. Create `HelpIntent`.

The following screenshot shows `HelpIntent`:

HelpIntent

19. For training phrases, enter `how do i use this`, `help me`, and `I need help`.

The following screenshot shows the `HelpIntent` training phrases:

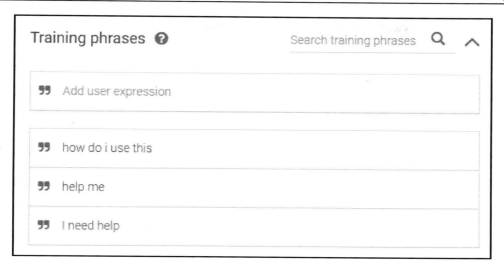

HelpIntent training phrases

20. For action name, enter input.help.

The following screenshot shows the HelpIntent action and parameters:

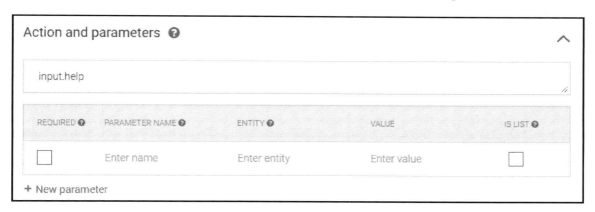

HelpIntent action and parameters

21. Enable a webhook on the **Fulfillment** section. Click **SAVE**.

Enabling a webhook

In the previous section, you created entities and intents. When you were creating intents, you enabled a webhook call in the Fulfillment section of each intent. A webhook for Dialogflow is similar to the service endpoint that you defined in Alexa. The webhook will allow Dialogflow to submit the mapped intents back to the server you specified and it would be the responsibility of your server code to fulfill the request:

1. Open Firefox or Chrome
2. Go to `https://console.dialogflow.com` and log in to the Dialogflow
3. If `HenrysKitchen` is not selected, click the down arrow in the top-left corner, and you should see `HenrysKitchen` agent
4. In the left menu, click **Fulfillment**
5. In the URL, enter `https://myhenrytestapp.azurewebsites.net/dialogflow/cookingApi`
6. In the **headers** section, enter `mysecret` as the key and `12345` as the value
7. Click **Save**

The following screenshot shows the enabled webhook:

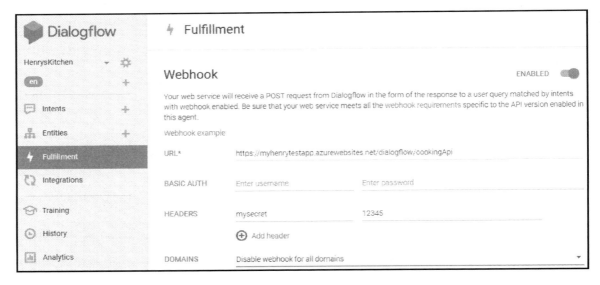

Enabled webhook

Alexa and Dialogflow take very different approaches to the security. In Alexa, your server code performs a series of steps in order to verify the request sent by Alexa. To simplify the verification, you used the Alexa verifier Node.js component. In Dialogflow, you will setting up the secret key and value that Dialogflow will be injecting into the header that you will be verifying in your server code.

Creating a webhook to handle Dialogflow

In the previous section, you successfully migrated the Henry's Kitchen Alexa skill to a Dialogflow agent. For the intents you created, you would need to fulfill the intents' requests from the Node.js server. You will be using the same Microsoft Azure App Service that you set up for handling the Alexa endpoint to also handle the Dialogflow webhook. Most of the code you wrote for the Alexa skill will be reused, but there is code that you must refactor in order to apply it to both Alexa skill requests and Dialogflow agent requests.

What code is reused?

Redis will be used for both Alexa and Dialogflow requests to maintain the conversational state. In the beginning of the code, you will be declaring the Redis authentication key, the host, and the port in order to establish a Redis connection later in the section, where you maintain the conversation state to handle `GetMoreRecipesIntent`.

The following code provides the Redis connection information:

```
var redis = require("redis");
var redisAuth = 'redis auth code goes here';
var redisHost = 'henrytest.redis.cache.windows.net';
var redisPort = 6380;
```

Then, you will be setting up `winston-azure-blob-transport`, which writes the logs to the Microsoft Azure Blob storage. You will be setting the log level, the blob key, the blob container name, and the blob name. You learned in detail about the Winston logger in the previous chapter.

The following code provides Winston logging information for the Microsoft Azure Blob storage:

```
var winston = require("winston");
require("winston-azure-blob-transport");
var loggingLevel = "info";
```

```
var logger = new winston.Logger({
    level: loggingLevel,
    transports: [
        new winston.transports.Console({
            stderrLevels: [loggingLevel],
            colorize: true
        }),
        new winston.transports.AzureBlob({
            account: {
                name: "henrytestlog",
                key: "blob key goes here"
            },
            containerName: "applog",
            blobName: "henrytestlog",
        })
    ]
});
```

You will also be setting up the express Node.js HTTP server that you will be using to host the REST API which can be called by Alexa and Dialogflow. Also, declare body-parser to parse incoming HTTP requests into JSON objects and declare unirest to easily create a REST API for the Alexa endpoint and Dialogflow webhook.

The following code declares express, http, body-parser, and unirest, which are essential for creating an Alexa endpoint and Dialogflow webhook:

```
var express = require('express');
var bodyParser = require('body-parser');
var http = require('http');
var unirest = require('unirest');
var app = express();
```

Finally, create a ping endpoint to quickly test whether the service is successfully deployed to Microsoft App Service.

The following code shows ping service:

```
app.use("/ping", function (req, res, next) {
    logger.info("ping service.");
    res.send('Welcome to Cooking Service');
});
```

Setting up a Dialogflow router

For Alexa, you created an Alexa router by declaring `app.use("/alexa", alexaRouter)`. Similarly, you will be creating a Dialogflow router to handle Dialogflow requests, `app.use("/dialogflow", dialogflowRouter)`, and then the body parser will be applied to the router to convert incoming HTTP requests to JSON objects. Finally, an HTTP server will be created using the routers for Alexa and Dialogflow.

The following code sets up Alexa and Dialogflow routers to handle incoming Dialogflow requests:

```
var verifier = require('alexa-verifier-middleware');
var alexaRouter = express.Router();
app.use("/alexa", alexaRouter);
if (!process.env.ISDEBUG) {
    logger.info("Setup Alexa verifier.");
    alexaRouter.use(verifier);
}
alexaRouter.use(bodyParser.json());

var dialogflowRouter = express.Router();
app.use("/dialogflow", dialogflowRouter);
dialogflowRouter.use(bodyParser.json());

var server = http.createServer(app);
var port = process.env.PORT || 8000;
server.listen(port, function () {
    logger.info("Server is up and running...");
});
```

Setting up a Dialogflow webhook entry point

For Alexa, you created an entry point by declaring `alexaRouter.post('/cookingApi', function (req, res)` so that the Alexa endpoint can point to `https://myhenrytestapp.azurewebsites.net/alexa/cookingApi`. For Dialogflow, you will be creating `dialogflowRouter.post('/cookingApi', function (req, res)` so that the Dialogflow webhook can point to `https://myhenrytestapp.azurewebsites.net/dialogflow/cookingApi`.

When the Dialogflow request comes in, you will need to authenticate the request by checking in the header that the secret is equal to `12345`, which is what you set up when enabling the webhook in Dialogflow web console. Also, you would need to check whether the request contains `req.body.queryResult` to ensure that it is a Dialogflow request.

The Dialogflow entry point handles four different requests, `input.cooking`, `input.more`, `input.help`, and `default`, which you set up in the **Action and parameters** sections of each intent that you created in the Dialogflow web console. `input.cooking`, `input.more`, and `input.help` correspond to `GetCookingIntent`, `GetMoreRecipesIntent`, and `HelpIntent` respectively.

The following code sets up the Dialogflow webhook entry point:

```
dialogflowRouter.post('/cookingApi', function (req, res) {
    try {
        logger.info(JSON.stringify(req.body, null, '\t'));
        var secret = req.get("mysecret");
        if (secret === "12345" && req.body.queryResult) {
            if (req.body.queryResult.action == 'input.cooking') {
                logger.info("input.cooking");
                BuildGetCookingInstruction(req, res);
            } else if (req.body.queryResult.action == 'input.more') {
                GetOffset(req, res, false);
            } else if (req.body.queryResult.action == 'input.help') {
                BuildHelpIntentResponse(req, res);
            } else {
                var responseJson = { fulfillmentText: "Welcome to Henrys
Kitchen" };
                res.json(responseJson);
            }
        } else {
            return res.status(403).end('Access denied!');
        }
    } catch (e) {
        logger.error(e);
    }
});
```

Refactoring the BuildGetCookingInstruction function

The `BuildGetCookingInstruction` function fulfills the `GetCookingIntent` request by querying the Spoonacular API, based on the food and diet type captured from the user request. In the case of an Alexa request, the food and diet type are stored in `request.intent.slots.Foods.value` and in `request.intent.slots.DietTypes.value`, whereas for a Dialogflow request, they are stored in `req.body.queryResult.parameters.Foods` and `req.body.queryResult.parameters.DietTypes`.

`queryObject` **contains** `offset`, `foodName`, **and** `dietType` **to handle special cases when the** **user requests more recipes.** `queryObject` **will be stored and then retrieved from Redis,** **where** `offset` **is incremented by** 3 **and then sent by the** `GetOffset` **function to** **the** `BuildGetCookingInstruction` **function. If the** `queryObject` **is empty, it means that** **the user made a new request to receive new recipes.**

The following code shows the first part of the `BuildGetCookingInstruction` function:

```
function BuildGetCookingInstruction(req, res, queryObject) {
    logger.info("BuildGetCookingInstruction");
    var url =
'https://spoonacular-recipe-food-nutrition-v1.p.mashape.com/recipes/search?
';
    url += 'number=3&instructionsRequired=true';
    var offset = queryObject ? queryObject.offset : 0;
    url += `&offset=${offset}`;
    if (req.body.queryResult) {
        var parameters = req.body.queryResult.parameters;
        if (queryObject || parameters.Foods) {
            var foodName = queryObject ? queryObject.foodName :
parameters.Foods;
            url += `&query=${foodName}`;
        }
        if (queryObject || parameters.DietTypes) {
            var dietTypes = queryObject ? queryObject.dietTypes :
parameters.DietTypes;
            url += `&diet=${dietTypes}`;
        }
    } else {
        var request = req.body.request;
        if (queryObject || request.intent.slots.Foods.value) {
            var foodName = queryObject ? queryObject.foodName :
request.intent.slots.Foods.value;
            url += `&query=${foodName}`;
        }
        if (queryObject || request.intent.slots.DietTypes.value) {
            var dietTypes = queryObject ? queryObject.dietTypes :
request.intent.slots.DietTypes.value;
            url += `&diet=${dietTypes}`;
        }
    }
```

In the second half of the `BuildGetCookingInstruction` function, `offset`, `foodName`, and `dietTypes` will be used to call Spoonacular API. Once the response is received from the Spoonacular API, a Dialogflow response is created by setting `fulfillmentText` similar to how an Alexa response is created. The way to find out whether to create a Dialogflow response is by looking at whether a Dialogflow response, `req.body.queryResult`, exists and if the Dialogflow response does not exist, an Alexa response can be created.

The following code shows the second part of the `BuildGetCookingInstruction`:

```
        logger.info("Executing spoonecular: " + url);
        unirest.get(url)
            .header("X-Mashape-Key",
"TTWRwOsRs6mshek89pL3XtbMhie9p10gT9ujsnCYKqafAWv5oF")
            .header("X-Mashape-Host", "spoonacular-recipe-food-nutrition-
v1.p.mashape.com")
            .end(function (result) {
                var responseText = "";
                if (result.error) {
                    logger.error('Error processing spoonacular.');
                    logger.error(result.body);
                    logger.error(result.error);
                    responseText = `I am sorry there was an issue processing
your request.`;
                } else {
                    logger.info("Successfully received results from
spoonacular.");
                    logger.info(result.body.results);
                    var dishTitle = '';
                    for (i = 0; i < result.body.results.length; i++) {
                        dishTitle += result.body.results[i].title + ', ';
                    }
                    responseText = `I found following dishes that you can cook.
                    ${dishTitle}`;
                }

                logger.info('BuildGetCookingInstruction Saving queryObject');
                if (!queryObject) {
                    GetOffset(req, res, true);
                }

                if (req.body.queryResult) {
                    var responseToDialogflow = { fulfillmentText: responseText
};
                    logger.info(JSON.stringify(responseToDialogflow, null,
'\t'));

                    res.json(responseToDialogflow);
```

```
        } else {
            var responseToAlexa = {
                "version": "1.0",
                "response": {
                    "shouldEndSession": true,
                    "outputSpeech": {
                        "type": "PlainText",
                        "text": responseText
                    }
                }
            };
            logger.info(JSON.stringify(responseToAlexa, null, '\t'));
            res.json(responseToAlexa);
        }
    });
};
```

By checking whether `req.body.queryResult` is empty, you can tell whether the request is from Dialogflow and Alexa. Using this technique, you can easily reuse the main fulfillment code, such as calling Spoonacular to get the recipes the user requested.

Refactoring the GetOffset function

The `GetOffset` function handles `GetMoreRecipesIntent` by retrieving the saved user request that contains `offset`, `foodName`, and `dietTypes`. They way you save the request to Redis is by using user identification as the key. In Alexa, you get the `userId` from `req.body.session.user.userId`, whereas in Dialogflow you get the `userId` from `req.body.originalDetectIntentRequest.payload.user.userId`. Next, you would need to build `queryObject` the very first time in order to save it to Redis, so that you can handle the user requesting more recipes based on the `foodName` and `dietTypes` the user previously requested. The first-time offset will be set to 0 and on consequent requests, the offset will be incremented by 3. For the Dialogflow request, `foodName` comes from `parameters.Foods`, and for the Alexa request, `foodName` comes from `request.intent.slots.Foods.value`. In the case of `dietTypes`, for Dialogflow `dietType` comes from `parameters.DietTypes`, and for the Alexa request, `dietTypes` comes from `request.intent.slots.DietTypes.value`.

The following code retrieves `userId` and creates `queryObject` from the appropriate request object:

```
function GetOffset(req, res, saveFromRequest) {
    logger.info('GetOffset');
    var client = redis.createClient(redisPort, redisHost,
        { auth_pass: redisAuth, tls: { servername: redisHost } });
    if (req.body.queryResult) {
        var parameters = req.body.queryResult.parameters;
        var key = req.body.originalDetectIntentRequest.payload.user.userId;
    } else {
        var request = req.body.request;
        var session = req.body.session;
        var key = session.user.userId;
    }

    var timeInSeconds = 60 * 10;
    if (saveFromRequest) {
        var queryObject = {
            offset: 0,
            foodName: req.body.queryResult
                ? parameters.Foods : request.intent.slots.Foods.value,
            dietTypes: req.body.queryResult
                ? parameters.DietTypes :
request.intent.slots.DietTypes.value
        };
        client.set(key, JSON.stringify(queryObject), 'EX', timeInSeconds);
    }
```

Finally, the second part of the `GetOffset` function remains the same, except the case where `queryObject` is not found in Redis. When it is not found in Redis, you would need to send a proper response back to the user. Again, after checking `req.body.queryResult` is not empty, you can create a Dialogflow response telling the user to ask for recipes again.

The following code shows the second half of the `GetOffset` function:

```
else {
        client.get(key, function (error, result) {
            if (error) {
                logger.error(error);
            } else if (result) {
                var queryObject = JSON.parse(result);
                queryObject.offset = queryObject.offset + 3;
                client.set(key, JSON.stringify(queryObject), 'EX',
timeInSeconds);
                BuildGetCookingInstruction(req, res, queryObject);
            } else {
```

```
                logger.info('GetOffset: queryObject is not found or
expired.');
                if (req.body.queryResult) {
                    var responseText = "You can say ok google ask henrys
kitchen
                    I want to cook burger to
                    get the list of recipes."
                    var responseToDialogflow = { fulfillmentText:
responseText };
                    res.json(responseToDialogflow);
                } else {
                    res.json({
                        "version": "1.0",
                        "response": {
                            "shouldEndSession": true,
                            "outputSpeech": {
                                "type": "PlainText",
                                "text": "You can say alexa ask henry's
kitchen I
                                            want to cook burger to
                                            get the list of recipes."
                            }
                        }
                    });
                }
            }
        });
    }
};
```

Deploying and testing Henry's Kitchen

Deploy the code to the same Microsoft Azure App Service where you deployed Alexa code
in the last chapter. Now you deployed Dialogflow agent and the web hook and you should
be able to test. Here are the steps to quickly test the Henry's Kitchen Dialogflow agent:

1. Open a browser, FireFox or Chrome.
2. Log in to `https://console.dialogflow.com`.
3. In the left menu, select **Integrations.**
4. On the right side, select **INTEGRATION SETTINGS** and the **Google Assistant**
   window will pop out.

The following screenshot shows the **Google Assistant** popup:

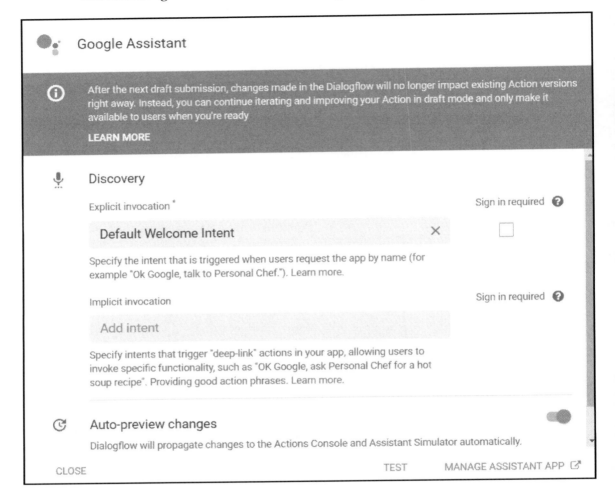

Google Assistant popup

5. Click **Test** and a new browser window will open to **Actions** on Google web page console.
6. In the left menu, click on **Invocation**.
7. On the right side, for **Invocation** name, put henrys kitchen.
8. For directory title, put henrys kitchen.

9. Choose **Female 1** as the Google Assistant voice.
10. Click **Save**.

The following screenshot shows the complete **Invocation** settings:

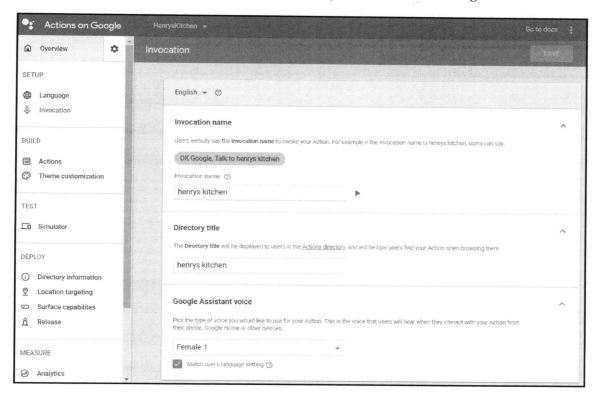

Invocation settings

11. Go to **Simulator**.
12. Test the Henry's Kitchen Dialogflow agent by typing in the following order: `Talk to henrys kitchen`, `I want to cook vegetarian burger`, and `get more recipes`. For each entry, you will hear the responses sent from the webhook.

The following screenshot shows the **Simulator**:

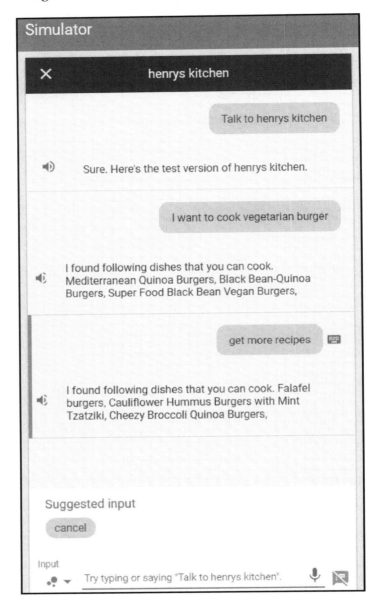

Testing in the simulator

Summary

In this chapter, you took the Henry's Kitchen Alexa Skill that you created in Chapter 7, *Using Advanced Alexa Features for the Cooking App*, and migrated it over to a Dialogflow agent. You also learned to reuse and refactor the Node.js server code written for the Alexa endpoint to handle Dialogflow requests. You learned subtle differences between the two platforms, and some major differences as well, while converting an Alexa Skill to a Dialogflow agent.

9
Building a Voice-Enabled Podcast for the Car

Every new car coming out today allows you to use your Android phone for navigation, messaging, calls, and playing music by using Android Auto. Although cars have their own dashboard, using Android Auto on your mobile phone has huge advantages:

- It allows addresses saved with Google Maps or Waze to be used without having to re-enter the addresses in the car's navigation system.
- You can use your favorite messaging application, such as WhatsApp.
- You can take advantage of Google Assistant and perform hands-free tasks, such as asking what the outside temperature is.
- You can use your favorite music players, such as Sound Cloud or Spotify.
- You do not have to learn a new car dashboard. For example, whenever I travel and get a new rental car, I plug in my phone and use Android Auto, and I am ready to go in a minute.

In this chapter, you will learn to develop a voice-enabled podcast for an automobile. You will attain important skills, such as setting up an Android Auto project in Xamarin and creating components such as MediaBrowserService, MediaPlayer, and MusicProvider, which are necessary for Android Auto. Then, you will learn to test, debug, and deploy the podcast application on your Android mobile phone to test its media features.

Here are the topics covered in this chapter:

- Learning about Xamarin
- Android Auto project setup in Xamarin
- Android Auto application development using Xamarin
- Building MediaBrowserService, MediaPlayer, and MusicProvider
- Building an Android media player UI
- Debugging and testing an Android mobile application

This chapter and Chapter 10, *Hosting and Enhancing the Android Auto Podcast*, will work towards creating the following final product for Android Auto, that is, playing your podcast:

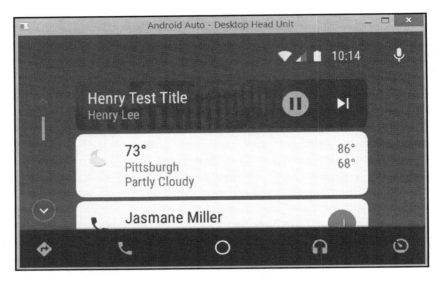

Android Auto podcast

Learning about Xamarin

Xamarin is a popular cross-platform mobile development tool for creating an application for iOS, Android, and Windows Phone. Typically, in order to create an iOS application, you will be using Objective-C in Xcode; to create an Android application, you will need to use Java in Eclipse or Android Studio; and to create a Windows Phone application, you will need to use C# in Visual Studio. As you can imagine, creating an application for all three major mobile platforms requires three different programming languages and their integrated development environments. With Xamarin, you only need to know C# and Visual Studio. Here are the advantages of utilizing Xamarin:

- Use only C# and Visual Studio to write an application for all platforms (iOS, Android, and Windows Phone).
- The code can be shared across all platforms.

- The user interface can be developed once and can be used on all platforms.
- C# is a very powerful object-oriented language with many advanced capabilities, allowing users to quickly create an application.
- There are large numbers of C# developers available, due to the popularity of Microsoft technology.
- The application performs at the native level because compiled code converts to native byte code.
- Xamarin does not hide platform APIs, but rather fully exposes all native platform APIs as is (iOS, Android, and Windows Phone). In fact, the method names and the programming namespaces exactly match those of native platforms.
- There are many available third-party UI components and libraries to help in development.
- It is free.

Setting up the development environment

In this section, you will learn how to set up a development environment for creating an Android Auto in Xamarin. I am using Windows 8.1 as my development operating system, but you can use Mac as well. Here are the steps you can follow:

1. Download Visual Studio Community 2017 (`https://visualstudio.microsoft.com/vs/`). It can be installed on Windows 7 or higher, or macOS.
2. Click on the downloaded installation file.
3. Go to the **Mobile & and Gaming** section and select **Mobile development with .NET**.

The following screenshot shows mobile development with .NET:

Mobile development with .NET

4. Click **Install**.

Creating a new Xamarin project

In this section, you will be creating an Android Auto Xamarin project in Visual Studio:

1. Start Visual Studio 2017.
2. Go to **File** | **New** | **Project**
3. Select **Blank App (Android)**
4. Name the project MyPodCast and click **OK**

The following screenshot shows the MyPoadCast Blank App (Android):

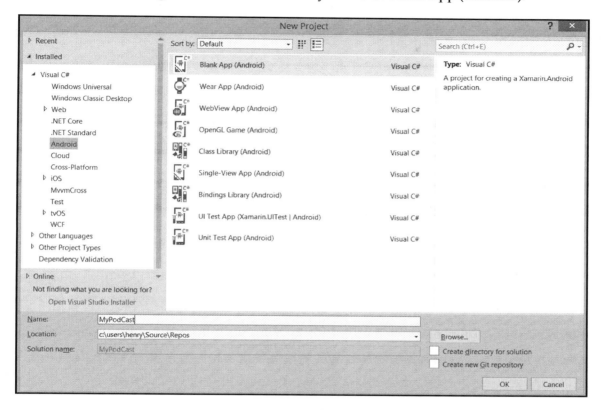

MyPodCast Blank App (Android)

5. Once the project is created, you will see **Solution Explorer** showing the project's structure.

The following screenshot shows the MyPodCast that we created and the project structure in **Solution Explorer**:

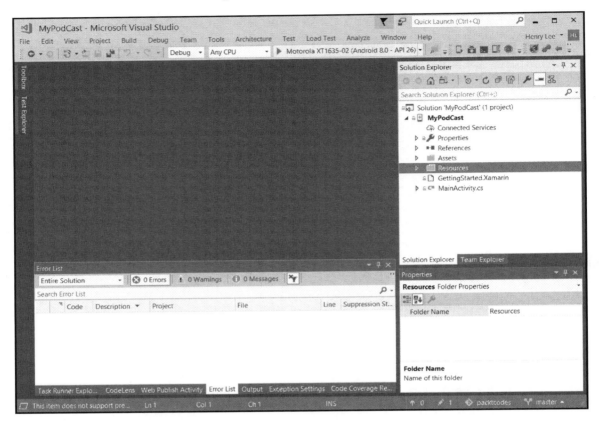

New MyPodCast project

6. Click on **Solution 'MyPodCast' (1 project)**, which is found in **Solution Explorer** and press *CTRL + S* to save the project.

7. Right-click on **MyPodCast** project | Open Folder in File Explorer and Windows File Explorer will open the MyPodCast folder. Here, you will find the files and directories that were created. Take note of this location and the MyPodCast.sln file, which you will need to open in Visual Studio 2017 to start the project.

The following screenshot shows the MyPodCast physical directory:

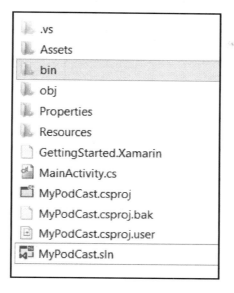

MyPodCast directory

In the next section, you will be setting up the MyPodCast Xamarin project to work with Android Auto.

Setting up the Xamarin project for Android Auto

Continuing from the previous section, you will be configuring the Xamarin project for Android Auto:

1. Open Visual Studio 2017.
2. Go to the project through **File** | **Open** | **Project / Solution,** go to the MyPodCast directory, and choose the MyPodCast.sln file.
3. Go to **Tools** | **Android** | **Android SDK Manager.**
4. In the **Platforms** tab, go to **Android 5.0 Lollipop** and select **Android SDK Platform 21.**
5. In **Tools** | **Extras** | **Android Auto API Simulators** and **Android Auto Desktop Head Unit (DHU)** emulator are selected.

6. Click **Apply Changes**.

The following screenshot shows the Android SDK manager for installing DHU:

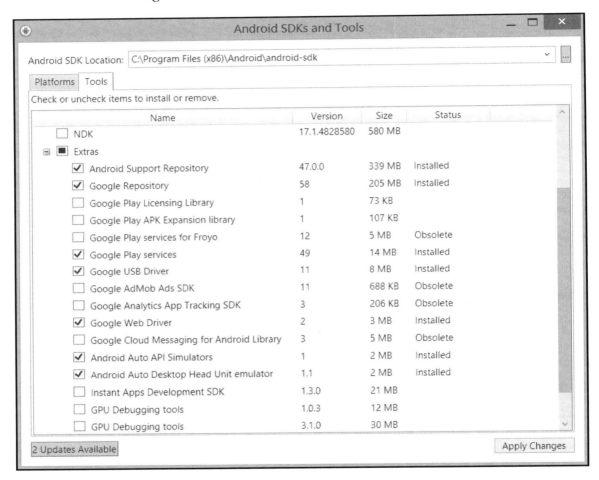

Name	Version	Size	Status
☐ NDK	17.1.4828580	580 MB	
⊟ ◼ Extras			
☑ Android Support Repository	47.0.0	339 MB	Installed
☑ Google Repository	58	205 MB	Installed
☐ Google Play Licensing Library	1	73 KB	
☐ Google Play APK Expansion library	1	107 KB	
☐ Google Play services for Froyo	12	5 MB	Obsolete
☑ Google Play services	49	14 MB	Installed
☑ Google USB Driver	11	8 MB	Installed
☐ Google AdMob Ads SDK	11	688 KB	Obsolete
☐ Google Analytics App Tracking SDK	3	206 KB	Obsolete
☑ Google Web Driver	2	3 MB	Installed
☐ Google Cloud Messaging for Android Library	3	5 MB	Obsolete
☑ Android Auto API Simulators	1	2 MB	Installed
☑ Android Auto Desktop Head Unit emulator	1.1	2 MB	Installed
☐ Instant Apps Development SDK	1.3.0	21 MB	
☐ GPU Debugging tools	1.0.3	12 MB	
☐ GPU Debugging tools	3.1.0	30 MB	

Installing DHU

7. Download and unzip (https://bit.ly/2JF8jMq) the file to the `MyPodCast\Resources` directory. The downloaded file contains all the images and icons you will need to build the MyPodCast application.
8. Go back to the Visual Studio MyPodCast project.
9. Click on the `MyPodCast` project.
10. Go to **Project | Show All Files**.

11. *Ctrl* + click on each of the folders that you unzipped from step 7 to select them.
12. Right-click on the selected folders and choose **Include in Project**.

The following screenshot shows the unzipped folders:

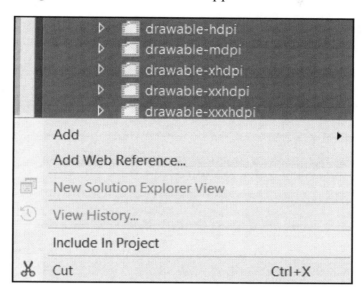

13. Expand the Resources/drawable, right-click on `icon.png`, and select **Include in Project**.
14. Right-click on **MyPodCast** project | **Properties**.
15. Click the **Application** tab.
16. From the **Compiling using Android version (Target Framework)** drop-down, choose Android 5.0 (Lollipop).
17. Click on the **Android Manifest** tab.
18. Enter the package name `com.henry.mypodcast`. This uniquely identifies the application.
19. For the Application icon, choose `@drawable/icon`.
20. For Minimum Android version and Target Android version, choose **Android 5.0 (API Level 21 - Lollipop)**.

21. In **Required permissions**, choose **INTERNET and WAKE_LOCK**. INTERNET permission allows your application to use the phone's internet connection and it is needed for streaming media. WAKE_LOCK permission stops the phone from going to sleep and is particularly required when you are streaming media.

22. *Ctrl + S* to save the changes.

23. Expand Properties and open `AndroidManifest.xml`.

24. Add `<meta-data android:name="com.google.android.gms.car.application" android:resource="@xml/automotive_app_desc" />` at the side of the application node. This will allow your application access to Android Auto features.

The following XML shows the completed AndroidManifest.xml:

```
<?xml version="1.0" encoding="utf-8"?>
<manifest
xmlns:android="http://schemas.android.com/apk/res/android"
        android:versionCode="1"
        android:versionName="1.0"
        package="com.henry.mypodcast"
        android:installLocation="auto">
    <uses-sdk android:minSdkVersion="21"
android:targetSdkVersion="21" />
    <uses-permission android:name="android.permission.INTERNET" />
    <uses-permission android:name="android.permission.WAKE_LOCK" />
    <application android:icon="@drawable/icon"
android:label="@string/app_name">
        <meta-data
android:name="com.google.android.gms.car.application"
            android:resource="@xml/automotive_app_desc" />
    </application>
</manifest>
```

25. Right-click on the `Resources` folder | **Add** | **New Folder** called `xml`.

26. Right-click on `xml` folder | **Add New Item**.

27. Select **XML File**, name it `automotive_app_desc.xml`, and click **Add**.

The following screenshot shows adding `automotive_app_desc.xml`:

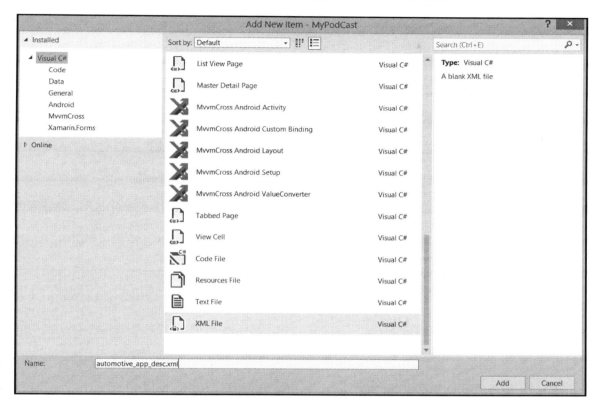

Adding an automotive_app_desc.xml

28. The `automotive_app_desc.xml` file is referenced in `AndroidManifest.xml` and it will contain the Android Auto feature `MyPodCast` will be using. Add `<automotiveApp> <uses name="media"/> </automotiveApp>` to `automotive_app_desc.xml`.

The following XML adds an Android Auto media feature that can be used by `MyPodCast`:

```xml
<?xml version="1.0" encoding="utf-8"?>
<automotiveApp>
    <uses name="media"/>
</automotiveApp>
```

29. Add `Helpers`, `MediaService`, and `UI` folders by right-clicking on **MyPodCast** project| **Add** | **New Folder**. You will be adding C# programming files under these folders in the following sections.

The following screenshot shows adding a new folder:

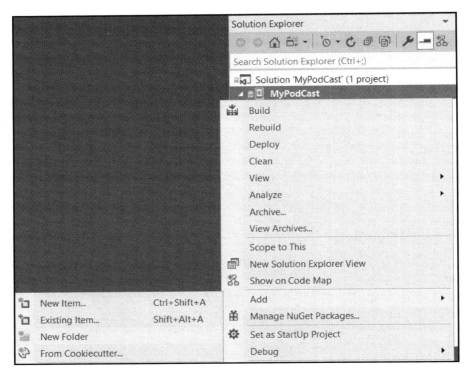

Adding a new folder

30. Right-click on **MyPodCast** | **Manage NuGet Packages**.
31. Add `Newton.Json` and `SkiaSharp.Views`. `Newton.Json` is used for working with JSON format and `SkiaSharp.Views` is needed for working manipulating the downloaded images like the media covers shown on the Android Auto.

The following screenshot shows added NuGet packages:

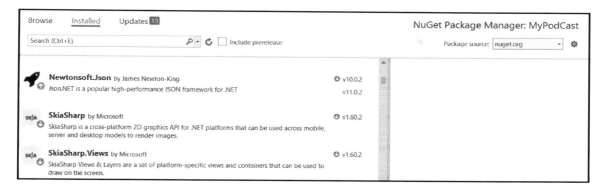

NuGet packages

You have now successfully prepared the MyPodCast Xamarin project for Android Auto. In the following section, you will be writing a program to serve media content to Android Auto.

Building Android Auto MyPodCast

MyPodCast contains two major parts:

- **MusicService**:
  This implements `Android.Service.Media.MediaBrowserService`, which provides media content such as mp3 podcast sources, cover images, and podcast information to Android Auto. MusicService also controls Android Auto's media player functions, such as play, pause, play next, play previous, and add a podcast as favorite. MusicService typically runs as a background service, does not need a UI, and will intercept requests coming from Android Auto to provide podcast sources and also help control the media player.

The following screenshot shows the Android Auto media player, which interfaces with your `MusicService`:

Android Auto interfacing with MusicService

- **Android mobile media player**: This application provides functionalities such as content browsing and media player functions by interfacing with `MusicService` in the same way as Android Auto. You want your users to play your podcasts not only on Android Auto while driving, but also simply by using their mobile phone.

The following screenshot shows the Android media player application you will be building:

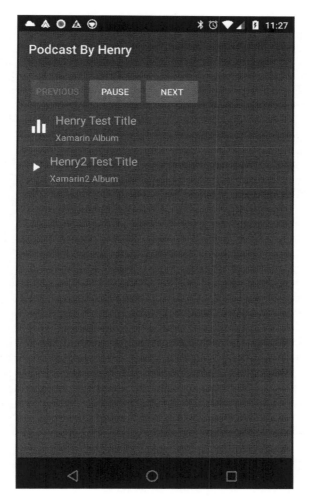

Android media player application

Building MusicService

This section is composed of three parts:

1. In the first section, you will be building `MusicService`, implementing `Android.Service.Media.MediaBrowserService`, which provides the Android Auto and Android mobile media player the ability to browse through your media contents and play podcasts. In the second section, you will be creating a `MusicPlayer` controller that implements `Android.Media.AudioManager.IOnAudioFocusChangeListener`, `Android.Media.MediaPlayer.IOnCompletionListener`, `Android.Media.MediaPlayer.IOnErrorListener`, `Android.Media.MediaPlayer.IOnPreparedListener`, and `Android.Media.MediaPlayer.IOnSeekCompleteListener`, which are responsible for controlling media player functions such as play, pause, next, and previous.

2. Then, you will be creating `MusicProvider`, which is responsible for delivering media content, such as sources that can be streamed; cover images; and media information such as title, genre, and `mediaId`.

3. Lastly, you will be building an Android media player application for an Android mobile phone using `MusicService`.

 There are many lines of code needed to make MyPodCast project work on Android Auto. Only the most important concepts for creating an Android Auto will be explained line by line, and you can look at the complete code in my GitHub repository for this chapter at `https://bit.ly/2uRdinX`.

Implementing MusicService (Android MediaBrowserService)

By implementing Android.Service.Media.MediaBrowserService, we are providing Android Auto the ability to browse through your media playlists. From the car dashboard, the user will be able to click through the playlists and select any podcast he or she wants to listen to:

1. Open Visual Studio 2017.
2. Go to **File | Open | Project/Solution**, go to your `MyPodCast` directory, and choose the `MyPodCast.sln` file.
3. Right-click on `MediaService` folder | **Add | New Item |** and select **Visual C# Class** and name the file `MusicService.cs`

4. Click **Add**

5. Open `MusicService.cs` by double-clicking the file.

6. Let the `MusicService` class implement
   `Android.Service.Media.MediaBrowserService`

7. Add the `MusicService` class's attributes:

   - Add the `Service` class attribute with Export set to `true`, `Label` set to
     `"Henry Podcast Service"`, and `Name` set to
     `"com.henry.mypodcast.service"`. The label will be displayed
     along with other media players such as Spotify or Google Play Music
     on your car dashboard .

   - Add `IntentFilter`, which contains `new[] {`
     `android.media.browse.MediaBrowserService}. IntentFilter`
     allows `MusicService` to provide service only to the application that is
     requesting the media browsing service.

The following is the completed code after steps 7 and 8:

```
[Service(Exported = true, Label = "Henry Podcast Service", Name =
"com.henry.mypodcast.service")]

[IntentFilter(new[] { "android.media.browse.MediaBrowserService"
})]

public class MusicService :
Android.Service.Media.MediaBrowserService
```

The following screenshot shows the Henry Podcast Service label in Android
Auto:

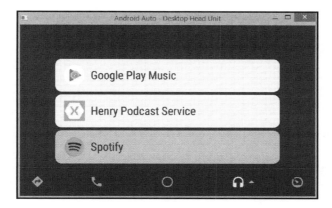

Label: Henry Podcast Service

8. Add the global `public` and `private` variables that you will be using throughout the `MusicService`.

9. The following describes the variables declared in `MusicService`:

   - `CustomActionFavorite` set to `"com.henry.mypodcast.FAVORITE"` will be used to reserve space in the Android Auto media player to handle custom actions.
   - `_playingQueue` will contain podcasts that will be played one after another.
   - `_isStarted` tracks whether or not `MusicService` has started.
   - `_session` contains `MediaSession`, which will interact with `MediaController`, which in turn controls media player functions such as play, pause, volume, next, and previous.
   - `_musicPlayer` contains the `MusicPlayer` class, which will be primarily used for creating an Android phone media player UI. `MusicPlayer` controls Android media player's play, pause, next, previous, and media browsing functions.
   - `_musicProvider` is an abstraction layer that provides streaming of media contents, cover images, and media information.
   - `_packageFinder` is a security layer that ensures that only the selected external application accesses your `MusicService`.

   The following code shows the declared variables for the `MusicService` class:

   ```
   private const string CustomActionFavorite =
   "com.henry.mypodcast.FAVORITE";
   private List<MediaSession.QueueItem> _playingQueue;
   private int _currentIndexQueue;
   private bool _isStarted;
   private MediaSession _session;
   private MusicPlayer _musicPlayer;
   private MusicProvider _musicProvider;
   private PackageFinder _packageFinder;
   ```

10. Create a `public override void OnCreate()` method that will get invoked whenever an external application such as Android Auto makes a request to use your `MusicService`.

11. The `OnCreate()` method instantiates the `_playingQueue`, `_musicProvider`, `_packageFinder`, `_musicPlayer`, and `_session` variables. To create `_musicPlayer`, the constructor takes `MusicService` and `_musicProvider` because `_musicPlayer` uses `MusicService` to browse and play media content, and `_musicProvider` provides media content sources.

The following code shows the variables being instantiated mentioned in step 11:

```
base.OnCreate();
_playingQueue = new List<MediaSession.QueueItem>();
        _musicProvider = new MusicProvider();
_packageFinder = new PackageFinder();
_musicPlayer = new MusicPlayer(this, _musicProvider);
```

12. `OnCreate()` instantiates object `mediaCallback`: `var mediaCallback = this.CreateMediaSessionCallback()`

13. Next, create a `private MediaSessionCallback CreateMediaSessionCallback()` method that returns `MediaSessionCallback`. `CreateMediaSessionCallback` handles all media interactions, such as browse, play, forward, previous, pause, search, add, and favorite.

14. The following media callbacks are implemented in the `private MediaSessionCallback CreateMediaSessionCallback()` method:

    - `OnPlayImpl`: On receiving a request to play media, it checks to see whether any podcasts are queued in `_playingQueue`. If no podcast is queued, then it will get a random podcast from `_musicProvider`. Otherwise, it will play the first podcast in the queue.

        The following code shows `OnPlayImpl`:

```
mediaCallback.OnPlayImpl = () => {
            if (_playingQueue == null ||
_playingQueue.Count != 0){
                _playingQueue = new
List<MediaSession.QueueItem>(_musicProvider.GetRan
domQueue());
_session.SetQueue(_playingQueue);
                _session.SetQueueTitle("Random
music");
                _currentIndexQueue = 0;
            }
            if (_playingQueue != null &&
_playingQueue.Count != 0)
                HandlePlayRequest();
```

```
};
```

- `OnSkipToQueueItemImpl`: It receives `QueueId_playingQueue`; when media with that specific `QueueId` is found, it plays that podcast.

The following code shows `OnSkipToQueueItemImpl`:

```
mediaCallback.OnSkipToQueueItemImpl = (id) => {
    if (_playingQueue != null && _playingQueue.Count != 0)
    {
        _currentIndexQueue = -1;
        int index = 0;
        foreach (var item in _playingQueue)
        {
            if (id == item.QueueId)
                _currentIndexQueue = index;
            index++;
        }
        HandlePlayRequest();
    }
};
```

- `OnSeekToImpl`: This is called when resume is clicked. The podcast will resume from this position.

The following code shows `OnSeekToImpl`:

```
mediaCallback.OnSeekToImpl = (pos) => {
                _musicPlayer.SeekTo((int)pos);
        };
```

- `OnPlayFromMediaIdImpl`: `MusicService` has two categories: All Podcasts and Month. All Podcasts is the top-level category and Month is the subcategory. Under Month, there will be a list of podcasts. Every podcast's media has a `mediaId` and this is encoded with category information and `mediaId`. For example, `mediaId` can contain `January/1`, which is decoded as `podcastId = 1` in the January subcategory. Using the decoded information, you can quickly search `_musicProvider` to extract all podcasts that belong to January and add them to `_playingQueue`.

The following screenshot shows the list of podcasts that belong to January; clicking any of the podcasts displayed will invoke `OnPlayFromMediaIdImpl`:

List of podcasts in January

The following code shows `OnPlayFromMediaIdImpl`:

```
mediaCallback.OnPlayFromMediaIdImpl = (mediaId, extras) => {
    _playingQueue = _musicProvider.GetPlayingQueue(mediaId);
    _session.SetQueue(_playingQueue);
    string[] hierarchies =
HierarchyHelper.GetHierarchy(mediaId);
    string month = hierarchies != null && hierarchies.Length ==
2 ? hierarchies[1] : string.Empty;
    var queueTitle = $"{month} Podcasts";
    _session.SetQueueTitle(queueTitle);
    if (_playingQueue != null && _playingQueue.Count != 0) {
        _currentIndexQueue = -1;
        int index = 0;
        foreach (var item in _playingQueue){
            if (mediaId == item.Description.MediaId)
                _currentIndexQueue = index;
            index++;
        }

        if (_currentIndexQueue< 0)
            Logger.Error($"OnPlayFromMediaIdImpl: media ID
```

```
{mediaId} not be found.");
        else
            HandlePlayRequest();
    }
};
```

- OnPauseImpl: **Pauses the currently playing media.**

The following code shows OnPauseImpl:

```
mediaCallback.OnPauseImpl = () => {
            OnPause();
        };
```

- OnStopImpl: **Stops the currently playing media.**

The following code shows OnStopImpl:

```
mediaCallback.OnStopImpl = () => {
            OnStop(null);
        };
```

- OnSkipToNextImpl: **Plays the next piece of media in the play list.**

The following code shows OnSkipToNextImpl:

```
mediaCallback.OnSkipToNextImpl = () => {
    _currentIndexQueue++;
    if (_playingQueue != null && _currentIndexQueue >=
_playingQueue.Count)
        _currentIndexQueue = 0;
    if (this.isIndexPlayable(_currentIndexQueue,
_playingQueue))
        HandlePlayRequest();
    else
        OnStop("Cannot skip");
};
```

- OnSkipToPreviousImpl: **Plays the previous media in the play list.**

The following code shows OnSkipToPreviousImpl:

```
mediaCallback.OnSkipToPreviousImpl = () => {
    _currentIndexQueue--;
    if (_playingQueue != null && _currentIndexQueue < 0)
        _currentIndexQueue = 0;
```

```
        if (this.isIndexPlayable(_currentIndexQueue,
_playingQueue))
            HandlePlayRequest();
        else
            OnStop("Cannot skip");
};
```

- `OnCustomActionImpl`: **Handles the favorite custom action by adding that specific podcast to the favorite list. This is to demonstrate how to create a custom action in Android Auto.**

The following code shows `OnCustomActionImpl`:

```
mediaCallback.OnCustomActionImpl = (action, extras) => {
    if (CustomActionFavorite == action)
    {
        var track = GetCurrentPlayingMusic();
        if (track != null){
            var musicId =
track.GetString(MediaMetadata.MetadataKeyMediaId);
            _musicProvider.SetFavorite(musicId,
!_musicProvider.IsFavorite(musicId));
        }
        UpdatePlaybackState(null);
    }
};
```

- `OnPlayFromSearchImpl`: **In Android Auto, when the user says** *"OK Google, play Henry test on Henry Podcast Service,"* **this call back will be invoked.** `_musicProvider.GetPlayingQueueFromSearch` **will search through the list of podcast titles and return a matching search** `query`.

The following code shows `OnPlayFromSearchImpl`:

```
mediaCallback.OnPlayFromSearchImpl = (query, extras) => {
    if (string.IsNullOrEmpty(query))
        _playingQueue = new
List<MediaSession.QueueItem>(_musicProvider.GetRandomQueue(
));
    else
        _playingQueue = new
List<MediaSession.QueueItem>(_musicProvider.GetPlayingQueue
FromSearch(query));
```

```
        _session.SetQueue(_playingQueue);
        if (_playingQueue != null && _playingQueue.Count != 0)
        {
            _currentIndexQueue = 0;
            HandlePlayRequest();
        }
        else
            OnStop("0 Found.");
};
```

15. Back in `OnCreate()`, instantiate `_session = new MediaSession(this, "HenryPodcast")`, where `this` is `MusicService` itself and `"HenryPodcast"` is the session name.

16. Next, in `OnCreate()`, set `MusicService SessionToken = _session.SessionToken`. Any time an external application requests `MusicService`, a session will be created with a unique session token.

17. Next, in `OnCreate()`, add the `mediaCallback` that you created in step 12 to the session: `_session.SetCallback(mediaCallback)`.

18. Next, in `OnCreate()`, add `pendingIntent` to `_session.SetSessionActivity`. `pendingIntent` allows the `_session` that you created in step 13 to control the media operation in the Android mobile media player. When Android Auto takes control, your Android phone will be locked and the Android media player that you will be creating later will be in the back ground. You want the `MusicService` session serving the request to Android Auto to also control the Android media player. For example, if Android Auto is playing the podcast, you want the Android media player to be in sync and doing the same thing, because if the user disengages from Android Auto and unlocks the Android phone, you want your Android media player to continue playing the same podcast.

The following code shows creating and setting `pendingIntent` to the session in `OnCreate`:

```
Context context = ApplicationContext;
var intent = new Intent(context, typeof(MainActivity));
var pendingIntent = PendingIntent.GetActivity(context, 99, intent,
PendingIntentFlags.UpdateCurrent);
_session.SetSessionActivity(pendingIntent);
```

19. Finally, `OnCreate()` creates `extraBundle`, which will reserve the actions in Android Auto that you can control by receiving a callback notification when those reserved actions are performed. For example, you may want to be notified when the play, previous, next, pause, and queue actions are performed. Then, add `extraBundle` to the `_session.SetExtras(extraBundle)` session.

The following reserved key words are set in `extraBundle`:

- `com.google.android.gms.car.media.ALWAYS_RESERVE_SPACE_FOR.ACTION_QUEUE`
- `com.google.android.gms.car.media.ALWAYS_RESERVE_SPACE_FOR.ACTION_SKIP_TO_PREVIOUS`
- `com.google.android.gms.car.media.ALWAYS_RESERVE_SPACE_FOR.ACTION_SKIP_TO_NEXT`
- `com.google.android.gms.car.media.ALWAYS_RESERVE_SPACE_FOR.ACTION_PLAY_PAUSE`

The following code shows the code reserving the play, previous, next, pause, and queue actions:

```
var extraBundle = new Bundle();
extraBundle.PutBoolean(
"com.google.android.gms.car.media.ALWAYS_RESERVE_SPACE_FOR.ACTION_Q
UEUE", true);
extraBundle.PutBoolean(
"com.google.android.gms.car.media.ALWAYS_RESERVE_SPACE_FOR.ACTION_S
KIP_TO_PREVIOUS", true);
extraBundle.PutBoolean(
"com.google.android.gms.car.media.ALWAYS_RESERVE_SPACE_FOR.ACTION_S
KIP_TO_NEXT", true);
extraBundle.PutBoolean(
"com.google.android.gms.car.media.ALWAYS_RESERVE_SPACE_FOR.ACTION_P
LAY_PAUSE", true);
_session.SetExtras(extraBundle);
```

20. Create `public override void OnDestroy()`, which will get called when `MusicService` is no longer needed. Here, you need to release the resources and stop `MusicService`:

The following code shows the `OnDestroy()` method:

```
public override void OnDestroy()
{
    Logger.Debug("OnDestroy");
    OnStop(null);
    _session.Release();
}
```

21. Create `public override BrowserRoot OnGetRoot(string clientPackageName, int clientUid, Bundle rootHints)`, which gets called the very first time when the user tries to browse through your podcast media. Here, you will be performing a security check to make sure the client requesting `MusicsService` has access by invoking `_packageFinder.Find(clientPackageName)`. If you verify that the client has access, you return `new BrowserRoot(HierarchyHelper.PodcastRoot, null)`, where you can start to browse your media list. `_packageFinder.Find` allows only two external clients to access Android Auto, `"com.google.android.projection.gearhead"` and your MyPodCast, `"com.henry.mypodcast"`.

The following code shows the `OnGetRoot` implementation:

```
public override BrowserRoot OnGetRoot(string clientPackageName, int clientUid, Bundle rootHints)
{
    Logger.Debug($"OnGetRoot:
clientPackageName={clientPackageName}");
    if (_packageFinder.Find(clientPackageName))
        return new BrowserRoot(HierarchyHelper.PodcastRoot, null);
    else {
        Logger.Warn($"OnGetRoot:
clientPackageName={clientPackageName} ignored");
        return null;
    }
}
```

The following code shows the `PackageFinder` class implementation:

```
public class PackageFinder
{
    private List<string> _allowedAppNames;

    public PackageFinder()
    {
        _allowedAppNames = new List<string>() {
```

```
                "com.google.android.projection.gearhead",
                "com.henry.mypodcast"
            };
    }

    public bool Find(string clientPackageName)
    {
        return _allowedAppNames.Contains(clientPackageName);
    }
}
```

22. Create `public override void OnLoadChildren(string parentId, Result result)`, which gets called when the user is clicking through the media categories. The categories start with All Podcasts, and All Podcasts has two child categories, January and March. When either January or March is clicked on, it will show the podcasts that the user can click to play. The very first time `OnLoadChildren` is called, `_musicProvider.RetrieveMedia` will be invoked to retrieve the play list and `LoadChildrenImpl` will handle all the browsing requests.

The following code shows the `OnLoadChildren` implementation:

```
public override void OnLoadChildren(string parentId, Result result)
{
    if (!_musicProvider.IsInitialized) {
        result.Detach();

        _musicProvider.RetrieveMedia(success => {
            if (success)
                LoadChildrenImpl(parentId, result);
            else {
                UpdatePlaybackState("Unable to get the data.");
                result.SendResult(new
JavaList<MediaBrowser.MediaItem>());
            }
        });

    }
    else
        LoadChildrenImpl(parentId, result);
}
```

23. Create `private void LoadChildrenImpl(string parentId, Result result)`, which will load categories while the user is browsing through the media categories. `LoadChildrenImpl` is composed of three sections: loading the root of the browsing category, loading All Podcasts, and loading monthly podcasts for January and March. On All Podcasts, January and March categories `MediaBrowser.MediaItems` are created with the title, the subtitle, and the `mediaId` set to the next category to load on click. Finally, the created `MediaItems` are sent using `result.SendResult(mediaItems)`.

The following table shows the category system of `MusicService` and which `LoadChildrenImpl` will load for each of the categories:

Root category	When application is initialized	When All Podcasts is clicked	When Month (January or March) is clicked
ROOT -> (Can be browsed)	All Podcasts -> (Can be browsed)	January -> (Can be browsed)	Henry1 Test (Playable music) Henry2 Test (Playable music) Henry3 Test (Playable music)
		March -> (Can be browsed)	Henry4 Test (Playable music)

- In ROOT, `MediaId` is set to `BY_MONTH` and title is set to All Podcasts. When the user clicks on All Podcasts, `LoadChildrenImpl` will send a `parantId` that contains `BY_MONTH`, which will instruct the method to build the correct month's list, January or March.

The following code shows the ROOT category loading All Podcasts:

```
if (HierarchyHelper.PodcastRoot == parentId) {
    mediaItems.Add(new MediaBrowser.MediaItem(
        new MediaDescription.Builder()
            .SetMediaId(HierarchyHelper.PodcastsByMonth)
            .SetTitle("All Podcasts")
            .SetIconUri(Android.NET.Uri.Parse(
"android.resource://com.henry.mypodcast/drawable/ic_by_genr
e"))
            .SetSubtitle("Podcasts By Month")
            .Build(), MediaItemFlags.Browsable));

}
```

The following screenshot shows the loaded ROOT category:

Loading ROOT category

- In BY_MONTH, MediaId is dynamically created using BY_MONTH/[month name] (for example, BY_MONTH/January). The title is set to the name of the month, and the subtitle is set to January Podcasts and March Podcasts.

The following code shows the section loading the BY_MONTH category:

```
else if (HierarchyHelper.PodcastsByMonth == parentId)
{
    foreach (var month in _musicProvider.Months) {
        var item = new MediaBrowser.MediaItem(
            new MediaDescription.Builder()
                .SetMediaId(HierarchyHelper.PodcastsByMonth
+ HierarchyHelper.CategorySeparator + month)
                .SetTitle(month)
                .SetSubtitle($"{month} Podcasts")
                .Build(), MediaItemFlags.Browsable);
        mediaItems.Add(item);
    }
}
```

The following screenshot shows the loaded list of months:

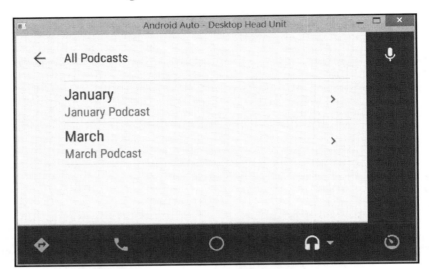

Loaded list of months

- In BY_MONTH/January and BY_MONTH/March, the MediaId contains a specially encoded value using By_MONTH/[month name]|[podcast trackId] (for example, BY_MONTH/January/1). MediaBrowser.MediaItem contains the playable podcasts' media content and it will be set to MediaItemFlags.Playable so that when the user clicks on the media, it will play the content.

The following code shows loading playable media content for the selected month:

```
else if
(parentId.StartsWith(HierarchyHelper.PodcastsByMonth))
{
    var month = HierarchyHelper.GetHierarchy(parentId)[1];
    foreach (var track in
_musicProvider.GetMusicsByMonth(month))
    {
        var hierarchyAwareMediaID =
HierarchyHelper.EncodeMediaID(
track.Description.MediaId, HierarchyHelper.PodcastsByMonth,
month);
        var trackCopy = new MediaMetadata.Builder(track)
        .PutString(MediaMetadata.MetadataKeyMediaId,
```

```
hierarchyAwareMediaID)
        .Build();
    var bItem = new MediaBrowser.MediaItem(
        trackCopy.Description,
MediaItemFlags.Playable);
        mediaItems.Add(bItem);
    }
}
```

The following screenshot shows loading the BY_MONTH/January playlist:

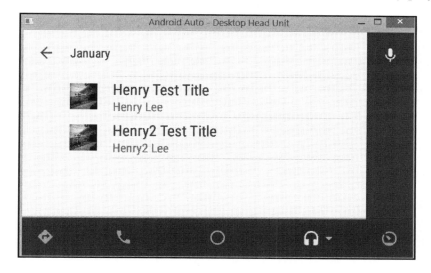

BY_MONTH/January|1 and BY_MONTH/January|2

Implementing MusicPlayer

`MusicService` invokes appropriate media player actions by calling media functions implemented in `MusicPlayer`. MusicPlayer will also contain a reference to MusicService so that it can notify MusicService if the media player's state changes.

Here are the steps to create MusicPlayer.

1. Open Visual Studio 2017.
2. Go to **File** | **Open** | **Project/Solution**, go to your `MyPodCast` directory, and choose the `MyPodCast.sln` file.
3. Right-click on the `MediaService` folder | **Add** | **New Item** | select **Visual C# Class** and name the file `MusicPlayer.cs`.
4. Click **Add**.
5. Open `MusicPlayer.cs` by double-clicking the file.
6. Create a public class, `MusicPlayer`, which implements `AudioManager.IOnAudioFocusChangeListener`, `MediaPlayer.IOnCompletionListener`, `MediaPlayer.IOnErrorListener`, `MediaPlayer.IOnPreparedListener`, and `MediaPlayer.IOnSeekCompleteListener`.

   The following code shows the `MusicPlayer` class inheriting `MediaPlayer` interfaces:

```
public class MusicPlayer :  Java.Lang.Object
      , AudioManager.IOnAudioFocusChangeListener
      , MediaPlayer.IOnCompletionListener
      , MediaPlayer.IOnErrorListener, MediaPlayer.IOnPreparedListener
      , MediaPlayer.IOnSeekCompleteListener
```

7. Declare the following global variables:

   - `_musicService`: Holds the `MusicService` object and sends various player states back to the `MusicService`
   - `_wifiLock`: Used for accessing Wi-Fi during media streaming
   - `_musicProvider`: Holds `MusicProvider`, which provides media metadata
   - `_mediaPlayer`: `MusicPlayer` will utilize this `MediaPlayer` object for the play, pause, seek, and resume functions
   - `_playOnFocusGain`: When set, `MusicPlayer` will play music; otherwise, the current media will be paused or the volume will be decreased or increased
   - `_currentPosition`: When the media is paused, the play position will be saved

- _currentMediaId: MediaId of currently playing media
- _audioFocusState: State of the current audio
- _audioManager: AudioManager, controls the audio focus
- MusicPlayerState: Contains player states such as none, stopped, Paused, playing, fast forwarding, rewinding, buffering, error, connecting, skipping to previous, skipping to next, and skipping to queue item
- IsPlaying: Set to true if media is playing currently: return _playOnFocusGain ||(_mediaPlayer != null && _mediaPlayer.IsPlaying)
- CurrentStreamPosition: Position of currently playing media: return _mediaPlayer != null ? _mediaPlayer.CurrentPosition : _currentPosition

The following code shows the declared global variables for MusicPlayer:

```
private MusicService _musicService;
private WifiManager.WifiLock _wifiLock;
private MusicProvider _musicProvider;
private MediaPlayer _mediaPlayer;
private bool _playOnFocusGain;
private volatile int _currentPosition;
private volatile string _currentMediaId;
private AudioFocusState _audioFocusState;
private AudioManager _audioManager;
public PlaybackStateCode MusicPlayerState { get; set; }
public bool IsPlaying {
     get {
          return _playOnFocusGain ||(_mediaPlayer != null &&
_mediaPlayer.IsPlaying);
     }
}
public int CurrentStreamPosition {
     get {
          return _mediaPlayer != null ?
_mediaPlayer.CurrentPosition : _currentPosition;
     }
}
```

8. Create the `MusicPlayer` constructor, `public MusicPlayer(MusicService service, MusicProvider musicProvider)`, which receives `MusicService` and `MusicProvider`. First, set `MusicPlayerState` to `PlaybackStateCode.None` if it is its first time being called and no media is selected to play. `_audioFocusState` is set to `AudioFocusState.NoFocusAndNoHide`, which means there is no focus on the audio and the audio is not in a hidden state. Set the `_musicService` and `_musicProvider` services, and `musicProvider`. Set `_wifiLock` to `((WifiManager) service.GetSystemService(Context.WifiService)).CreateWifiLock(WifiMode.Full, "mywifilock")`. `_wifiLock` will obtain the current Wi-Fi settings from your phone, if any, and this is required for streaming media. Finally, create `_mediaPlayer` with `SetWakeMode` using `_musicService.ApplicationContext` and `Android.OS.WakeLockFlags.Partial`. `SetWakeMode` will allow your media player continue to utilize `MusicService` even after your phone locks. On `_mediaPlayer` set listeners to MusicPlayer: `SetOnPreparedListener`, `SetOnCompletionListener`, `SetOnErrorListener` and `SetOnSeekCompleteListener`.

The following code shows the `MusicPlayer` constructor:

```
public MusicPlayer(MusicService service, MusicProvider
musicProvider)
{
    MusicPlayerState = PlaybackStateCode.None;
    _audioFocusState = AudioFocusState.NoFocusAndNoHide;
    _musicService = service;
    _musicProvider = musicProvider;
    _audioManager =
(AudioManager)service.GetSystemService(Context.AudioService);
    _wifiLock =
((WifiManager)service.GetSystemService(Context.WifiService))
        .CreateWifiLock(WifiMode.Full, "mywifilock");
    if (_mediaPlayer == null)
    {
        _mediaPlayer = new MediaPlayer();

        _mediaPlayer.SetWakeMode(_musicService.ApplicationContext,
            Android.OS.WakeLockFlags.Partial);
        _mediaPlayer.SetOnPreparedListener(this);
        _mediaPlayer.SetOnCompletionListener(this);
        _mediaPlayer.SetOnErrorListener(this);
        _mediaPlayer.SetOnSeekCompleteListener(this);
```

```
        }
    }
```

9. Implement IOnAudioFocusChangeListener, which is responsible for handling the lost focus on the current audio. Currently playing audio can lose a focus if another application takes control of the audio. For example, while listening to your podcast, Google Maps might be giving you directions, and you might want to either pause the podcast or lower the volume. When another application takes control, _audioFocusState can have two different states: AudioFocusState.NoFocusAndNoHide, which means to lose audio focus and pause the current media, and AudioFocusState.NoFocusAndCanHide, which means to lose audio focus and lower the volume. After setting proper _audioFocusState property call ConfigMediaPlayerState().

   The following code shows OnAudioFocusChange:

```
public void OnAudioFocusChange(AudioFocus focusChange)
{
    if (focusChange == AudioFocus.Gain)
        _audioFocusState = AudioFocusState.Focused;
    else if (focusChange == AudioFocus.Loss ||
        focusChange == AudioFocus.LossTransient ||
        focusChange == AudioFocus.LossTransientCanDuck)
    {
        bool canDuck = focusChange ==
AudioFocus.LossTransientCanDuck;
        _audioFocusState = canDuck ?
AudioFocusState.NoFocusAndCanHide :
AudioFocusState.NoFocusAndNoHide;

        _playOnFocusGain |= MusicPlayerState ==
PlaybackStateCode.Playing && !canDuck;
    }
    ConfigMediaPlayerState();
}
```

10. Depends on _audioFocusState method ConfigMediaPlayerState() will play, pause, seek, or lower the volume of the media. After performing the action, it will notify MusicService of the changed state, _musicService.OnPlaybackStatusChanged(MusicPlayerState).

The following code shows `ConfigMediaPlayerState`:

```
private void ConfigMediaPlayerState()
{
    if (_audioFocusState == AudioFocusState.NoFocusAndNoHide) {
        if (MusicPlayerState == PlaybackStateCode.Playing)
            Pause();
    }
    else {
        if (_audioFocusState == AudioFocusState.NoFocusAndCanHide)
            _mediaPlayer.SetVolume(0.2f, 0.2f);
        else
            _mediaPlayer.SetVolume(1.0f, 1.0f);

        if (_playOnFocusGain) {
            if (_mediaPlayer != null && !_mediaPlayer.IsPlaying) {
                if (_currentPosition ==
_mediaPlayer.CurrentPosition) {
                    _mediaPlayer.Start();
                    MusicPlayerState = PlaybackStateCode.Playing;
                }
                else {
                    _mediaPlayer.SeekTo(_currentPosition);
                    MusicPlayerState = PlaybackStateCode.Buffering;
                }
            }
            _playOnFocusGain = false;
        }
    }
    if (_musicService != null)
        _musicService.OnPlaybackStatusChanged(MusicPlayerState);
}
```

11. Implement `IOnCompletionListener.OnCompletion`, which gets called when the podcast finishes playing. It will notify `MusicService` that the media has finished playing.

The following code shows `IOnCompletionListener.OnCompletion`:

```
public void OnCompletion(MediaPlayer mp)
{
    if(_musicService != null)
        _musicService.OnCompletion();
}
```

12. Implement `IOnErrorListener.OnError`, which will send an error message to `MusicService`.

    The following code shows `IOnErrorListener.OnError`:

    ```
    public bool OnError(MediaPlayer mp, MediaError what, int extra)
    {
        if (_musicService != null)
            _musicService.OnError("MediaPlayer error " + what + "(" +
    extra + ")");
        return true;
    }
    ```

13. Implement `IOnPreparedListener.OnPrepared`, which is called when the media is being prepared in order to be played. Any special logic that needs to be done before playing the media can be handled here.

    The following code shows `IOnPreparedListener.OnPrepared`:

    ```
    public void OnPrepared(MediaPlayer mp)
    {
     ConfigMediaPlayerState();
    }
    ```

14. Implement `IOnSeekCompleteListener.OnSeekComplete`, which notifies `MusicService` when the media player has found its position in the media.

    The following code shows `IOnSeekCompleteListener.OnSeekComplete`:

    ```
    public void OnSeekComplete(MediaPlayer mp)
    {
        _currentPosition = mp.CurrentPosition;
        if (MusicPlayerState == PlaybackStateCode.Buffering) {
            _mediaPlayer.Start();
            MusicPlayerState = PlaybackStateCode.Playing;
        }
        if (_musicService != null)
            _musicService.OnPlaybackStatusChanged(MusicPlayerState);
    }
    ```

15. Create the `Stop` method, which will be called by `MusicService`. When the media stops `MusicPlayerState` will be set to `PlaybackStateCodeStoped` and then `_currentPosition` is set to `CurrentStreamPosition` in case the media needs to resume.

The following code shows the `Stop` method:

```
public void Stop(bool notifyListeners)
{
    MusicPlayerState = PlaybackStateCode.Stopped;

    if (notifyListeners && _musicService != null)
        _musicService.OnPlaybackStatusChanged(MusicPlayerState);

    _currentPosition = CurrentStreamPosition;
    GiveUpAudioFocus();
    CleanUp(true);
}
```

16. Create the `Pause` method. When the media is paused using the function `_mediaPlayer.Pause()`, `_currentPosition` is set to `_mediaPlayer.CurrentPosition` in order to resume from the pasued position. It will notify `MusicService` of the paused state.

The following code shows the Paused method:

```
public void Pause()
{
    if (MusicPlayerState == PlaybackStateCode.Playing) {
        if (_mediaPlayer != null && _mediaPlayer.IsPlaying) {
            _mediaPlayer.Pause();
            _currentPosition = _mediaPlayer.CurrentPosition;
        }
        CleanUp(false);
        GiveUpAudioFocus();
    }
    MusicPlayerState = PlaybackStateCode.Paused;
    if (_musicService != null)
        _musicService.OnPlaybackStatusChanged(MusicPlayerState);
}
```

17. Create the `SeekTo` method, which will get invoked when the player resumes or fast forwards to a certain position in the media. In order to resume playing, the player must buffer to the new position by invoking `_mediaPlayer.SeekTo(position)`.

The following code shows the `SeekTo` method:

```
public void SeekTo(int position)
{
    if (_mediaPlayer == null)
        _currentPosition = position;
```

```
        else
        {
            if (_mediaPlayer.IsPlaying)
                MusicPlayerState = PlaybackStateCode.Buffering;
            _mediaPlayer.SeekTo(position);
            if (_musicService != null)
    _musicService.OnPlaybackStatusChanged(MusicPlayerState);
        }
    }
```

18. Create the `public void Play(MediaSession.QueueItem item)` method, which will get invoked when the user hits the play button. `item` contains `MediaId`, which can be used to get `MediaMetadata` from `_musicProvider.GetMusic`. `MediaMetadata` contains the media streaming source, `PodcastSource`. The following methods will be invoked in order to initialize the media player:

   - `_mediaPlayer.Reset`: Resets the media player since you will be playing a new podcast
   - `MusicPlayerState`: Set this to `PlaybackStateCode.Buffering` and the player will buffer the steam for few seconds
   - `_mediaPlayer.SetAudioStreamType`: Set it to `Android.Media.Stream.Music`
   - `_mediaPlayer.SetDataSource`: Set it to the podcast source URL
   - `_mediaPlayer.PrepareAsync`: Invoke to prepare the media, which will trigger `IOnPreparedListener.OnPrepared` when finished preparing the media
   - `_wifiLock.Acquire`: A Wi-Fi lock needs to be acquired so that the player can stream data using Wi-Fi
   - `_musicService.OnPlaybackStatusChanged`: Notify the `MusicService` of the status of the player

The following code shows the `Play` method:

```
public void Play(MediaSession.QueueItem item) {
    var mediaHasChanged =
InitPlayerStates(item.Description.MediaId);
    if (MusicPlayerState == PlaybackStateCode.Paused &&
!mediaHasChanged && _mediaPlayer != null)
        ConfigMediaPlayerState();
    else {
        MusicPlayerState = PlaybackStateCode.Stopped;
        CleanUp(false);
        MediaMetadata track = _musicProvider.GetMusic(
```

```
HierarchyHelper.ExtractMusicIDFromMediaID(item.Description.MediaId)
);
        string source =
track.GetString(MusicProvider.PodcastSource);
        try {
            _mediaPlayer.Reset();
            MusicPlayerState = PlaybackStateCode.Buffering;
_mediaPlayer.SetAudioStreamType(Android.Media.Stream.Music);
            _mediaPlayer.SetDataSource(source);
            _mediaPlayer.PrepareAsync();
            _wifiLock.Acquire();
_musicService.OnPlaybackStatusChanged(MusicPlayerState);
        }
        catch (Exception ex) {
            _musicService.OnError(ex.Message);
        }
    }
}
```

Building MusicProvider

MusicProvider will be responsible for building the media sources. In this section, you will be creating the media sources from static content, but in Chapter 10, *Hosting and Enhancing the Android Auto Podcast*, you will be generating the media sources from the backend server hosted on Microsoft Azure Cloud:

1. Open Visual Studio 2017.
2. Go to **File** | **Open** | **Project/Solution**, go to your MyPodCast directory, and choose the MyPodCast.sln file.
3. Right-click on MediaService folder | **Add** | **New Item** | select **Visual C# Class**, and name the file MusicProvider.cs.
4. Click **Add**.
5. Open MusicProvider.cs by double-clicking the file.
6. Create a public class, MusicProvider, and add the following global variables to it:
   - Add a PodcastSource constant set to "PODCASTS_SOURCE". This is the name of the podcast source key that you will be using to save and retrieve podcast media from MediaMetadata.
   - Add Dictionary<string, List<MediaMetadata>> _musicListByMonths, which contains retrieved media sources saved by month.

- Add `Dictionary<string, MediaMetadata> _musicListById`, which contains media sources by mediaId.
- Add `List<string> _favorites`, which contains media that has been marked favorite by the user.
- Add `State _currentState = State.NonInitialized`, where it will maintain the current state of the `MusicProvider`: `State _currentState = State.NonInitialized`, Initializing and Initialized.
- Add Month, which returns a list of the months, `_currentState != State.Initialized ? new List<string>() : new List<string>(_musicListByMonths.Keys)`.
- Add `IsInitialized`, which checks to see whether `MusicProvider` is in an initialized state: `_currentState == State.Initialized`.

The following code shows the declared `MusicProvider` global variables:

```
public const string PodcastSource = "PODCASTS_SOURCE";
private Dictionary<string, List<MediaMetadata>> _musicListByMonths;
private Dictionary<string, MediaMetadata> _musicListById;
private List<string> _favorites;
private volatile State _currentState = State.NotInitialized;
public List<string> Months
{
    get
    {
        return _currentState != State.Initialized
                ? new List<string>() : new
List<string>(_musicListByMonths.Keys);
    }
}
public bool IsInitialized {
    get {
        return _currentState == State.Initialized;
    }
}
```

7. Add the `MusicProvider` constructor, which initializes `_musicListByMonths`, `_musicListById`, and `_favorites`.

The following code shows the `Musicprovider` constructor:

```
public MusicProvider()
{
    _musicListByMonths = new Dictionary<string,
```

```
List<MediaMetadata>>();
    _musicListById = new Dictionary<string, MediaMetadata>();
    _favorites = new List<string>();
}
```

8. Create `public void RetrieveMedia(Action<bool> callback)`, which will be called by `MusicService` to obtain the media sources. Upon acquiring the media sources callback function will be called with the `MusicProvider` state. Two things will happen during this call: `GetSource()` to get the media sources and `BuildListsByMonths()` to re-group the media sources by month for quick retrieval.

   The following code shows the `RetreiveMedia` method:

```
public void RetrieveMedia(Action<bool> callback)
{
    Logger.Debug("RetrieveMedia");
    if (_currentState == State.Initialized) {
        callback(true);
        return;
    }

    try
    {
        if (_currentState == State.NotInitialized) {
            _currentState = State.Initializing;
            GetSource();
            BuildListsByMonths();
            _currentState = State.Initialized;
        }
    }
    catch (Exception e) {
        _currentState = State.NotInitialized;
    }

    callback(_currentState == State.Initialized);
}
```

9. Create the `GetSources` method, which will build media sources and save them to _musicListById. You will create `List<PodcastData> sources = new List<PodcastData>()`, which creates static `PodcastData` sources. Then, you will loop through sources, generate `MediaMetadata`, and add it to _musicListById.

The following code shows the GetSource method:

```
private void GetSource()
{
    List<PodcastData> sources = new List<PodcastData>()
    {
        new PodcastData() {
            Id = "1",
            PodcastSource =
"http://storage.googleapis.com/automotive-media/Jazz_In_Paris.mp3",
            AlbumName = "Xamarin Album", Artist = "Henry Lee",
Month = "January",
            AlbumCoverSource =
"http://storage.googleapis.com/automotive-media/album_art.jpg",
            Title = "Henry Test Title",
        },
        new PodcastData() {
            Id = "4",
            PodcastSource =
"http://storage.googleapis.com/automotive-media/Jazz_In_Paris.mp3",
            AlbumName = "Xamarin Album", Artist = "Henry Lee",
Month = "March",
            AlbumCoverSource =
"http://storage.googleapis.com/automotive-media/album_art.jpg",
            Title = "Henry4 Test Title",
        }

    };

    foreach (var data in sources)
    {
        List<Bitmap> images = GetImage(800, 480, 128, 128,
data.AlbumCoverSource);
        _musicListById.Add(data.Id, new MediaMetadata.Builder()
            .PutString(MediaMetadata.MetadataKeyMediaId, data.Id)
            .PutString(PodcastSource, data.PodcastSource)
            .PutString(MediaMetadata.MetadataKeyAlbum,
data.AlbumName)
            .PutString(MediaMetadata.MetadataKeyArtist,
data.Artist)
            .PutString(MediaMetadata.MetadataKeyGenre, data.Month)
            .PutString(MediaMetadata.MetadataKeyAlbumArtUri,
data.AlbumCoverSource)
            .PutString(MediaMetadata.MetadataKeyTitle, data.Title)
            .PutBitmap(MediaMetadata.MetadataKeyAlbumArt,
images[0])
            .PutBitmap(MediaMetadata.MetadataKeyDisplayIcon,
images[1])
```

```
                    .Build());
    }
}
```

10. Create `GetMusicsByMonth`, **which returns podcasts for the month.**

    The following code shows `GetMusicsByMonth`:

```
public IEnumerable<MediaMetadata> GetMusicsByMonth(string month) {
    if (_currentState != State.Initialized ||
!_musicListByMonths.ContainsKey(month))
        return new List<MediaMetadata>();
    return _musicListByMonths[month];
}
```

11. Create `GetMusic`, **which returns podcasts by** `mediaId`.

    The following code shows the `GetMusic` **method:**

```
public MediaMetadata GetMusic(string musicId) {
    return _musicListById.ContainsKey(musicId) ?
_musicListById[musicId] : null;
}
```

12. Create `SetFavorite`, **which will add or remove** `mediaId` **from** `_favorites`.

    The following code shows the `Setfavorite` **method:**

```
public void SetFavorite(string musicId, bool favorite) {
    if (favorite)
        _favorites.Add(musicId);
    else
        _favorites.Remove(musicId);
}
```

13. Create `SearchMusic`, **which will search** `_musicListById` **by title.**

    The following code shows the `SearchMusic` **method:**

```
public IEnumerable<MediaMetadata> SearchMusic(string titleQuery) {
    if (_currentState != State.Initialized)
        return new List<MediaMetadata>();
    var result = new List<MediaMetadata>();
    titleQuery = titleQuery.ToLower();
    foreach (var track in _musicListById.Values) {
        if
(track.GetString(MediaMetadata.MetadataKeyTitle).ToLower().Contains
(titleQuery))
```

```
            result.Add(track);
        }
        return result;
    }
```

14. Create `BuildListsByMonths`, which will take `_musicListById` and create `_musicListByMonths`, which is organized by month.

The following code shows the `BuildListsByMonths` method:

```
private void BuildListsByMonths() {
    _musicListByMonths = new Dictionary<string,
List<MediaMetadata>>();
    foreach (var m in _musicListById.Values) {
        var month = m.GetString(MediaMetadata.MetadataKeyGenre);
        if (_musicListByMonths.ContainsKey(month))
            _musicListByMonths[month].Add(m);
        else
            _musicListByMonths.Add(month, new List<MediaMetadata> {
m });
    }
}
```

15. Create `GetRandomQueue`, which generates a random playlist. It will be used by `MusicService` the very first time `MusicService` is requested.

The following code shows the `GetRandomQueue` method:

```
public List<MediaSession.QueueItem> GetRandomQueue() {
    List<string> months = this.Months;
    if (months.Count <= 1)
        return new List<MediaSession.QueueItem>();
    string month = months[0];
    IEnumerable<MediaMetadata> tracks =
this.GetMusicsByMonth(month);
    return ConvertToQueue(tracks, HierarchyHelper.PodcastsByMonth,
month);
}
```

16. Create `GetPlayingQueue`, which returns recently played media. It will be utilized by `Musicservice` when the media player tries to resume the last played media.

The following code shows the `GetPlayingQueue` method:

```
public List<MediaSession.QueueItem> GetPlayingQueue(string mediaId)
{
    string[] hierarchy = HierarchyHelper.GetHierarchy(mediaId);
    if (hierarchy.Length != 2)
        return null;
    string categoryType = hierarchy[0];
    string categoryValue = hierarchy[1];
    IEnumerable<MediaMetadata> tracks = null;
    if (categoryType == HierarchyHelper.PodcastsByMonth)
        tracks = this.GetMusicsByMonth(categoryValue);
    else if (categoryType == HierarchyHelper.PodcastsBySearch)
        tracks = this.SearchMusic(categoryValue);
    if (tracks == null)
        return null;
    return ConvertToQueue(tracks, hierarchy[0], hierarchy[1]);
}
```

17. Create `GetPlayingQueueFromSearch`, which returns media based on the search request sent by `MusicService`.

The following code shows the `GetPlayingQueueFromSearch` method:

```
public List<MediaSession.QueueItem>
GetPlayingQueueFromSearch(string query) {
    return ConvertToQueue(this.SearchMusic(query),
HierarchyHelper.PodcastsBySearch, query);
}
```

18. Create the `ConvertToQueue` method, which will convert `MediaMetadata` to `MediaSession.QueueItem`. The media sources are in `MediaMetadata` format, but when MediaPlayer plays a podcast, it needs to be in `MediaSession.QueueItem`.

The following code shows the `ConvertToQueue` method:

```
private List<MediaSession.QueueItem> ConvertToQueue
                (IEnumerable<MediaMetadata> tracks, params string[]
categories) {
    var queue = new List<MediaSession.QueueItem>();
    int count = 0;
    foreach (var track in tracks) {
```

```
        string hierarchyAwareMediaID = HierarchyHelper
                .EncodeMediaID(track.Description.MediaId,
categories);
        MediaMetadata trackCopy = new MediaMetadata.Builder(track)
            .PutString(MediaMetadata.MetadataKeyMediaId,
hierarchyAwareMediaID)
            .Build();
        var item = new
MediaSession.QueueItem(trackCopy.Description, count++);
        queue.Add(item);
    }
    return queue;
}
```

Building an Android Media Player UI

For Android Auto, building an Android media player UI is not necessary; only MusicService is required. However, it is very convenient to troubleshoot MusicService using the Android media player installed on your phone. You can find the Android media player UI code on GitHub at `https://bit.ly/2LALL4N`. You can copy files from `ch9/MyPodCast/UI` and `ch9/MyPodCast/Helpers` to the respective folders in your current working project.

Testing Using Android Phone

In this section, you will learn to test what you have created so far using your Android phone and Visual Studio. There are a few steps you need to perform before you can deploy and test what you created on your phone:

1. On your Android phone, go to **Settings** | **System** | **About.**
2. Hit the Build number seven times, until you come to a prompt asking you whether you want to make your phone into a development phone.

The following screenshot show Build number, which you need to hit seven times to make your phone into a development phone:

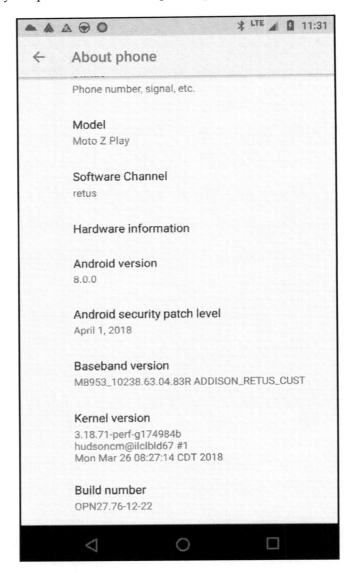

Build number

3. Go to **Settings** | **System** | **Developer options.**
4. Make sure the USB debugging option is enabled.

The following screenshot shows enabling USB debugging:

USB debugging

5. Open Visual Studio 2017.
6. Go to **File** | **Open** | **Project/Solution**, go to your `MyPodCast` directory, and choose the `MyPodCast.sln` file.
7. Connect your USB to your computer and then to your Android phone.
8. Click **OK** at the Allow USB debugging prompt.

The following screenshot shows the Allow USB debugging prompt:

Allow USB debugging prompt

9. In your Visual Studio, which you just opened up, you will notice that your Android phone name shows up.

The following screenshot shows Visual Studio showing the connected Android phone:

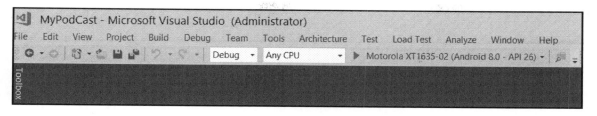

Visual Studio showing connected Android phone

10. Press *F5*.

11. On your Android phone, you will notice the MyPodCast application will be running, showing the All Podcasts category.

The following screenshot shows MyPodCast running on the Android phone:

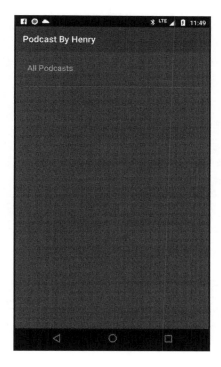

MyPodCast running on Android phone

12. Click on **All Podcasts** and you will see the list of months, January and March.

13. Click on **January** and you will see the list of podcasts, **Henry Test Title**, **Henry2 Test Title**, and **Henry3 Test Title**

14. Click on **Henry Test Title** and you will see media player playing **Henry Test Title**.

The following screenshot shows the media player playing **Henry Test Title**:

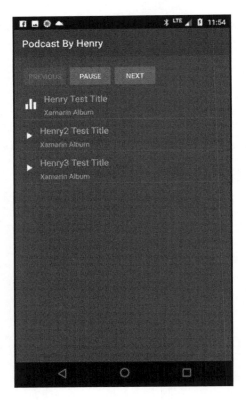

MyPodCast playing "Henry Test Title"

You just successfully ran `MyPodCast` utilizing `MusicService` and `MediaPlayer` to play the test media.

Summary

In this chapter, you built MusicService, MediaPlayer, and MusicProvider, which Android Auto will be using to allow the user to browse through the media content categories and select media to play. Also, you created an Android mobile media player application that you can use to test MusicService, MediaPlayer, and MusicProvider. In the next chapter, you will learn to create a backend service to serve the media content from Microsoft Azure, and most importantly you will learn to simulate your MusicService using the Android Auto desktop header unit and then you will be running your Android Auto podcast application using the real car.

10
Hosting and Enhancing the Android Auto Podcast

In the previous chapter, you created MusicService, MusicProvider, and MediaPlayer, and ran the Android media application on the mobile. In this chapter, you will use the experience you gained by utilizing the Microsoft Azure cloud offerings to develop the podcast backend using Node.js for MusicProvider and store streaming media sources in Microsoft Azure Storage. Then, you will learn how to configure and test MusicService on Android Auto using the desktop-header unit simulator and then run it in a real car. You will also learn some basic voice commands to interact with your Android Auto application. Finally, you will learn about the Android Auto certification process.

In this chapter, we will cover the following topics:

- Creating the Node.js media's metadata provider
- Refactoring MusicProvider to retrieve the media metadata from the Node.js server
- Setting up streaming media sources in Microsoft Azure Storage
- Configuring and testing on the desktop-header unit (DHU) to simulate Android Auto
- Testing Android Auto in the real car
- Basic voice commands
- Android Auto certification process

Enhancing a MusicProvider

In the previous chapter, static media content was used. In this section, you will be creating a Node.js server that returns the media contents. In the real world, you would want the media contents to be sent from the backend server so that you can save and manage the media information in the database. You will not be learning about storing and retrieving media from the database in this chapter, but you can refer to the technique used in Chapter 4, *Hosting, Securing, and Testing Fortune Cookie in Cloud*, where the data is saved and retrieved from CosmoDB. Finally, the podcast music files and the cover image are saved to the Microsoft Azure blob storage.

The following shows the media content dataflow:

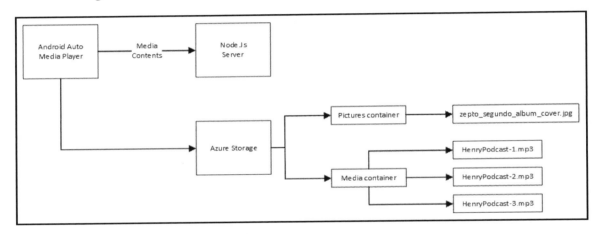

Media content dataflow

Creating a Node.js backend server

You will be creating a Node.js backend server that will return a list of `PodcastData` elements. Here are the steps to create a Node.js backend server:

1. Open Visual Studio Code for writing the Node.js server.
2. Go to **File** | **Open Folder** and select the directory where you will be working with the Node.js server codes. The following shows the folder in Visual Studio Code:

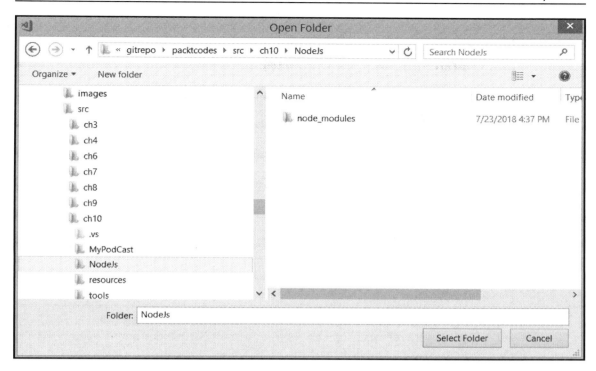

Open folder in Visual Studio Code

3. **Create three files:** `package.json`, `server.js`, **and** `web.config`.

4. **In** `package.json`, **add** `name:"podcasts"`, `description:"podcast service"`, `version:"0.1.0"`, `author:"Henry Lee <henry@henrylee.link>"`, `dependencies: body-parser": "^1.9.0"`, `"express": "^4.0.0"`, `"jsonpath": "^0.2.0"`, **and** `script: "./server.js"`. **The following shows the** `package.json` **content:**

```
{
    "name": "podcasts",
    "description": "podcast service",
    "version": "0.1.0",
    "author": "Henry Lee <henry@henrylee.link>",
    "dependencies": {
        "body-parser": "^1.9.0",
        "express": "^4.0.0",
        "jsonpath": "^0.2.0"
    },
    "script": "./server.js"
}
```

5. `web.config` is needed in order to allow the Microsoft Azure App Service to host the Node.js server. The following shows `web.config`:

```
<? xml version = "1.0" encoding = "utf-8" ?>
<configuration>
    <system.webServer>
        <handlers>
            <add name="iisnode" path="server.js" verb="*"
modules="iisnode" />
        </handlers>
        <rewrite>
            <rules>
                <rule name="DynamicContent">
                    <match url="/*" />
                    <action type="Rewrite" url="server.js" />
                </rule>
            </rules>
        </rewrite>
    </system.webServer>
</configuration>
```

6. Create server.js, which is responsible for sending the JSON object of the `PodcastDat` list. First, declare the `express` REST server, `body-parser` for parsing request-and-response objects as JSON, and `http` for creating the HTTP server. The following shows declaring the `server.js` global variables:

```
var express = require('express');
var bodyParser = require('body-parser');
var http = require('http');

var app = express();
var server = http.createServer(app);
app.use(bodyParser.json());

var port = process.env.PORT || 8000;
server.listen(port, function () {
    console.log("Server is up and running...");
});
```

7. Create a `ping` service that simply returns, `Welcome to Podcasts Provider`. This is very useful for testing whether your Node.js server is deployed successfully and running in Microsoft Azure App Service. The following shows the `ping` service:

```
app.use("/ping", function (req, res, next) {
    res.send('Welcome to Podcasts Provider');
});
```

8. For the GET `podcasts` method, you will be creating static `PodcastData` where the podcast sources and album cover point to the Microsoft Azure blob storage. Also, GET `podcasts` to check for a security header called `mysecret` to ensure it will only respond to the request with the correct `mysecret` value. The following shows the GET `podcasts` method:

```
app.get('/podcasts', function (req, res) {
    var secret = req.get("mysecret");
    if (secret === "12345") {
        res.json([
            {
                id: "1",
                podcastSource:
"https://henrypodsstorage.blob.core.windows.net/media/HenryPodcast-
1.mp3",
                albumName: "Andromeda", artist: "Zepto Segundo",
month: "January", title: "Andromeda",
                albumCoverSource:
"https://henrypodsstorage.blob.core.windows.net/pictures/zepto_segu
ndo_album_cover.jpg"
            },
            {
                id: "2",
                podcastSource:
"https://henrypodsstorage.blob.core.windows.net/media/HenryPodcast-
2.mp3",
                albumName: "Andromeda", artist: "Zepto Segundo",
month: "January", title: "Morir con
Honor",
                albumCoverSource:
"https://henrypodsstorage.blob.core.windows.net/pictures/zepto_segu
ndo_album_cover.jpg"

            },
            {
                id: "3",
                podcastSource:
"https://henrypodsstorage.blob.core.windows.net/media/HenryPodcast-
3.mp3",
                albumName: "Andromeda", artist: "Zepto Segundo",
month: "March", title: "Ars Chimica",
                albumCoverSource:
"https://henrypodsstorage.blob.core.windows.net/pictures/zepto_segu
ndo_album_cover.jpg"
            }
        ]);
    }
```

```
        else {
            return res.status(403).end('Access denied!');
        }
    });
```

9. Hit *F5* to run `server.js`.

10. Open Postman to test GET `http://localhost:8000/ping` and GET `http://localhost:8000/podcasts` with the 12345 mysecret header. You can refer to `Chapter 4`, *Hosting, Securing, Testing Fortune Cookie in Cloud*, if you need a refresher on how to use Postman to debug and test your Node.js server.

11. Once tested, refer to `Chapter 4`, *Hosting, Securing, Testing Fortune Cookie in Cloud*, for deploying your Node.js server to Microsoft App Service.

12. Using Postman, you can test GET `https://myhenrytestapp.azurewebsites.net/ping` and GET `https://myhenrytestapp.azurewebsites.net/podcasts`, just like in step 10.

Creating and adding the podcasts to the Microsoft Azure blob storage

The Microsoft Azure blob storage is an excellent choice for streaming your podcasts, as it provides a large amount of storage capacity and also provides reliable and fast disk spaces for streaming podcasts. In this section, you will learn to set up podcast-streaming using the Microsoft Azure blob storage.

Here are the steps to create podcast-streaming in the Microsoft azure blob storage:

1. Using FireFox, go to `https://portal.azure.com`.

2. In `Chapter 4`, *Hosting, Securing, Testing Fortune Cookie in Cloud,*, you learned how to work with Microsoft Azure and created the account. Using the same account, log into the Microsoft Azure portal.

3. In the top-left corner, click the **All services** link.

4. On All services, filter the text box type in `storage`.

5. Select **Storage accounts** from the filtered list.

The following shows the Storage accounts from the filtered list:

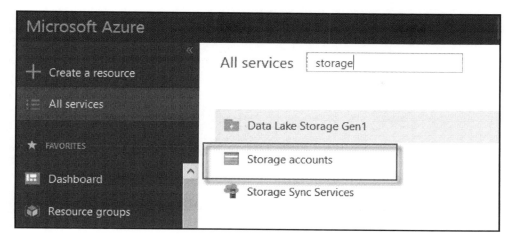

Storage accounts

6. Click **+Add**.
7. Create a storage account with the following properties and the rest of the properties take the default values:
   - **Name**: henrypodstorage
   - **Account kind: Blob storage**
   - **Replication: Locally-redundant storage (LRS)**
   - **Resource group**: User existing -> HenryResourceGroup

The following image shows the Create storage account settings:

Create storage account settings

8. Click on **Create**.

9. Go to this book's GitHub repository (`https://github.com/henrywritesbook/VoiceUserInterfacesProjects`) and download `HenryPodcast-1.mp3`, `HenryPodcast-2.mp3`, and `HenryPodcast-3.mp3`. From `ch10\resources zepto_segundo_album_cover.jpg`.

10. Come back to the Microsoft Azure portal and re-execute steps 2 through 5.

11. Click on **henrypodstorage** from the list.

12. Click on **Containers**.

13. Click **+Container**, put `media` as the **Name**, choose the Public-access level to be Container (anonymous read access for containers and blobs), and then click **OK**.

14. Click **+Container**, put `pictures` as the **Name**, choose the Public-access level to be Container (anonymous read access for containers and blobs), and then click OK.

15. Click on **Media**.

16. Click **Upload**.

17. From the Upload blob screen, click on the folder, go to the folder where you download MP3 files, and select all three files: `HenryPodcast-1.mp3`, `HenryPodcast-2.mp3`, and `HenryPodcast-3.mp3`.

18. Click **Upload**.

The following image shows the uploaded MP3 files:

Uploaded MP3 files

19. Go back to the list of the containers, click **Pictures**, and upload
`zepto_segundo_album_cover.jpg`.

You have successfully uploaded the cover image and the podcasts that you will be streaming from Android Auto. You can access the files using the following format: `https://[storage name].blob.core.windows.net/[container name]/[uploaded file name].`

The following shows an example of accessing one of the MP3s you uploaded:

`https://henrypodsstorage.blob.core.windows.net/media/HenryPodcast-2.mp3`

Refactoring the GetSource() method in MusicProvider

In this section, you will be modifying the `GetSource` method in `MusicProvider` that you wrote in previous chapter. `GetSource` is responsible for returning `MediaMetaData` to `MusicService` so that the user can browse and play from the list. Instead of hardcoded static content, you will be getting the media content from the Node.js backend server that you created in previous section.

Here are the steps to modify `GetSource`:

1. Open Visual Studio 2017.
2. Go to **File** | **Open** | **Project/Solution**, go to your `MyPodCast` directory, and choose the `MyPodCast.sln` file.
3. Open `MusicProvider.cs`.
4. Retrieve the JSON object from your Node.js server, hosted on Microsoft Azure App Service at `https://myhenrytestapp.azurewebsites.net/podcasts`, by using `HttpClient`.

The following shows the `GetSource` method:

```
private void GetSource() {
    JsonConvert.DefaultSettings = () => {
        var settings = new JsonSerializerSettings();
        settings.NullValueHandling = NullValueHandling.Ignore;
        settings.DefaultValueHandling =
DefaultValueHandling.Ignore;
        settings.ContractResolver = new
CamelCasePropertyNamesContractResolver();
        return settings;
```

```
            };
        using (var httpClient = new HttpClient()) {
            httpClient.DefaultRequestHeaders.Add("mysecret", "12345");
            var message =
httpClient.GetAsync("https://myhenrytestapp.azurewebsites.net/podca
sts").GetAwaiter().GetResult();
            var result =
message.Content.ReadAsStringAsync().GetAwaiter().GetResult();
            var sources =
JsonConvert.DeserializeObject<List<PodcastData>>(result);
            foreach (var data in sources) {
                List<Bitmap> images = GetImage(800, 480, 128, 128,
data.AlbumCoverSource);
                _musicListById.Add(data.Id, new MediaMetadata.Builder()
                    .PutString(MediaMetadata.MetadataKeyMediaId,
data.Id)
                    .PutString(PodcastSource, data.PodcastSource)
                    .PutString(MediaMetadata.MetadataKeyAlbum,
data.AlbumName)
                    .PutString(MediaMetadata.MetadataKeyArtist,
data.Artist)
                    .PutString(MediaMetadata.MetadataKeyGenre,
data.Month)
                    .PutString(MediaMetadata.MetadataKeyAlbumArtUri,
data.AlbumCoverSource)
                    .PutString(MediaMetadata.MetadataKeyTitle,
data.Title)
                    .PutBitmap(MediaMetadata.MetadataKeyAlbumArt,
images[0])
                    .PutBitmap(MediaMetadata.MetadataKeyDisplayIcon,
images[1])
                    .Build());
            }
        }
    }
```

Testing Android Auto using the Desktop-Header unit

The **desktop-header unit (DHU)** is a tool provided by Google to simulate Android Auto on your computer. It allows your phone to connect to your computer via USB and then allows DHU to directly interface with the Android Auto installed on your phone.

Here are the steps to test Android Auto using DHU:

1. On your Android phone, download and install Android Auto from the Google Play Store:

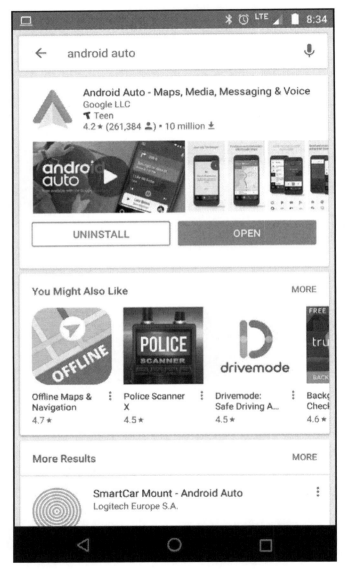

Android Auto on Google Play Store

2. Open Android Auto.
3. Click on the hamburger menu and go to About.
4. Click on **About Android Auto** until you get a message saying that the developer mode is enabled.

The following image shows About Android Auto:

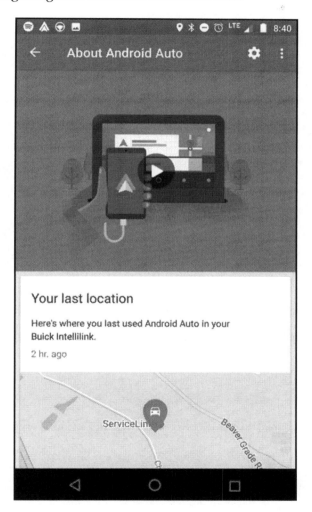

About Android Auto

5. Once developer mode is enabled, Android Auto is activated. Go to the top-right corner, click on the three vertical dots, and choose **Start head-unit server**.

The following image shows starting the header-unit server on Android Auto:

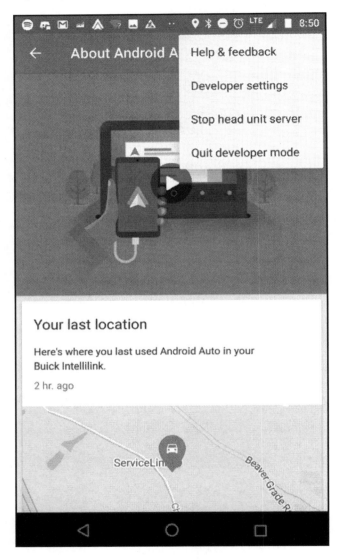

Started header-unit server

6. Click on the three vertical dots in the top-right corner and choose **Developer settings**.

7. Set **Application Mode** to **Developer**, enable **Unknown sources**, and exit out by hitting the back button on your phone.

The following image shows the Android Auto developer settings:

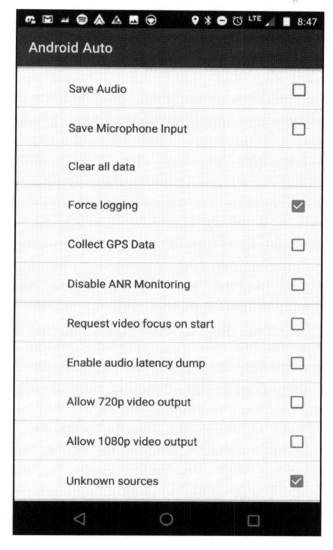

Android Auto developer settings

8. Open Visual Studio 2017.

9. Go to **File** | **Open** | **Project/Solution**, go to your MyPodCast directory, and choose the MyPodCast.sln file.

10. Connect your Android phone to your computer using USB.

11. Go to **Tools** | **Options** and choose **Xamarin** | **Android Settings**. Take note of the **Android SDK Location**:

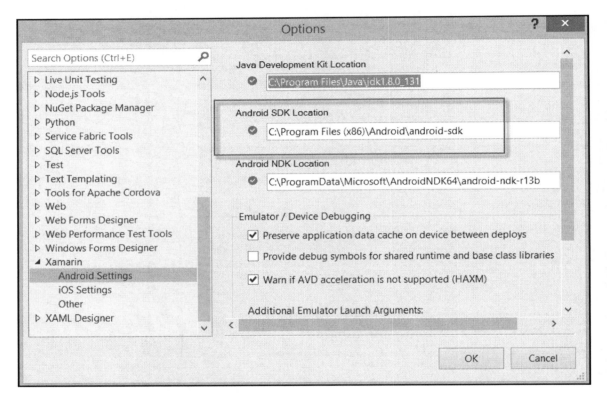

Android SDK Location

12. Go to **Tools** | **Android** | **Android Adb Command Prompt**.

13. On the command prompt, go to [location from step 12]\extras\google\auto directory by typing cd [location from step 13]\extras\google\auto directory

14. On the command prompt, type adb forward tcp:5277 tcp:5277.

15. On the command prompt, type `desktop-head-unit.exe`.
16. On your phone, you will be getting Android Auto setup prompts about **What will Android Auto do?** Click **Continue**:

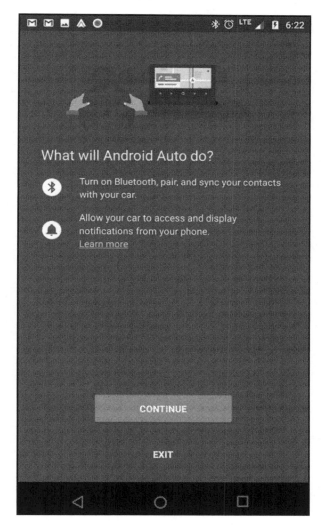

Android Auto setup prompt

17. On your phone, Android Auto setup will prompt you to use Google Assistant. Click **CONTINUE**:

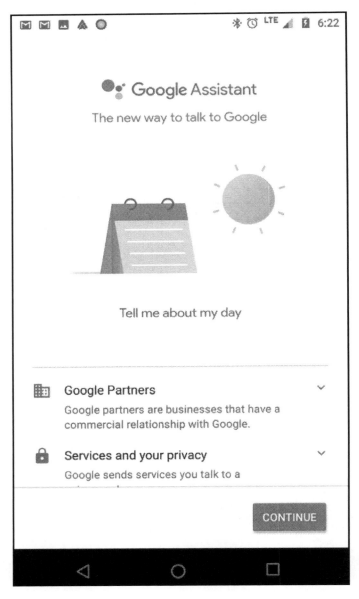

Android Auto and Google Assistant

18. On your computer, you will see the DHU. Click **SKIP**:

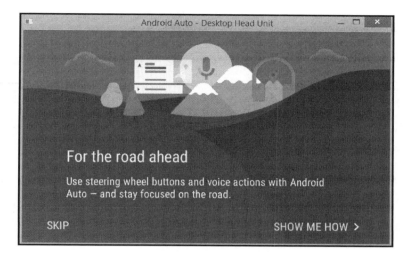

Desktop header unit setup

19. In Visual Studio, click *F5* to run the MyPodCast project. It will deploy MyPodCast to your phone but it will run on Android Auto.

20. Once the MyPodCast project is deployed, go to the DHU. Click on the headphone icon until the list of music services is displayed:

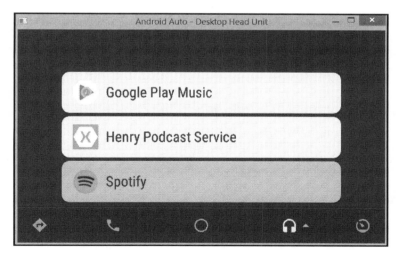

DHU music service list

21. You will see the list of music services for Android Auto, such as Google Play Music, Spotify, and the Henry Podcast Service that you created. Click on **Henry Podcast Service**.

22. Click on the **Podcast by Henry** menu in the top right | **All Podcasts** | **January** | **Morir con Honor**.

The following image shows the DHU playing podcast-streaming from the Microsoft Azure blob storage:

DHU playing podcast

In the next section, you will be deploying your podcast and playing it in your car.

Testing the Podcast's Application in the Car

In this section, you will learn to deploy your project and play the podcast in your car using Android Auto. In this example, I will be using a 2018 Buick Regal Sportback, but the Android Auto setup should be similar in other cars.

Here are the steps to set up and test your Android podcast project:

1. Start your car
2. On the car's dashboard, go to **Settings** | **Android Auto**
3. Enable **Android Auto**

The following image shows the Android Auto settings in the car:

Android Auto car settings

4. Connect your phone to the car using the USB.
5. From the car dashboard, find Android Auto and select it.

The following image shows the Android Auto start button on your car's dashboard:

Android Auto in the car

6. On your phone, you will be getting Android Auto setup prompts about What will **Android Auto do?** Click **Continue**:

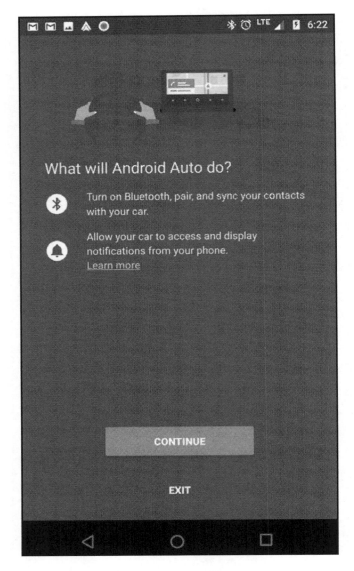

Android Auto setup prompt

7. On your phone, the Android Auto setup will prompt you to use Google Assistant. Click **CONTINUE**:

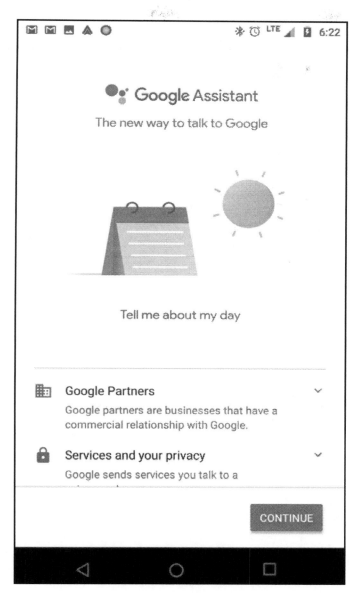

Android Auto and Google Assistant

8. On the car's dashboard, you will see the Android Auto setup prompt. Click **SKIP**:

Android Auto setup for the car

9. You should be able to browse through the podcast menu by clicking the top-left corner menu.

The following image shows the All Podcasts root menu:

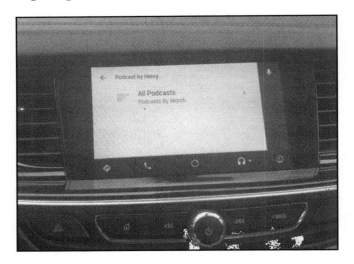

Android Auto podcast menu

10. Select a podcast to play and your car will play the podcast you selected by streaming it from the Microsoft Azure blob storage:

Car playing the podcast

Basic Voice Commands

In this section, I'll cover some voice commands that you can use to interact with your Android auto podcast. Essentially, Android Auto uses Google Assistant, so to activate the voice command, you initiate with the "OK Google" wake word.

Then you can use following voice commands.

- **Play Andromeda on Henry podcast service**: "Henry podcast service" is the label that you applied in the `MusicService` class of the MyPodCast project. "Andromeda" is the title of the song. When this command is invoked, it will invoke the `OnPlayFromSearchImpl` search from `MusicService`.
- **Stop playing**: Stops playing podcast.
- **Resume**: Resumes playing.
- **Play next**: Plays next podcast.
- **Play previous**: Plays previous podcast.

You can discover more Android-Auto-related commands at `https://support.google.com/androidauto`.

Certifying Android Auto

When this book was written, in August 2018, Android Auto was not open to all developers. The Android Auto application was only available in the marketplace to tier-one approved vendors, such as WhatsApp, Spotify, Waze, Pondora, and ABC News. You can easily check out some of the available Android Auto apps by going to **Android Auto** | **Apps for Android Auto**.

The following image shows the Android Auto applications:

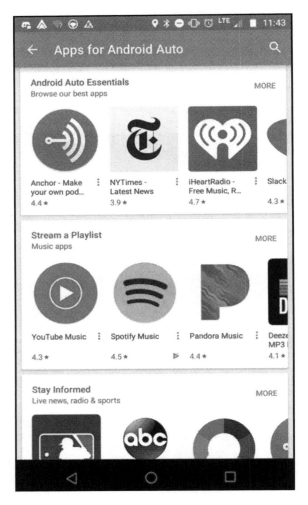

Android Auto applications

Google has not yet to announce when the Android Auto development will be open to all developers so that third-party applications can be created and available for all Android Auto users. But it is important to be on the breeding edge and at least develop Android application in development mode and learn to interface with Android Auto now, so that when the Android Auto marketplace is open, you will be way ahead of your competition.

Summary

In this chapter, you learned to get the media contents from the Node.js backend server and stream the podcast content from the Microsoft Azure blob storage. You also learned how to simulate your Android Auto podcast application on the DHU and then ran the application using a real car. Finally, you learned some basic Android voice commands to interact with your podcast application.

Other Books You May Enjoy

If you enjoyed this book, you may be interested in these other books by Packt:

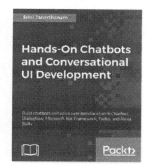

Hands-On Chatbots and Conversational UI Development
Srini Janarthanam

ISBN: 9781788294669

- Design the flow of conversation between the user and the chatbot
- Create Task model chatbots for implementing tasks such as ordering food
- Get new toolkits and services in the chatbot ecosystem
- Integrate third-party information APIs to build interesting chatbots
- Find out how to deploy chatbots on messaging platforms
- Build a chatbot using MS Bot Framework
- See how to tweet, listen to tweets, and respond using a chatbot on Twitter
- Publish chatbots on Google Assistant and Amazon Alexa

Alexa Skills Projects
Madhur Bhargava

ISBN: 9781788997256

- Understand how Amazon Echo is already being used in various domains
- Discover how an Alexa Skill is architected
- Get a clear understanding of how some of the most popular Alexa Skills work
- Design Alexa Skills for specific purposes and interact with Amazon Echo to execute them
- Gain experience of programming for Amazon Echo
- Explore future applications of Amazon Echo and other voice-activated devices

Leave a review - let other readers know what you think

Please share your thoughts on this book with others by leaving a review on the site that you bought it from. If you purchased the book from Amazon, please leave us an honest review on this book's Amazon page. This is vital so that other potential readers can see and use your unbiased opinion to make purchasing decisions, we can understand what our customers think about our products, and our authors can see your feedback on the title that they have worked with Packt to create. It will only take a few minutes of your time, but is valuable to other potential customers, our authors, and Packt. Thank you!

Index

Printed in Great Britain
by Amazon